Gameplay Mode

ELECTRONIC MEDIATIONS

KATHERINE HAYLES, MARK POSTER, AND SAMUEL WEBER, SERIES EDITORS

(continued on page 225)

Gameplay Mode

War, Simulation, and Technoculture

PATRICK CROGAN

Electronic Mediations 36

UNIVERSITY OF MINNESOTA PRESS

MINNEAPOLIS • LONDON

An earlier version of chapter 4 was published as "Logistical Space: Flight Simulation and Virtual Reality," in *The Illusion of Life 2: More Essays on Animation,* ed. Alan Cholodenko (Sydney: Power Publications, 2007); copyright Power Institute Foundation for Art and Visual Culture. An earlier version of chapter 5 was published as "Gametime: History, Narrative, and Temporality in *Combat Flight Simulator 2,*" in *The Video Game Theory Reader,* ed. Mark J. P. Wolf and Bernard Perron (New York: Routledge, 2003); reproduced with the permission of the publisher. Portions of chapter 6 were published as "The Experience of Information in Computer Games," *Scan* 1, no. 1 (January 2004), http://www.scan.net.au. An earlier version of chapter 8 was published as "Playing Through: The Future of Alternative and Critical Game Projects," in *Changing Views: Worlds in Play,* ed. Suzanne de Castell and Jennifer Jenson (New York: Peter Lang Publishing, 2007).

Published by the University of Minnesota Press
111 Third Avenue South, Suite 290
Minneapolis, MN 55401-2520
http://www.upress.umn.edu

Library of Congress Cataloging-in-Publication Data

Crogan, Patrick.
    Gameplay mode: war, simulation, and technoculture / Patrick Crogan.
        p. cm. — (Electronic mediations; 36)
    Includes bibliographical references and index.
    ISBN 978-0-8166-5334-8 (hardback) — ISBN 978-0-8166-5335-5 (pb)
    1. Computer games—Social aspects. 2. Video games—Social aspects.
    3. Computer war games. 4. Computer flight games. I. Title.
    GV1469.17.S63C76 2011
    793.93´2—dc23

                                        2011017085

Printed in the United States of America on acid-free paper

The University of Minnesota is an equal-opportunity educator and employer.

17 16 15 14 13 12 11   10 9 8 7 6 5 4 3 2 1

Dedicated to the memory of

RONNI REDMAN

(1966–2007)

CONTENTS

ACKNOWLEDGMENTS

The original research for this book was completed with the assistance of an Australian Research Council Discovery Project grant for 2005–2007. An internal research grant from the Faculty of Humanities and Social Sciences at the University of Technology, Sydney, supported its early development in 2001–2003. Several small grants from the University of Adelaide also contributed to its progress.

Several individuals deserve my warm gratitude for their help in the development of the work from which this book subsequently emerged. Sam Weber provided incisive critical engagement with some of the original research. Helen Kennedy has maintained a dialogue with my research around the theme of war and technoculture. Joost Raessens and Tanya Krzywinska read the original manuscript thoughtfully, offering valuable suggestions for its revision. Dan Ross brought his rigorous efficiency to a review of the project. Janna Poole did graphic design work for the simulation design diagram in the conclusion.

On a personal note, I would like to express my thanks to Yvonne Chun for her patience and care throughout this long procedure. Thanks to Cassandra and Tiernan Chun-Crogan, my principal gameplay researchers. To Melissa and Max Emanuel: you were there for us when we really needed you. Thanks also to the Duthy Street Deli in Adelaide, where much of the original version of this book was written over a continuous supply of fresh coffee. Last, I would like to thank Ronni Redman, one of my oldest friends, whose highly valued support for my endeavors started long before this project. Her lifetime commitment to inspiring intellectual inquiry, social justice, and peace will not be forgotten quickly by those who knew her.

Introduction

Technology, War, and Simulation

Maxis's 2008 computer game *Spore* (Electronic Arts) offers a world of interactive play that tells us much about the world in which it jostles for position among competing digital entertainments. Designed by Will Wright, legendary designer of video game classics *Sim City* (Maxis, 1989) and *The Sims* (Maxis, 2000), it is a game of many modes. Single-player play (including first-person, tactical, realtime, and turn-based strategy), asynchronous interactivity, user-generated content creation, and publishing are all built into the downloadable or packaged commodity. The player controls the development of a species from its beginnings as a single cell organism through stages of biological, then sentient, socioeconomic development up to and beyond global technocultural forms. The final phase is one of space exploration and colonization. Players compete against game- or user-created species, first to achieve phase victories and ultimately to make one of the game-winning moves: be first to reach a star in the center of the galaxy, or to defeat the cyborg species defending it. The game package encourages players to spend time on creating new species. The developers run Web sites supporting user communities for sharing, testing, and celebrating creatures and for developing new applications around these activities.

Key elements of today's digital media technoculture are immediately readable in *Spore*'s release and the buzz of both enthusiastic and annoyed user responses to the game. A virtual world and virtual history simulator, its ambit was global in the way that Western media conglomerates envisage the globe. It was released internationally in September 2008 and was then available globally for download from the publisher, Electronic Arts, one of the largest multinational game publisher-distributors. Although essentially a single-player game, it sought to compete with multiplayer virtual game-worlds by building in user creation and sharing of content, managed by EA and the developer, Maxis. This immediately brought angry responses from buyers because the game's digital rights management software lodged itself unannounced on their computer registries and restricted their ability to play the game online from more than one registered computer. This led to a rights management hack version of the game becoming the record peer-to-peer download in the months after the game release before EA modified the copy protection software to better match the online usage the developers wanted to encourage.

Global solicitation of player-consumers in simulated virtual environments, problematic appropriation of user creativity, copyrighting and negotiation of intellectual property, ever-expanding packages targeting player participatory and community involvement—these themes have all attracted attention in digital media studies. From a more specifically games studies perspective, *Spore* also offers its grand mobilization of artificial life and procedural generation software as significant developments in game design and animation technology.

What is not recognizable in *Spore* when approached from the perspective of digital media and games studies is its adoption of the military technoscientific legacy forged in the face of total war and the nuclear age inaugurated by the cold war. This has nonetheless had a profound impact on the development of computer games. It is there in the permanent warring across biological and sociocultural phases of *Spore* gameplay, in the routine terms for these modes (tactical realtime strategy), and in the game victory conditions (win the race to an objective or defeat the ultimate enemy). It is also to be found in less explicit ways, inhabiting the technological lineages of digital computing, visual displays and interactivity, virtual space simulation, and software development. It is there in the teleological tweaking of evolutionary principles that inform the key game dynamic of competitive creature evolution: game goals dictate the direction and prerogatives of evolution, whereas in biological theory, evolution is not teleological. Something deeply embedded in the cold war development of simulational technologies, at the center of which was the digital computer, is playfully explored in *Spore*: the impulse to model phenomena by hypothetically extending and extrapolating its future to see how that future may be predicted, modified, and controlled. *metaverse that we control our future — (our designer)*

This book is about this military technoscientific legacy and its shadow in contemporary technoculture. It may be better to think of contemporary technoculture as the shadow. This is closer to the perspective I take in the chapters that follow, but I look at many of the ways in which other futures for technocultural becoming are sought and experimented with in adopting this weighty legacy. I examine this theme through computer games because they and the practices that have developed around their use are especially privileged technocultural forms for this purpose. Computer games are the first major global technocultural form native to the computer, and they are a defining technology of the contemporary digital information age. This is why I generally prefer to call them *computer games,* as opposed to the more common term *video games,* although for the sake of variety I use both terms interchangeably.

In many respects, these computer-based entertainments represent a point of generational division between those brought up in recent media contexts that contain video games as a matter of course, and those who are older. This partly explains their habitual appearance in mainstream media as a focus of (and even a scapegoat for) anxieties about adolescent behavior and the deleterious effects of media exposure for children. Simplistic, misinformed discourse about the nature of video games, which frequently focuses on their obvious relation to their military origins as simulation training aids, tends to fill the space of what should be a more rigorous and reasoned examination of these relations. Most media studies and video game researchers either outright reject or avoid engaging the mainstream moral panic approach to video games and their relation to violence. They throw the baby out with the bathwater, avoiding the question concerning technoculture's relation to war and the military that computer games pose so insistently beyond the media effects debate, which itself is unable to articulate it adequately in these terms.

I will approach computer games differently for the purposes of this study, with the aid of some exceptional guides, because as I just suggested, contemporary media and video games studies tend not to recognize just how significant this military technoscientific legacy has been and continues to remain for our world of mediated digital culture and communications. Whereas media technology historians identify the military funding and developmental contexts in which digital computing and simulational technologies first emerged, media studies, and video game studies in its wake, seem to prefer neither to dwell on the legacies of these beginnings nor to follow the story forward too closely. This may strike one as particularly strange today in the wake of the large-scale military involvements of the United States, the United Kingdom, and so many other Western and developing states around the world in the first part of the twenty-first century. On the other hand, this perhaps better explains what I would call the elective naivety of much media and games studies, which avoid a frank consideration of computer games as forms that emerge out of ongoing interchanges between war, simulation, and contemporary technoculture. In this formulation, naivety is not meant to signal ignorant immaturity but to indicate the stubborn popularity of notions of culture and technology that ignore the profound connections of each to war in both their origin and ongoing development.

There have emerged some significant exceptions to this state of affairs in recent years. Roger Stahl's *Militainment, Inc.: War, Media and Popular Culture* and Nick Dyer-Witherford and Greig de Peuter's *Games of Empire: Global Capitalism and Video Games* are the most substantial of these. Stahl examines in detail across several forms of media entertainment (reality television, sports coverage, toys, and computer games) the expansion and transformation of the relations between the military and entertainment spheres since the war in the Persian Gulf of 1991. He argues that in this period, which corresponds with the rise of computer-based media technologies, interactive war developed out of the previously dominant (and still significant) spectacular packaging of war in mainstream Western media. In this solicitation of the citizen for entertainment purposes, the provision of an explosive, spectacular (but always sanitized) vision of the battlefield gives way to a "projection into the action" via the interactive situating of the viewer in a more experiential, immediate, and realtime virtual war.[1] He identifies military-themed video games as the most representative of militainment's cultural manifestations of "the emerging politics of the virtual citizen-soldier, produced by the changing configurations of electronic media, social institutions, and world events."[2] A central theme for Stahl is the contradictions of a more involved, embodied, and immediate (if virtual) experience of war that nonetheless wants to secure the insulation of the citizenry from a deliberative social and political engagement in the interminable war on terror prosecuted in their name.

Dyer-Witherford and de Peuter also explore the post–cold war period via their focus on video games as products and active contributors to the latest phase of global capital's empire theorized in a critical modification of Michael Hardt and Antonio Negri's influential 2000 book of the same name. They identify video games as originating from the same military technoscientific efforts as the computer itself.[3] The U.S. military–industrial complex was the "nuclear-armed core of capital's global domination," and games remain "umbilically connected" to it.[4] Dyer-Witherford and de Peuter examine the emergence of commercial video games from out of this core before going on to analyze their contemporary role in the "immaterial" political economy and in the maintenance and dissemination of global capitalist hegemony.

While Stahl and the *Games of Empire* authors concentrate on the post–cold war era of American technoculture and geopolitical adventure, I seek to make more substantial theoretical connections with the period in which the computer develops from out of the total mobilization of World War II to explore the longer lines of becoming of the changing configurations of media, social institutions, and the world associated with global capital, digital technoculture, and the current crisis of the political in American civil society. Simulation will emerge as central to the virtualization of the citizen in the contemporary moment (with all its contradictions). The complex connections between war and technoculture made concrete in the lineage of computer-simulational technologies from this period have implications for critically approaching today's situation. My consideration of these may add another dimension to the valuable and substantial work on the political and economic critique of computer games in relation to war and the military accomplished in these studies.

War

War, simulation, and technoculture are the three principal terms I address here, but first I must emphasize their interrelatedness. A schematic map of this book would have computer games at the center of a triangle, the points of which are war, simulation, and technoculture. The historical, techno-logical, and conceptual connections between these three corners of the triangle, each with the other two, pass through the history, technology, and conceptual development of computer games. The latter are constituted out of these passages.

Gilbert Simondon, the mid-twentieth-century philosopher of technol-ogy whose work has been rediscovered in anglophone contexts in recent years, has an influential concept for the kind of relational dynamics I am sketching out here: transductivity. Simondon described it as

> a process—be it physical, biological, mental or social—in which an activity gradually sets itself in motion, propagating within a given domain, by basing this propagation on a structuration carried out in different zones of the domain: each region of the constituted structure serves as a constituting prin-ciple for the following one, so much so that a modification progressively extends itself at the same time as this structuring operation.[5]

This ontogenic process involves a reciprocal, rebounding effect rather than a linear enchainment of causes and effects from a single original cause. Simon-don developed the notion in order to account for technical evolution and its interaction with social change. Adrian Mackenzie states that Simondon later generalized transduction to name any process "in which metastability emerges."[6] Transduction, argues Mackenzie, "aids in tracking processes that come into being at the intersection of diverse realities."[7] Our examination of computer games, therefore, is best thought of as an attempt to track the transductivities between war, simulation, and technoculture.

War's place is crucial in this book's framing of video games. The absence of substantial critical examinations of the central, ongoing role played by military technoscience in the development of computer games in recent scholarship is readily apparent to anyone scanning the indexes, content pages, and abstracts of the growing body of published work in game studies

and related subareas of media and cultural studies. We will encounter many
instances of this in the course of our second look at influential theorizations
of computer game phenomena. To compensate for this, I devote substantial
effort in what follows to considering military-led and -funded technological
research and development in terms of its influence on computer game hardware and software. This is certainly necessary, but more fundamental to the
aim of this study is the reconsideration of war as no longer simply opposed
to peace as an exceptional, temporary interruption. Peacetime and wartime
cannot, if they ever could, be neatly separated into discrete durations, as
seemed to be the case during and after World War II. While this may, and
indeed should, be a fairly obvious and noncontroversial assertion—for both
the United Kingdom and the United States, not to mention the other victors
of that conflict, the number of days since that they have had no armed forces
on active duty in some part of the globe is negligible—the assumption that
brackets war off from peace, and the military from the domestic or the civilian spheres, is still tenaciously held in mainstream discourses surrounding
politics, economics, and social and cultural life.

There are some important critical and cultural theorists for my project
who have undermined this assumption, none more so than Paul Virilio,
who has not ceased to question its distorting effects across the interpretation of art, architecture, media, culture, history, and politics. His notion of
pure war describes the tendency toward the undermining of any definitive
separation of wartime and peacetime existence. This tendency crystallized
in the passage to total war traversed in the course of World War II and gained
momentum in the cold war era. The cold war continued the processes and
technics of total mobilization beyond the end of the "hot war" under the
decisive stimulus provided by the advent in 1945 of the nuclear weapon.
The impact of the latter continues to be underestimated today.

Virilio has characterized the essential feature of this pure war tendency
as the increasing ascendancy of logistics over strategic and political prerogatives in the organization of life. In *Pure War*, Virilio cites a definition of
logistics that issued from the Pentagon in the early postwar era: "Logistics is
the procedure following which a nation's potential is transferred to its armed
forces, in times of peace as in times of war."[8] The transfer of a nation's potential to its armed forces in this guise of a generalized policy and procedure

would amount to the transformation of a nation into logistical potential and a concomitant blurring of the distinction between times of peace and war. To bring it back to video games, *Spore* players play in this blurred time, getting pleasure from their hypothetical creatures designed to evolve into successful species in a hypothetical historical technoscientific contest leading to a space operatic conclusion. They play through various modes adopted from tactical and strategic political training and simulation practices traceable back to the technoscientific think tanks and research teams of the 1940s and 1950s. These were first assembled in the government-led reinvention of the scientific interface with industry during World War II and consolidated in postwar arrangements. One cannot hope to critically comprehend contemporary computer simulation–based technoculture without taking account of this historical development and its ongoing unfolding.

Simulation

That technoculture is productively understood as computer simulation based, and that computer games provide a valuable gauge of this situation, is articulated neatly in this quote from influential interactive media and games theorist Espen Aarseth: "The question is what is the essence of computing? If there is such an essence we could say it is simulation: that is the essence from Turing onwards. Games of course are simulations and computers are a prime platform for doing simulations."[9] Aarseth has in mind Alan Turing's vision of the modern digital computer as a universal machine capable of imitating other machines when he identifies simulation as the essential constituent of computing and therefore of computer gaming.[10] We will examine in some detail, in particular in the first chapters of this study, the wartime and postwar logistical contexts in which both the technologies and the conceptualization of computer simulational practices flourished. Understanding the simulational milieu in which computer-based technoculture has developed since the 1940s is key to any substantial critical account of that development.

Simulation is a process by which a phenomenon is representatively modeled by another phenomenon. The process involves a selective reduction in the representative model of the complexity of elements composing the simulated phenomenon. Gonzalo Frasca puts it in the language of postwar systems theory: "Simulation is the act of modeling a system A by a less complex system B, which retains some of A's original behaviour."[11] As technique and complex of technical devices, or rather as their combination, computer simulation was invented to deal with natural, sociopolitical, economic, cultural, tactical, strategic, and logistical phenomena. Of course, technology itself pervades these phenomena. Simulational technics immediately became a factor in the phenomena their development was dedicated to address.

As the now-pervasive "prime platform for doing simulations," computers have had a major impact on history and society over the last sixty years. It is a difficult task to find the right scale to assess this impact without missing something of its scope and extent, even while it is problematic to overgeneralize about the "information," "digital," or "computer" age. If these terms, as well as the critical work done under these names, designate general conditions or developments in this period differently, it is evidence of these difficulties as much as it is of differing assessments of what is most essential or determining in the technological changes of the recent past. I want to focus on how simulation has been and remains a crucial motivating and enabling factor of these changes. The electronic digital computer promised a greatly enhanced capacity for this technique—or, better, technical tradition of a family of techniques, including games of all kinds, military training devices and exercises, probabilistic statistics, and so forth. The digital computer offered a reconfigurable platform for simulating different phenomena, the calculating power to model complex interactions, and the speed to do so in real time. This is the assumed ground of the designed activities and experiences promised by a game like *Spore*.

Developing computer simulation in a military technoscientific context of the logistical drive toward a permanent preparation for the eventuality of thermonuclear conflict, it is no wonder the calculative power and speed of the digital computer forged pathways leading toward preemption. The modeling of real-world physical or human behavior to experiment with its hypothetical futures amounts to a technics of anticipating what has not yet happened. This needs to be considered as both an extension and an exacerbation of the purposive quality of technics in general; the technical instrument or system is always taken up in a gesture aimed toward the future its use will influence. The development of the digital computer as simulational system since the late 1940s tends to spiral the engagement with what is out there and what is to come toward a cybernetic, looping, preemptive regulation of the future's emergence—at least, that is the intent, if not the effect, of the simulational gesturing I wish to trace in this study. The gesture and its accidental consequences will be uncovered in this tracing.

Technoculture

This exacerbated extension of the dynamics of human–technical becoming is the unstable milieu in which people live today. If modernity is the installation of change as the only permanence, then we appear to be approaching the limits implied in that oxymoronic formulation on a number of fronts: environmental, economic, strategicopolitical. The term *technoculture* emerged around the early 1990s in media and cultural studies at a moment where the rapid advance of high-speed transport, communications, and representational and virtualizing technologies seemed to correspond with major geopolitical and cultural changes around the globe. In a collection of essays titled *Technoculture,* the task outlined by the editors, Constance Penley and Andrew Ross, was to look for appropriations and strategic, local adoptions of cultural technologies that were rolled out by global capitalist enterprises complete with designed patterns of use by their consumers. Researched and developed "mostly under military auspices," these technologies have tended to become increasingly more pervasive as the conditions in which social, political, and cultural interactions happen.[12] The local struggle against the englobing forces of economic and social control is central to the concerns the editors had with the technocultural future of this phase of (post)modernity.

Philip K. Lawrence states, "Modernity seeks to colonise the future; its watchword is control."[13] If the latest phase of technological modernity is significantly different, as I believe it is, along with those cited above and so many others, it is because it moves beyond control toward the new watchword of *preemption.* Computer-based simulational technics are a privileged vector of this movement. *Spore* is an exemplary instance. It is like an executive summary of tactical, strategic, and logistical simulation games. Experimental development of a superior virtual life form best suited to the game's phased challenges is the metagameplay. In addition, the conflicts noted above between player and publisher, move and countermove between controlled and unregulated download, and use and modification of the game are all readable in terms of this passage from control toward preemption.

As we explore the history and contemporary state of play of technocultural dynamics through the perspective provided by computer games—as both privileged example of and significant contributor to these dynamics—it is crucial to keep in mind that we are dealing with both an historical and an historically singular situation. In other words, if technoculture names a particularly extreme configuration of the technological conditioning of culture, this is on the basis that all culture is technoculture in a sense. As philosopher of technology Bernard Stiegler makes apparent, there is no cultural life without the cultivation of practices and forms that are significant to the collective or collectives to which individuals belong. These practices and forms are lived through and as gestures, techniques, objects, records, and so forth that enable transmission, preservation, repetition, and reinvention. Today, technocultural development tends to undermine the viability of this vital dynamic. The drive to foreclose the future shuts off the future as such. According to Stiegler, this amounts to an increasingly toxic cultural milieu of extreme eventualities corresponding to the destabilizing disintegration of the individuating dynamic of individual and collective. Preservation of the very possibility of the continuation of cultural becoming seems increasingly to depend on a reinvention of technical conditions that model and anticipate rather than support its emergence.

What Follows

In chapter 1, I put in place the most important themes for our study of the relation between war, simulation, and technoculture. I discuss three influential developments in the emergence of the computerized platform for simulational practices: Norbert Wiener's invention in the 1940s of cybernetics on the back of work toward an antiaircraft weapons system: the U.S. Air Force's 1950s–1960s Semi-Automated Ground Environment project, which kick-started the American computing industry in its flawed effort to shield America from nuclear attack by virtualizing it in real time; and the 1980s development of SIMNET as a networked simulation training system that put in place much of the technology and expertise subtending the 1990s explosion in realtime networked games. Three key developments, three key elements—the cybernetic approach to modeling complex phenomena, realtime interactive control through virtualization, and the convergence of simulated and real events. Computer games have played an integral part in the dissemination of the logistical tendencies that animate our contemporary technoculture. It is important for my effort to rehabilitate critical discourse on the latter to situate these tendencies historically and conceptually, and this is what I attempt in this chapter.

In chapter 2, I address the challenge this development poses to critical engagement with computer games inasmuch as they are part of this contemporary technoculture in which war and simulation play such co-constitutive roles. After situating this challenge in relation to other important accounts of the information age, postmodernity, and simulation, I will explain the significance and critical potential of a games-centered response to this challenge. This revolves around the fact that computer games play with the playing out of what I will call the war on contingency. This has been an animating force throughout the course of the development of computers as simulation platforms capable of modeling the future as virtually accessible to preemption. The way games put this in play is the source of the critical potential of games as signal examples and proponents of this development.

The following two chapters are devoted to flight simulation, one of the key avenues for technoscientific innovations in the visualization of computer-simulated space. When one recalls that a flight simulation game was routinely shipped with the MS-DOS-based personal computers sold during the 1980s expansion of the home computer market, the duration of the connection between the military invention of computerized flight simulation and domestic use of the computer as entertainment technology becomes apparent.[14] These two chapters deal in turn with what game versions of the virtual reality technologies pioneered in flight simulation can tell us about our contemporary technocultural engagements in space and in time. Chapter 3 concerns itself principally with the simulation of virtual space developed in flight simulation. I examine how a powerfully effective system for reenvisioning geographical space enacts a logistical transformation of the perception of the exterior world. The influence innovations in flight simulation's scene generation in real time had on computer visualization cannot be overestimated. This chapter will reexamine some of these developments by means of analysis of a flight simulation game in order to trace their dissemination via personal computing and its interactive entertainments. Flight simulation's virtual space will be considered as a form of animation—one that, like all animation, operates by bringing to life another mode of being in the world as it deanimates others.

In chapter 4, "Military Gametime," the difference between simulational and narrative deployments of fictional space will be discussed in order to develop a meditation on the specific temporality of computer game simulations of events. A comparison between a ludic and a filmic representation of the World War II air war in the Pacific will be the means for developing this account of the temporal engagements of the player in a computer game relying on the visual simulation of event sequences. Drawing on games and narratological theories from Espen Aarseth to Paul Ricoeur, I will argue that the co-option of narrative and historical forms in games reliant on this kind of contextualization of gameplay is an exemplary instance of a reorientation to temporal experience I would identify with the logistical transformations affecting contemporary technoculture. Central to this is the ludic redeployment of narrative form from a hermeneutic-based experience to a performative orientation toward interactive navigation and mastery of game challenges.

In chapter 5, I discuss the game genre of the first-person shooter—or, rather, its gameplay mode, so extensive is its deployment across a variety of game genres. I argue that it crystallizes in ludic form key principles of the cybernetic model of information processing that underpinned the historical development of digital computing. Both the playing out of and the playing with the "man in the middle" conundrum of classic cybernetic thought can be seen in the generic history of the first-person shooter game. I will also address in this context the question of the link between shooter games and real-life passages to violent acts by children seemingly well trained in marksmanship. This will enable me to situate my approach in this study to those mainstream media effects discourses on computer games and related accounts of the connections between games and violent conflict. These tend to shoot the messenger, failing to see the wider logistical dynamics of which computer games are certainly a part. A more appropriate critical practice in regard to the relations between media such as computer games and violence in society would have to begin with the relations between war, simulation, and technoculture that are writ large in computer games as fruits of these transductive relations.

Chapter 6, "Other Players in Other Spaces," examines online gaming from a perspective that deliberately avoids the more conventional perspectives established in game studies, perspectives that focus on the potential (or lack of potential) for new forms of sociality and community represented by online gaming. Instead, I develop an account from a phenomenological—or, better, postphenomenological—position on the technological dependence of all forms of community and the continuities between online gaming sociality and real-world communities in their contradictory struggle to produce themselves. It is from this basis that the online gaming phenomenon can be more rigorously interrogated for its potential to invent new forms of sociality, subjectivity, participatory culture, and the political economy of media production. A systemic tension between the individual and the collective is configured in the very technics supporting the realtime networked communications enabling the various virtual worlds around which communities of online players assemble. I will argue that the history of Western modernity's development of the principle of the (Western, humanist) subject-centered world is readable in the computer network, even as the network's potential to grow new, more horizontal and lateral associations opens paths to other kinds of possible worlds. The network itself, while often adopted as a neutral description of computer-linked association and communication today, needs to be carefully interrogated before approaching a term like *networked community*. If the networked communities around virtual worlds are, as many researchers argue, important new phenomena presaging the future of the digital age, this chapter seeks to lay a better foundation for assessing their significance as portents.

Chapter 7 looks at several alternative and critical game projects for their potential to interrogate and detour the predominant concretization of computer game technology and routinization of gameplay. These include critical or art games such as Newsgaming's *September 12th: A Toy World* (2002) as well as art-based projects like the *Painstation* (/////////fur//// art entertainment interfaces, 2002) that adopt cultural and technical elements of computer gaming differently in order to interrogate the conventional taking place of computer games as media entertainment forms. Drawing on the work of Samuel Weber, I will examine how these works theatricalize gameplay in different ways, destabilizing its usual placement in the everyday rhythms of technocultural experience. In doing so, they raise crucial questions about how that experience is conditioned by simulational technics. This will lead me to develop a critique of influential games studies work— for instance, that of Gonzalo Frasca and Espen Aarseth—addressing the notion of critical simulation. This work identifies the centrality of a simulational configuration of experience in computer games but tends to treat this as an interesting new tool for cultural, political, or artistic experimentation, without attending to the logistical trajectories that have overdetermined the emergence of this tool.

In the concluding chapter, I again take up the question of simulation and criticality—always in its transductive relation to war and technoculture—to work toward a concluding perspective for my inquiry concerning computer games in the contemporary technocultural moment. I characterize computer simulation as a fictioning of the future that bears the ongoing legacy of the deterrent anticipatory impetus of its logistical origins. I move between wider contemporary developments, such as the war on terror and the rise of the security industry in which computer simulation and war continue to condition the technocultural future, and the field of computer games as the entertaining expression of these compositional dynamics. If this deterrent, preemptive tendency remains a powerful factor in contemporary technoculture, this is not to say that the results are predictable. On the contrary, the book concludes on the theme of accidentality as the necessary corollary of this effort to foreclose future eventuality, because this preemptive tendency is paradoxically the very opposite of a conservative program, however much it seeks to guarantee order. The cultural and political potential of play, and of the players, will be articulated from this perspective. With this potential resides the possibility of other kinds of accident, other detours of the technocultural program, turning it toward more viable futures.

A final note on the contents of this study is in order. The games I discuss here are preponderantly (but not exclusively) the more explicitly war- and conflict-based games. One could object that I am giving only a selective view of the range and diversity of commercial computer gaming. I would not disagree with this, but I would add that every account of computer gaming is selective in one way or another. As I have already argued, the majority of these go out of their way to deemphasize the kinds of transductive connections between war, simulation, and technoculture that are nonetheless apparent in any examination of the ongoing history of computer games. Having said that, I would add two further points in support of my selective encounter with contemporary computer gaming.

First, my interest in the connections between war and technoculture and war and simulation tend to make explicitly conflict-based games the most amenable forms for consideration. In these, the continuities and transductivities can be discerned more readily than in games that are not so explicitly grounded in virtual war, such as sport simulations, puzzle games, nonmilitary simulation games such as *Sim City* (Maxis, from 1989) or *The Sims* (Maxis, from 2000), or children's games involving doll-like activities such as the *Barbie Dress Up* games available online.[15] I am concerned in this study, however, with dynamics animating the broad development of computer-based technoculture, such as the influence of cybernetic principles of the regulation of processes through the medium of information; the virtual, remote management of events via the power of calculative anticipation and communication delivered in the form of digital computing; and the growth of simulation as a central form of technocultural practice. Consequently, many of the observations that are drawn from my consideration of conflict-based games are not irrelevant to consideration of the nature and significance of other less explicitly war-related computer games.

Second, and on this last point, conflict-based games are arguably the major proportion of commercial computer games, even beyond those game genres that explicitly market themselves as such. Levels of realism in depicting violent conflict differ greatly, and in many nonviolent games, the results of conflict may be reduced to simple (temporary) disappearance of the player avatar or opponent from the gamespace, or to some mild, anodyne euphemism for virtual destruction. In many action games with scenarios that do not seem to center on conflict, the basic engine of gameplay is nonetheless some variation of tracking, targeting, and shooting/acquiring interactions, usually while navigating through a challenging environment. Most platform games can be characterized in this way, from the *Super Mario Bros.* franchise to *The Simpsons Game* (Electronic Arts, 2007). Navigating, solving puzzles revolving around obstacles to progress through the terrain, and targeting and striking various objects and opponents are the core of gameplay.

My point is not to denounce computer games as (all or mostly) dedicated to warlike scenarios and action analogs, however sublimated by different design metaphors. Such a denunciation is tantamount to shooting the messenger of the larger transductive dynamics that computer games instantiate, exemplify, and in some cases innovate. I see computer games as providing a valuable opportunity to reflect on today's technocultural becoming. As we will see, many games and adoptions of game technologies open up spaces for insightful reflection on this engagement. Rather, my goal is to show that the possibility for play, for the ludic adoption of computer technoculture that is always underway, emerges out of an encounter with technological systems, which, as Friedrich Kittler so acutely reminds us, "unambiguously revealed themselves as hardware for the destruction of Iraqi hardware" during the air-to-ground Desert Storm campaign in 1990–1991.[16] These systems are called computers, and playing with them is one of our best chances to adopt them for other ends. The less naive our encounter with the givens of these systems, the more potential exists for gameplay mode to anticipate a different future for their and our becoming.

1 From the Military-Industrial to the Military-Entertainment Complex

Mainstream media commentary on the carefully orchestrated "highlights packages" released daily to the international press during the U.S.-led 1991 Desert Storm campaign in Kuwait and Iraq registered the striking resemblance between the "missile cam" and spotter plane footage of targets being destroyed and the screens of contemporary combat-based video games. Media theorists typically responded in the wake of the war by exposing the highly selective and unrepresentative nature of U.S. military–controlled media briefings. The rhetoric of a war of precision weapons delivering surgical strikes obscured the fact that the vast majority of military ordnance was not precision guided; that area bombing was more prevalent than precision targeting; and that in any event, many of the "smart" weapons (like the Patriot antimissile missiles) were far less effective than was made out in the press briefings.

In a similar vein, games theorist Mia Consalvo criticized the mainstream identification of the second Gulf war as another video game war, arguing that it was an ideological construction that served in part to reduce the need for American telespectators to confront the real horror of the war's effect on the Iraqi and Kuwaiti populations subject to it. At the same time, this identification profited from the uneasy, ambivalent charge video gaming carried in mainstream media as a marginal, transgressive, nonproductive, and potentially dangerous youth.[1]

While I would not disagree with these critical responses to the extraordinarily successful efforts of the coalition forces to direct the media representation of Desert Storm and Operation Iraqi Freedom, I think something important was missed in the effort to uncover the lie and the ideological function of the military representation of its operations. The immediate recognition of the relationship between the vision of simulated execution of high-tech warfare in virtual spaces and that of the leading edge of real weapon systems—some of them being deployed for real for the first time—spoke volumes about the homologies between the technoculture where this vision was produced commercially as entertainment and the military technoscientific milieu where its operational effectiveness was being presented as the new face of war. In the blurred zone of news infotainment, this military-industrial vision provided the spectacular payoff that combat video game players sought through successful manipulation of the game interface. If war was, and remains, unlike the virtualized, simulated experience of instrumental efficiency for much of the time and for most who fall within its theater, this vision of controlled, precise, clean war has been and remains a powerful animating tendency of technocultural becoming. Computer simulation is at the heart of this tendency, the technical thread connecting war and contemporary technoculture.

In this chapter, I will discuss three influential developments in the emergence of the computerized platform for simulational practices: Norbert Wiener's invention of cybernetics as a by-product of his wartime efforts to invent an antiaircraft weapons system; the development by the U.S. Air Force of the Semi-Automated Ground Environment, a cold war air defense project that helped to build the American computing industry; and the Defense Advanced Research Projects Agency (DARPA) development of SIMNET, a networked military simulation training system responsible for much of the technology and expertise subtending the 1990s explosion in realtime networked games. Each of these developments is more than an important contributor to the technics and established practices of design and use of computers in our digital technoculture. Each also exemplifies the logistical dynamic I described in the introduction, whereby specific military research and development exceeded its initial context and application to participate in the wider transformation of the technocultural milieu—three key developments, three key elements: the cybernetic approach to modeling complex phenomena, realtime interactive control through virtualization, and the convergence of simulated and real events. Computer games have played an integral part in their subsequent dissemination, providing a powerful impetus to the logistical tendency animating contemporary technoculture. It is important for our effort to rehabilitate critical discourse on the latter to situate these developments historically and conceptually.

Calculating the Enemy: Computers and Cybernetics

The birth of the modern digital electronic computer is attributed to efforts directed toward two major military goals during World War II: breaking enemy codes, and improving the performance of artillery through more rapid and accurate ballistic trajectory calculation.[2] They exemplify the activity that came to be known as technoscience, a new regime of research and technological innovation that arose in the belligerent countries out of the total mobilization of scientific research toward military goals such as these.[3]

The path to the computer age emerges in this coordinated military technoscientific quest for the means to be in advance of the enemy's means. To be able to decipher the enemy's coded messages is to know what they intend to do before they have done it. It is widely accepted that the success of Allied efforts in this regard greatly affected various actions during the war, including Atlantic convoy protection, the Battle of Midway, and subterfuges surrounding the D-day Normandy landings.[4] Similarly, to shoot shells more accurately in a dynamic environment is premised on knowing how to reaim your gun more quickly by means of reliable calculations that can be used to affect the ballistic trajectory of the shell. Norbert Wiener, the founder of cybernetics, was addressing this very task with his contribution to the war effort at MIT. The inception of cybernetics as method and theory is inextricably linked to these efforts to respond to this anticipatory imperative. The influence of cybernetics on the development of computing—as theory of organized entities, as methodology for the mathematical expression of phenomena, and for interaction design—is widely acknowledged. Paul N. Edwards states that in the immediate postwar period, "Norbert Wiener's cybernetics seemed to offer a comprehensive theory capable of encompassing issues in government and society as well as in science, engineering and factory production. The Shannon–Wiener theories of information and communication unified a wide range of concepts in language, data analysis, computation and control."[5]

Peter Galison examines Wiener's project for an antiaircraft artillery system aimed at automating targeting and firing procedures and how it led to his discovery of the more general science of cybernetics. [6] Wiener's proposed antiaircraft (AA) predictor drew on established servomechanism technologies, modifying these with innovative and ambitious mathematical and statistical models of control. The goal was to invent a calculating device that would "characterize an enemy pilot's zigzagging flight, anticipate his future position, and launch an antiaircraft shell to down his plane."[7] This early work, despite failing to result in a viable antiaircraft weapons system improvement, was crucial in the theoretical development that led to cybernetics. For Wiener, the predictor represented a prototype for a technical system capable of modeling the interactions of connected but independently acting elements. He envisaged a new science of the modeling of the systemic characteristics and behaviors of these elements. Cybernetics would "embrace intentionality, learning, and much else within the human mind," before its ultimate expansion toward a modeling of the entire universe.[8]

This expansion of the model of a protocyborgian weapons system toward a universal cybernetic model of all dynamic phenomena is an exemplary instance of the logistical tendency's expansion outward from specific military technoscientific projects. These projects were initiated as part of the military mobilization of all sectors of society during and immediately after World War II. Cybernetics grew into what I would describe as an ur-simulation capable of modeling natural and social organizations. Galison's research traces it back to the project of attaining predictive control of the deadly contingency represented by the (enemy) other. Wiener's abstract characterization of his work on the AA predictor in a letter to a friend makes this clear. Discussing his preoccupation with the analysis of the "intrinsic possibilities" of certain types of behavior, he goes on to say that this "has become necessary for me in connection with the design of an apparatus to accomplish specific purposes in the way of the repetition and modification of time patterns."[9] After the war, in a written debate with philosopher Richard Taylor over the validity of the emerging cybernetic cosmology, Wiener (with colleague

Arturo Rosenbleuth) described the ideal cybernetic, self-regulating system as "governed by time-reversible causal stories." Galison adds this parenthetical explanation of Wiener's curious formulation: "(The AA predictor, for example, makes its statistical forecast on the basis of the *history* of the pilot's past performance)."[10]

In embryonic form here are the elements of the well-known ludology versus narratology (or narrativism) debate over the nature of computer games and the gaming experience. This debate revolved around how to understand the way computer games both appropriated and modified the narrative structures of older media forms like cinema and literature. The intervention in the timeline of a sequence of events that characterizes interactive engagement with(in) a cybernetic system is described here by Wiener as being governed by a form of story, a particularly peculiar form that challenges the conventional notion of a story as unidirectional in its ordering of events in time. This question of the relation between narrative forms and computer games as cybernetically conceived computer simulations is one that will concern us throughout this book, and I will return to it. Later in this chapter, I will look at how the U.S. military's SIMNET developers enthusiastically embraced the potential of simulation to supersede historical (narrative-based) recordings of exemplary battles.

For now, I want to underline the importance of the anticipatory impulse driving the development of cybernetics that is in evidence in Wiener's vision for his new science. It is central to the rise of the electronic digital computer itself and the realtime, interactive technoculture that proliferated around it. The formulation of the cybernetic desire to design technical systems capable of providing control over time patterns—that is, over the likely direction of future events without the preemptive intervention of the control apparatus—is a major theoretical and technical vehicle for the passage of total war into its pure war phase in the cold war period.

The conception and modeling of all manner of complex processes and phenomena as dynamic systems is the most pervasive indication today of this impulse. We live in a world anticipated by our computer-based predictive and preemptive systems. Emerging from military projects to continue the wartime work of applying instrumental scientific approaches to the conduct of operations, the improvement of training methods, logistical supply flows, and so forth, the logistical expansion of these processes received its definitive enabling generalization in the cybernetic gesture of rendering all dynamic phenomena as complex interactions governed by communicational networks and predictable flows of information. Built on historical records and story-making techniques of selecting and ordering records to interpret their significance, these systems enable the transformation of these story forms of understanding into the hypothetical, extrapolatory, and experimental running of future eventuality made possible by the calculation of the possibilities of the system being modeled. Computer games like *Spore*, discussed in this book's introduction, are the ludic entertainment form of this default mode of the contemporary technocultural temporalization of experience.

SAGE, Computing, and Virtualization

If cybernetics developed out of weapons targeting systems, virtualization was concretized as an operational goal in the major military-sponsored projects from the 1950s onward. The management and control of eventuality through virtualization techniques made possible through digital electronic computing systems remains a pervasive phenomenon today. It was defined in the major U.S. Air Force project of the late 1950s and 1960s: SAGE. The Semi-Automated Ground Environment air defense project was one of, if not the, most important digital computer research and development projects in the 1950s–1960s. For one thing, as Paul N. Edwards has shown, computer programming effectively commenced as a profession in response to the demands for programmers to work on the immense task of implementing a nationwide command, control, and communications system linking radar facilities, Air Force bases, and other operational units to a hierarchy of command centers. The Rand Corporation, a major U.S. Air Force–sponsored think tank and research and development body, won the contract for programming SAGE in the mid-1950s. Rand originally assigned twenty-five programmers to the task, then devolved its Systems Development Division into a separate company, the SDC (Systems Development Corporation), to handle the mountain of programming development and innovation. The SDC, Edwards tells us, "grew to four times Rand's size and employed over 800 programmers at its peak."[11] SAGE trained the leading figures of the emerging computer programming profession.

Edwards also lists the major technical advances in computing and electronic communication technology made as part of SAGE, including such things as innovations or major improvements in magnetic core memory, graphic display techniques, simulation techniques, digital data transmission over telephone lines, and computer networking.[12] Personal computing and the contemporary networked computer system in general, including the Internet, the graphical user interface, and of course the possibility of computer gaming in realtime, simulated environments, cannot be envisaged without the innovations listed here. The major commercial firms developing computer and communications technology, such as IBM, Bell Laboratories, and Western Electric, received the bulk of their income from contracts and research funding associated with SAGE and other high-tech weapons system projects for which SAGE was the model.

The SAGE project started life as MIT's Whirlwind project to develop a computer to enhance military flight simulation training systems, another critical vector of the transductivity between war, simulation, and technoculture. The Whirlwind project commenced as an analog computer design, but by 1946, it was reconceived as an electronic digital computing device that could serve as a general flight simulator capable of taking advantage of the protean potential of digital computing proclaimed by Turing.[13] Indeed, this shift toward a generalizable machine altered the very conception of the project, which evolved—in the mind of its chief designer, Jay Forrester—from a general flight simulator device into a general digital computation device with a range of possible applications. In evidence here is another important instance of the logistical expansion of a specific technoscientific project outward toward a more general program of development and application. The project was transformed from a flight training equipment development to become U.S. Air Force Project 416L for a realtime command and control network coordinating the response to air attack of the U.S. mainland by a foreign nuclear power.[14]

SAGE was not fully operational until 1961. It was thus already obsolete as a result of the appearance of intercontinental ballistic missiles (ICBMs) as a viable nuclear weapons delivery system by the end of the 1950s. Nonetheless, SAGE ran its system of radar surveillance, command center monitoring, and communications to air bases and, later, surface-to-air missile posts, into the 1980s. In concert with other sector command centers, each base commanded, in real time, fighter interception vectors and missile-firing control in the event of an enemy air attack. Edwards says that "SAGE barely worked" because of the emergence of ICBMs and a host of important technical and design failings, but he is right to point out how successful the project was in terms of its influence on the growth of the military-industrial complex, on strategicopolitical discourse generally, and more specifically, on military command and control philosophy and procedures. The cybernetic-influenced model of centralized command and control enabled by realtime communications networking together of computer systems, military and political commanders, and armed forces overthrew traditional military command structures and their interface with the political sphere. SAGE became "the pattern for at least *twenty-five* other major military command-control systems of the late 1950s and early 1960s (and, subsequently, many more)."[15]

In other words, the SAGE project was logistically crucial, if strategically and tactically useless. The SAGE ground environments were each rendered metonymically by the constantly updated map screens in the various control centers of the air defense system. These screens were fed data from a range of surveillance systems, such as radar and, later, networks of satellite monitoring technologies (photographic, video, and infographic). Radar had been one of the key cutting-edge technologies at the outset of World War II, not least because it was the major focus of the initial U.S. mobilization of scientists and engineers for military research, above all at MIT's Radiation Lab. Its contribution to fighting an enemy lay in its ability to provide early warning of the enemy's movements, allowing for a response adequate to the increased speed of assault in the era of motorized warfare. Later, this capacity was exploited as a component of weapons systems so that they could carry the assault beyond the scope of the geographical location of one's own forces. As Andy Pickering states, radar "produced maps," not death and destruction.[16]

The maps on the screens of the SAGE control centers were, from our perspective, the most significant and influential harbinger of the technocultural future toward which they opened a path. They were from the beginning animated maps that delivered what was called a "situation picture" (Figure 1).[17] This is perhaps better described as a situation movie, or better yet, a situation simulation. If the term *movie* suggests a predetermined sequence of images (and sounds) that can be played and replayed, a simulation runs a program that determines a particular outcome for each run on the basis of its modeling of particular contingencies and the interactions between these. While the SAGE system and its progeny were designed as real control systems, not merely simulations of hypothetical (if realistic) scenarios, they are in many respects comprehensible as simulations of the total, absolute, and almost unimaginable possible eventuality of large-scale nuclear conflict. They are comprehensible as simulations inasmuch as they operate by modeling thermonuclear war as, precisely, comprehensible and therefore manageable. The reality of their operational lives as systems dedicated to the potentiality of a war that has (so far) never taken place, and maintained through regular simulation drills of their actual functioning, supports this perspective.

At this operational level, the symmetry is evident between these systems and the nuclear war simulation practices that developed and expanded so rapidly in the same period across the agencies and associated think tanks and university research institutes of the military-industrial complex. At both

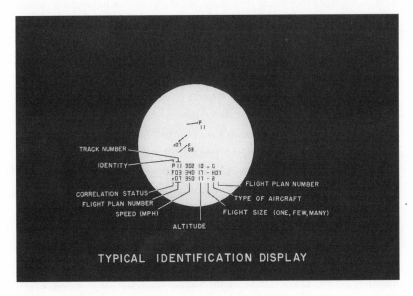

FIGURE 1 The SAGE situation picture, courtesy of the MITRE Corporation.

the "sharp end" of nuclear war fighting and the logistical and strategicopolit-ical structures that designed and prepared for it, the hypothetical ruled. As Edwards and others have pointed out, total thermonuclear war is a "fabulous" concept, one whose material impact lies not in actual death and destruction, but in the efforts to imagine and implement a viable response to its possible eventuality.[18]

In the command and control centers of SAGE and its progeny, hypothet-ical renderings created by radar and other electronic surveillance technolo-gies were displayed on screens. The "ground environment" was effectively virtualized on these displays. They presented a schematic map of a more complex territory of cultural, political, ethnic, individual, ecological, and biological diversity. Operators used a light gun interface device to target particular flight trajectories on the screens for further evaluation (Figure 2). Benjamin Woolley recounts that the light gun was first invented to aid in the testing procedures of Project Whirlwind. It was used to select one dot on the oscilloscope display, thereby identifying the corresponding memory device—that is, a particular vacuum tube component of the original Whirl-wind computer.[19] The adoption of this diagnostic instrument in the SAGE interface system represents one of the most significant innovations of the SAGE project for the subsequent history of virtualization: the discovery of the possibilities of this precision mapping of the technical componentry of the virtual display for the mapping of the virtual onto the real for precision, realtime control.

The virtualization of the real that in other quarters has occupied the attention of theorists of technoculture, postmodernity, and the information age was first undertaken as a key plank of the technoscientific solution to the problem of defense from nuclear attack. What was key in the SAGE project was the (desired) realtime, semiautomated control of the response to a jet airborne attack. The map display, constantly updated with the latest informa-tion on the projected trajectories of incoming enemy forces, was the primary command interface with the networked digital computer and communica-tions system through which the response was managed and monitored. Pro-tection of the ground environment was to be achieved in and through the doubling of that environment by the virtual display. This doubling aimed to make possible the preemptive realtime control of eventuality within the

FIGURE 2   The SAGE light gun interface device; courtesy of the MITRE Corporation.

parameters of the real space mapped on screen. Like the smart weapons and the tactical and strategic simulation training technologies also being developed in this era, the success (however imagined) of the system rested on the effectiveness of its advance mapping of the real environment's potential eventuality—in this case, the very destruction of that real environment—and the execution of a controlling, preemptive gesture based on that mapping.

The design and deployment of digital computing and of video and communications technology in this realtime virtual control system was a crucial development for both military conceptions of nuclear war and for the future course of digital computing applications in the domestic sphere. When one recalls the enormous influence of these projects on the development of computing technology and its dissemination into the commercial sector, it is not difficult to accept the suggestion of Andy Pickering that the constitution of postmodernity can best be traced in the outcomes of the military technoscientific assemblage from World War II onward.[20] The postmodern concern with simulation and the virtual can be seen to be in no small part the fallout of projects such as SAGE aimed at the realtime, virtual control of eventuality. Rather than an ironic or cynical response to the modernization project arising from a sense of the exhaustion of its possibilities, a critique of its rationalist underpinnings, or boredom with its aesthetic doctrines of purity and functionalism, the postmodern turn is perhaps better envisaged as arising from a productive anxiety about the hypermodern military technoscientific future.

SIMNET: The Training Vehicle of the Future

Having discussed virtualization and cybernetics as important military-led innovations in technoscientific research and development that have had a profound effect on shaping the emergence of computerized technoculture, I now turn to the third element of most relevance to our concerns in this study: the development of networked simulation training in the 1980s–1990s by the U.S. Department of Defense. This is significant for a number of reasons, not least of which is for the way it leads into and then forms a central part of what has become known recently as the military-entertainment complex. This term designates the modification of the existing military-industrial complex installed in the Eisenhower administration as the predominant model for the logistical organization of American society and the American economy to serve the nation's strategic ends. As the term indicates, the relations between commercial enterprises, in particular media and entertainment firms, and government funding and development agencies shifted significantly in the reformation of military technical innovation in the post–cold war period. SIMNET—the principal simulation networking project funded by the U.S. Department of Defense in this period—has been an important transitional vector for this shift. It also brought together elements of the two earlier developments in crystallizing a technics and rationale for computer simulation that mark much contemporary video game and digital technoculture.

From the 1950s to the 1980s the Department of Defense, through agencies such as the Defense Advanced Research Projects Agency (DARPA, formerly ARPA, the Advanced Research Projects Agency), funded the majority of advanced research in realtime computer simulation and associated technologies, such as computer graphics and networking. In the post–cold war period, however, a more entrepreneurial approach by the Department of Defense toward the computer industry at large (and the graphics and entertainment sectors in particular) was mandated by federal government policy. This was partly a fiscally motivated shift that the early Clinton administration saw as necessary in the wake of the excessive military spending of the Reagan presidency. However, it was also a change demanded by the new industrial landscape where the computing technology developed in the cold war era was now part of the wider industrial-technological landscape.

This shift, combined with the massive increase in commercial computer research and development after the expansion of personal computing from the late 1970s, has led to a situation in which defense-funded research is not the principal source of technical innovation in the same way it was in the cold war period. Timothy Lenoir and Henry Lowood point out that if the groundwork for computing and simulation technology was laid by military research and development in the 1950s–1980s, since then, the traffic between military and nonmilitary innovations has been increasingly significant in driving cutting-edge developments.[21]

SIMNET was the major DARPA simulation training technology project of the 1980s–1990s and made critical innovations leading to remotely networked computer simulation in real time. SIMNET made groundbreaking developments both for military simulation training and for realtime multiuser simulation practices, including contemporary online gaming in networked virtual environments. These include the development of economically viable distributed interactive simulation hardware and software and associated computer graphics and communications advances. Lenoir and Lowood also note the significance for design and implementation of the shift to "selective functional fidelity" principles of interface design (instead of the goal of complete realism, which was the orthodoxy in stand-alone simulators).[22] The "distributed net architecture" of SIMNET was used to construct local and "long haul nets" of simulators for moving and operating tanks and other vehicles, combat support elements, and the range of logistical and command communications facilities for two opposing simulated forces.[23]

SIMNET was in use by the U.S. armed forces by the end of the 1980s. Tank and armored vehicle units had extensive simulator training in preparation for the 1990–1991 Gulf war. This war provided a highly valued opportunity to the U.S. military to test and review the effectiveness of its weapons technologies and simulation training regimes. Indeed, as Lowood and Lenoir, among others, have pointed out, the entire Desert Storm campaign was based on plans developed in a war-gaming simulation of the crisis that ran during the period after the occupation of Kuwait by Iraqi forces.[24]

In this manner, SIMNET technology, first used to anticipate the conflict and prepare combat units to fight it, was utilized immediately after its conclusion as a means of recording its actual eventuality. It is more accurate to say that the conflict was used by SIMNET developers to review, refine, and improve its functioning as a training simulator. Lenoir and Lowood examine the postwar efforts to develop a simulated reconstruction of an important tank battle from the short ground campaign of the Gulf war. The Battle of 73 Easting, named after a military map grid reference, took place early in the ground campaign between armored units of the U.S. and Iraqi armies and resulted in a decisive victory for the U.S. forces. The battle took place in a swirling sandstorm, but only U.S. units were equipped with infrared vision systems. This was one of the important determinants of the resulting destruction of Iraqi forces by U.S. armor that remained largely unscathed.[25]

Having trained soldiers for hundreds of hours on SIMNET simulators as part of their preparation for the battle, the U.S. Army saw an opportunity to analyze the effectiveness of such training through a detailed simulation of the battle. Led by the Institute for Defense Analyses Simulation Center (IDA), a team composed of SIMNET project principals and contractors and assisted by the Army's Engineer Topographical Laboratories began to "record" the battle.[26] This process involved the acquisition of every possible form of material record of the battle (at least, from the side of the victors) for the purpose of constructing the simulation's database, including debriefings with U.S. Army participants, battle site surveys, action logs, recordings of radio transmissions, tape recordings and diaries made by soldiers, overhead reconnaissance photography before and after the battle, observation records of battle wreckage locations, black box recordings from U.S. Army vehicles, tracks in the sand of vehicle and missile trajectories, and digital mappings of the terrain captured by radar and lasers.[27]

The simulation that was created on the basis of this recording effort could replay the course of the actual battle as one of its possibilities. It is the very raison d'être of simulation techniques, however, to provide for the projection forward from initial conditions toward hypothetical futures. The value of the project was essentially as projective technique, not in its capability as a virtually enhanced staff ride over the battle space, illustrating what happened at different points in the timeline of the battle. "As a computer simulation with programmable variables," Lowood and Lenoir state, "the scenario could be replayed with different endings."[28] They have this to say about how the project was seen by the IDA and the U.S. military:

> The Battle of 73 Easting was viewed as confirmation of Jack Thorpe's original vision for the SIMNET of using networked simulation technology to use history to prepare for the future. It set the standard of a future genre of training simulations. The simulation provided a link with history, but at the same time a dynamic interactive training vehicle for the future.[29]

In other words, the 73 Easting simulation would work toward the cybernetic ideal of a system (war) "governed by time-reversible causal stories." The past event, the actual battle—at least, the battle as accessible through the database of the victors—would be transformed into a model time pattern, control over which is to be taught to soldiers, whose future will form part of the pattern. An implicit claim is being made here about the superiority of simulation over the historical rendering of the battle record as forms of preparation for the future. A series of questions arises in attempting to understand the purport of this affirmation of simulation's value by its proponents: What was history's use before its adoption by networked simulation technology? Is not history itself another form dedicated toward the encounter with the future? As a recording and interpretation of past events, history is always produced for others to examine. As such, it is always a future-oriented production. Indeed, it is only on this basis that simulation can utilize its techniques for selectively recording and arranging the available materials and accounts of the event in the construction of its database. What, then, is the impact on history of its modification in and as simulation? Is the "link with history" provided by simulation—through its translation of historical records into the simulation database—fatal to historical discourse as a hermeneutic, critical process? Moreover, if simulation is a "dynamic interactive training vehicle for the future," what is its impact on the future as such? Is this vehicle one that determines in advance the terrain of the future through the virtualization of that terrain?

These questions concerning the relation between history and simulation are absolutely central to our concern in this book to understand the animating principles of the logistical tendency so influential in the ongoing development of contemporary digital technoculture. I will return to consider these in the following chapters to examine the part video games play in that technoculture. For now, I think the most important point to note is the way that simulation was, and is, promoted as a new and superior form of anticipatory engagement in the future through a more or less explicit comparison with history. This comparison tended to relegate history to the past by implying that only simulation concerns itself with the future. History becomes a resource for this preferred, proactive, and instrumental orientation to a future whose decisive characteristic in this military technoscientific frame is as potential threat.

The degree to which simulation is integral to both the planning and execution of the military operations of the wealthy industrialized states today is indicated by the trajectory of the 73 Easting project. In relation to the logistical dissemination of this technics and manifesto of the simulational future beyond narrowly military contexts, writers such as Lenoir and Lowood, J. C. Herz, Ed Halter, Roger Stahl, and Nick Dyer-Witherford and Greig de Peuter have been astute in observing the increased interactions between military and commercial research and development efforts in simulation, realtime networking, and related areas since the 1990s.[30] The shifts in Department of Defense project funding policy, the research and development culture, and the education and career trajectories of important innovators have been well documented. Some key milestones along the way toward the military-entertainment complex include the U.S. Marine Corps' experimental adaptation of the classic first-person shooter game *Doom II* (id Software, 1994) as a training system for squad tactics. This was arguably the first official military licensing of a commercial off-the-shelf (COTS) game. *Falcon 4.0* (Spectrum Holobyte, 1998) was the first COTS flight simulator to be adapted by the U.S. Air Force for pilot training. After 9/11, in the context of the Bush administration's massive boost to military and homeland security budgets, the Institute for Creative Technologies was established at the University of Southern California with funds from the U.S. Army to facilitate collaboration from entertainment industry creatives in the development of more believable and sophisticated military training simulation scenarios.[31] Military, entertainment, and education partnerships such as these revivified and diversified the linkages between these sectors of the American national logistical potential. From this point of view, the military-entertainment complex is the logical—or logistical—consequence of the military-industrial complex.

The significance of these developments is clear: the cross-fertilization of military and entertainment prerogatives and applications of computer simulational technics and practices is a true complex, where the two strands are folded together in such a way that it does not make any sense to oppose them. While they can be distinguished from each other in their specifrc fields of pertinence, practice, sociopolitical and cultural significance, and legal framing, they must be approached in their complexity as composed together in their mutual codevelopment. A truly viable critical engagement with the entertainment forms of our contemporary technoculture must proceed on the basis of this complexity. Indeed, it must understand its task as making a difference in the course of the unfolding of this compositional dynamic.

In this chapter I have examined three important moments in the military-technoscientific emergence of the computerized simulational practices that have become the platform for video gaming, which is today a major military-entertainment form, commercial application, and expanding social, educational, and training technology. The cybernetic approach to modeling complex phenomena, realtime interactive control through virtualization, and SIMNET's expansion of computerized networked simulation toward the integration of simulated and real events have each greatly influenced the contemporary technocultural framing of existence. They should not be understood simply as moments in the completed history of computerization. They are better approached as tendencies—the cybernetic, the virtualizing, and the converging of real and simulation—that continue to play their part in the ongoing compositional dynamics driving the evolution of technoculture, war, and simulation. They lead us toward the value of computer games in the midst of these dynamics. As computer simulational forms native to this milieu and this process, computer games offer a privileged view of these developmental dynamics.

2 Select Gameplay Mode

Simulation, Criticality, and the Chance of Video Games

Alternative reality games (ARGs) have grown in popularity since the turn of the most recent century. Players are engaged to uncover some mystery or puzzle by searching for clues in documents, on Web sites, via communication with other players or game-created automatic agents ("bots"), and so forth. The multimodal means by which ARGs are played is key to their appeal: the games are played not on a screen like a video game, but in and among the spaces and routines of everyday life.

By mapping a game over the real space of normal activity, alternative reality games virtualize reality for the players who play the game where their everyday nongame lives usually take place. While they can be established and played through Internet access at fixed locations—home, office, Internet café—the possibilities offered by more recent locative media (mobile Internet and geographical positioning communications) are especially felicitous for the design and play of these kinds of multimodal games. In a manner symmetrical to how persistent virtual worlds such as *Second Life* (Linden Labs, 2003) pose the question of the reality of the virtual online life, alternative reality games pose the question of the virtuality of the real world. In the tradition of the treasure hunt and the domestic murder mystery game, they convert real life for a time into a space for play, suspending its normal character as milieu of the player's serious activities. In the words of T. L. Taylor and Beth E. Kolko's account of a 2001 game, *Majestic* (Electronic Arts,

2001), the "boundary work" required by a technocultural milieu increasingly negotiated by means of digital informational and simulational forms is exemplified in alternative reality games.[1]

Alternative reality games are a further instance, and indeed a further complication, of the uncertain status of computer games today. Within the field of digital games studies, efforts to define the essential characteristics of video games have not ceased after more than a decade of research. This is despite efforts to move on from the major debate about the core of the video game object of study between theorists approaching games as continuous with existing media forms (sharing narrative, iconographic elements, and appeal) and those seeking a more game-centered approach to the significance of video games in their specificity. What alternative reality games raise, arguably more explicitly than games played on a console or on stationary computer screens, is the relation between simulated game space, and game time, and the apparently real space and time that they seem to suspend, relativize, and render less real as a function of their taking place.

This chapter asks what video games are and why they are important factors in our shifting sense of space and time in the contemporary digital age. I want to explain how my framing of the object under consideration responds to existing theories of technoculture and technocultural forms. The analysis and interpretation of video games from a cultural and media studies perspective is a relatively recent enterprise. I thus hope to contribute something to games studies' ongoing groundwork of defining its object among those other emerging media phenomena of digital technoculture. At the same time, as I demonstrated in the previous chapter, video games continue and transform technoscientific and technocultural developments going back to the early post–World War II period. Beyond that, games themselves have a much longer backstory; indeed, some claim that game playing goes right back to before the conjectural origins of human being as such.

Definitions and theoretical approaches to the topic in question are always selective and must decide where they will begin tracing the origins of the phenomenon and what for them is most significant to include in the analysis. They are part of the argument rather than a neutral gesture of delineating a preexisting object for consideration. As I situate video games in theoretical and contextual terms, it is important to keep in mind that this is done vis-à-vis other positionings. I will speak of the ambition and the stakes of these efforts to name video games and delineate the field of pertinence for describing, interpreting, developing, and using them.

Simulation and Postmodern Critical Thought

I approach video games as computer simulational forms, emphasizing their historical pedigree in postwar military technoscientific research and development, and in the overarching logistical trajectory of the reorganization of all spheres of society as potential resources for war. Moreover, as hinted at in the previous chapter, this approach responds to more familiar accounts of the social and technocultural change that made itself apparent in the 1980s. These accounts addressed various aspects of phenomena commonly thematized from the 1980s under the rubric of postmodernism. The significations of this term are legion, from socioeconomic approaches influenced by Daniel Bell's notion of the postindustrial system of production, to those following Jean-François Lyotard's account of the collapse of the grand narratives of the West's cultural legitimation, to Fredric Jameson's Marxist critique of postmodernism as the cultural form of late capitalism.[2] Simulation was prominent in many writings dedicated to understanding the crisis of modernity and modernist art and culture in the 1980s. Jean Baudrillard's thematization of simulation as leitmotif of a collapse of the circuits through which cultural forms of expression and signification come to mean something was undoubtedly the most influential, if often poorly understood, conceptualization of simulation in much postmodern critical discourse and artistic practice.[3]

To understand simulation, and video games as the major computer simulational form of today's technoculture, differently from this postmodern account of simulation is part of the project and argument of this study. But it is also to make connections to this phase of critical and cultural analysis that from today's perspective can be seen as the first major wave of work struggling to understand the emerging computer-based technoculture. Its key concerns, for example, include the following: simulation, media-led saturation and preemption of real politics and cultural expression, the end of history, virtual reality, emergent globalization of manufacturing and consumption, and recombinatory, citational aesthetics. These are the parents of today's critical work on globalizing, realtime, convergent digital technocultures. To a significant extent, however, the early media studies work on video games tended to take them as new forms needing a new conceptualization distinct from existing media forms. This is nowhere more evident than in the way writers such as Espen Aarseth and Gonzalo Frasca identified games as simulations on a computer platform. Aarseth was at pains to point out the inappropriateness of approaches used for conventional noninteractive media forms, while Frasca drew on systems theory to define games as simulational forms with a radically different nature from traditional representational forms.[4]

While both have something important to say about how the specificity of video games can and has been defined, my point here is that thinking about how games bear out or challenge 1980s conceptions of a soon-to-be-pervasive simulational state of technocultural reality was not on their agenda. Rather, what was on the agenda was approaching video games as new kinds of interactive experiences emerging from commercial entertainment sectors but with artistic, educational, and critical potential. The status of the reality of video game experience did become a focus of research when online multiplayer networks were analyzed as forms of social network and community. T. L. Taylor's *Play between Worlds* led the field here.[5] This work tended to rely on ethnographic and social science approaches in its efforts to deny mainstream opinion about the antisocial nature of extended engagements in online virtual worlds. It argued convincingly that electronically mediated social relations were neither wholly separate from real-world social networks nor illusory because ungrounded in real-world spatial proximity.

This work to establish the legitimacy of examining the growth of game-centered online sociality against simplistic mainstream media accounts of the isolation of young players in virtual realities was not without merit. I would argue, however, that it shared a somewhat positivist approach to video game phenomena with the work of ludologists such as Aarseth and Frasca. This is most evident in its forgetting of the critical reflexive questioning that the best of postmodernist work inaugurated in coming to terms with the first stage of digital technocultural changes. Mark Poster gives a highly pertinent example of this challenge of postmodern critical discourse to conventional framings of media phenomena when he states that virtual reality systems, exemplified by flight simulators "in their military and game varieties," both continue and exacerbate the "Western trend of duplicating the real by means of technology" for the purposes of better controlling it.[6] "Yet this doubling, as many have noted, puts the original into question: the virtual upsets the stability of the real in ways that were perhaps unintended but certainly unwanted by proponents of the modern."[7] The modern is usually associated with progress toward an ever-improving state of social existence via rational application of science and technology, leading to better levels of education, health, and wealth, and in their wake increased political participation, all reflected in cultural production showing greater functional efficiency and aesthetic coherence. Poster identifies the desire for and design of control as pervasive in this technological rationale. Paradoxically, it is the effort made toward technical realization of this control—through the development of virtual reality systems for Poster, and of computer simulation more generally—that produces an unanticipated destabilizing of reality, the very object of this controlling desire and design.

What is meant here by *reality?* This was a highly significant question for postmodern critical thought, one that has become less urgent in more recent times as Western technoculture habituates people to socializing and working in and across virtual and real spaces, encountering local and distributed networks of friends and colleagues. Indeed, I would venture that the question of the reality of the virtual has become less a critical concern and more a part of the amusement or entertainment value of innovations in digital media forms. For example, the interest that sustains participants in the virtual online persistent world *Second Life* could be characterized as a fascination (monetized by many inhabitants) with the reality of their virtual lives, homes, goods, property speculation, social interactions, and so forth. In the emerging field of augmented reality and pervasive gaming, the fascination is with the digitally enabled virtualization of real space as resource or affordance for the game's taking place.

This kind of musing about what reality is—both as amusement and, it must be said, in much of the consideration of virtualizing technics disseminated from the more critically acute postmodern theorists—misses the most significant aspects of what the rise of simulation means for reality. The ontological inquiry about whether the virtual duplication of something is real or not is a more simplistic and comfortable question because it leaves untroubled the status of the real as a stable category for interpreting and placing phenomena. The question critical postmodernism was articulating in different registers was, on the other hand, about whether reality can retain its established modernist character as a state of social, cultural, political, and aesthetic amelioration in progress. Can it still be understood as such, using those modernist assumptions and rationales, in the face of the major changes that are now identified with the passage toward digital technologically mediated globalization? Or has the expansion and sophistication of the rational technical instrumentalization of control technics in fact altered the real, its developmental trajectory, and its capacity to support human individual and cultural becoming?

For Baudrillard, this was articulated as a question about whether established critical or analytic discourse in the humanities or social sciences could say anything significant about reality anymore. This questioning was conducted reflexively, through meditations on changing social, cultural, and economic phenomena. As Rex Butler has made apparent in his insightful commentary on Baudrillard's project, most of those who have responded to Baudrillard's pronouncements on hyperreality and simulation have tended to underestimate, ignore, or completely miss this important dimension of his work as a provocation to critical work seeking to define and produce knowledge about its real-world object of study.[8]

Baudrillard's most influential analysis for the wider field of postmodern critical and cultural work—notwithstanding the fact that he never used this description of either his work or of the phenomena he concerned himself with—was of the simulational hyperreal. This was characterized as a shift in the existing relations between reality and its representation. Simulation upsets these relations, opening a passage from the representational logic of the original and its copy to a situation in which the precedence or priority of an original, preexistent reality is undermined by the preeminence given to the modeling of phenomena that then function in place of the former original. Baudrillard uses cybernetic and computer terminology to elaborate how simulation operates this transformation of representation:

> The real is produced from miniaturized units, from matrices, memory banks and command models—and with these it can be reproduced an indefinite number of times. It no longer has to be rational, since it is no longer measured

against some ideal or negative instance. It is nothing more than operational. In fact, since it is no longer enveloped by an imaginary, it is no longer real at all. It is a hyperreal, the product of an irradiating synthesis of combinatory models in a hyperspace without atmosphere.[9]

This characterization of the hyperreal as the new reality produced by operational, computerized, interactive command models is redolent with the cybernetic approach to phenomena examined in the previous chapter. In play here is an elegantly inferred critique of how cybernetics and the computerized society it fostered are the extreme exacerbation of modern rational desire and design. This has led paradoxically to the very collapse of the collective imagining of a future better than the past that was the condition of the modern rationale.

Taken as an analysis of historical sociocultural phenomena, Baudrillard's account of a hyperreal ushered in by simulation has distinct parallels with other critical projects going on around the same time. Lyotard's account in *The Postmodern Condition* of information society and the erosion of the orienting grand narratives of modern sociality, and Virilio's analysis in *Pure War* of a logistical corruption of traditional strategicopolitical logics both share aspects of this overview of a major crisis in modern ways of understanding reality and how to critically evaluate its development.[10] Even more than in these and similar projects to understand a dynamic contemporary situation that did not seem to make sense according to the usual frameworks of interpretation, Baudrillard pushed the implications of his analysis to the limit. This was also to push back against the enabling assumption that analytical work could represent and interpret the real. The simulation of reality according to models of audiovisual representation on television and other mainstream media, social science modeling of social phenomena, political and marketing solicitation, surveying and polling of the masses, and so forth were all submitted to provocative performative meditations on the very possibility of legitimately establishing a viable position from which to define and analyze the object of study.[11] The former Marxist sociologist challenged the discourses producing knowledge about society and culture to show how they were not functioning parts of the simulational hyperreal deterring people from disbelieving its reality.

This challenge to the very possibility of representing external, experienced events and phenomena became, inevitably, a mise-en-abyme where simulation and its representation in writing tended to collapse into each other. Baudrillard himself has said that his speculations about simulation started to drive him mad.[12] The ontological undecidability between what is theoretical projection and what is empirical, independent phenomenality overtook the critical purport of his writing on simulation. We are still left with the challenge of what to make of the unfolding of exterior events and how to intervene in, support, or oppose them.[13] This has led some working with the legacy of postmodern critical inquiry toward a renewed engagement with the materiality of simulational forms. Poster, for instance, points out that Baudrillard's consideration of the material specificities of computer-based media such as virtual reality systems is limited.[14] Of course, materiality as an established Marxist critical concept was included in Baudrillard's challenge to theory's purchase on its object. Poster calls for a "new materialism" that would be competent to account for the "installation of interfaces that unite humans and machines in new configurations of agency."[15]

Paying attention to the specificities of new mediations of social and cultural expression and experience is certainly a necessary element in renewing a viable critical encounter with contemporary technoculture. Much of the work on video games has focused on these specifics of online sociality and virtual experience. It is a mistake, however, to completely forget the questions that Baudrillard, and postmodern critical work more generally, posed to classic modernist interpretive models of reality's nature and developmental dynamic. Consequently, any new materialism of digital technoculture must think again about what materiality means in the era of simulational forms that have developed and proliferated on the basis of a revision of the reality of matter in cybernetic and informational theories and technics. This amounts to more than the provision of newer forms of representational and communications technologies that enable more extended and more instantaneous interactions. These do not simply update the means of production and amend the relations of production that emerge on the basis of the former. They have remodeled the expectations, intentions, and recollections of the people who are part of both the production and consumption of reality. This has not only blurred the production versus consumption distinction, as many have noted about the information economy. Understanding this remodeling of the real would be considered a task of ideological analysis in classic Marxist theory, but the very opposition of matter and ideology is in question today in the era of virtual materiality. As theorists such as Jameson and Bill Nichols showed, the affordances of the material technics of digital media and communications have destabilized the relations of production and distribution and rendered them indeterminate, putting into crisis both the workings and the interpretation of political economy.[16] Because immaterial things like ideas, innovation, and experience are now central to the information economy, it is crucial to include these in any critical conceptualization of what is material to an understanding of contemporary technoculture.

Computer Games within Technocultural Facticity

In order to formulate an approach to video games as key elements of the digital remodeling of technoculture, it is necessary to think about games materially and technically, but in a way that does not reduce their use in gameplay to an ideological artifact of consumption. Computer games— how they are designed, played, and modified—are material practices involving complex technical objects operating in concert with each other and with humans via networked communications channels. They both enable and challenge our efforts to say something significant about them and the world they form part of today. As existent elements of what Martin Heidegger called the facticity of world historiality, they are part of a realized ensemble of sociocultural and technical elements that go together in systems of usability and intelligibility.[17] They are given to the player and to anyone to use, modify, and consider on the basis of this coherence—that is, as elements of a wider everydayness that they instantiate and perpetuate.

Of course, debates rage about the scope, nature, dynamics, and prospective development of this systematicity. For in no place is this systematicity the same as it is elsewhere, even if the prevailing tendency of globalization is precisely toward this end. Moreover, the ethnic, political, and technocultural coherence underpinning this system in any given place is fictional, desired rather than actual. It is a possibility opened by a particular factical heritage rather than something ever experienced even by those who gave us these objects and techniques. Indeed, there is no us, no culture, that is not fictional in this sense.

However imaginary or disputed, this coherence through which one encounters computer games has a determining influence on the nature and potential of that encounter. Each instantiation of the coherence of facticity, however, always has the potential to perpetuate it differently, to change the dynamic of the procedures for adopting the complex of interactions between the existent elements. That is, each concretization of the system of objects, people, and the relations between these has what Bernard Stiegler has called an "idiosyncratic" potential to alter and reinvent the system's ongoing reproduction of itself.[18] A theory dedicated to mapping the system through its concrete examples always runs the risk of missing this idiosyncratic potential and its implications for the theory.

Stiegler proposes that ethnic differentiation in the human should be understood as a process whose motor has been the idiosyncratic adoption of technical innovations for a very long time. It has been so long, in fact, that the development of humans since the stabilization of the cortical evolution of human brains can only be explained as what he calls epiphylogenesis, a biological–cultural process of differentiated development of the human. The epiphylogenetic passes through lineages of the factical adoption of technical prosthetic supports that humans used to live longer and then better. Here is Stiegler:

> Epiphylogenesis, a recapitulating, dynamic, and morphogenetic (phylogenetic) accumulation of individual experience (epi), designates the appearance of a new relation between the organism and its environment, which is also a new state of matter. If the individual is organic organized matter, then its relation to its environment (to matter in general, organic or inorganic), when it is a question of a *who*, is mediated by the organized but inorganic matter of the *organon*, the tool with its instructive role (its role *qua* instrument), the *what*. It is in this sense that the *what* invents the *who* just as much as it is invented by it.[19]

Our efforts to understand the nature, meaning, and purpose of computer games both derive from and are challenged by this ensemble of practices and experiences composing our epiphylogenetic technocultural facticity.

This ensemble coalesces in what Stiegler characterizes as the "metastable" connection between the individual and his or her sociotechnical milieu, a dynamic connection constitutive of human being as technical being. The interiority of human consciousness and the exteriority of his or her social and cultural milieu are, in this view, radically co-constitutive. That is, no interiority of human thought, reflection, or memory can exist without the exteriority of technically mediated interaction with the external world—no theory of culture without the human and technically constituted milieu of cultural existence; no theory of history without what he calls the mnemotechnical archive of objects, tools, rituals, texts, and other recordings of past human experience; no theory of the image without fabricated images, and so on.

This perspective on the co-constitutive relation between exteriority and interiority is more appropriate than conventional Marxist materialism to tackling the challenge to critical thought posed by the virtualization of materiality. It also provides an answer of sorts to Baudrillard's reflexive mise-en-abyme where theory finds itself trying decide whether it is itself part of the simulation of reality. Baudrillard's theory of the end of the real in simulation depends on his examples of this (cybernetic models, hyperreal images, and digital sound, for example) as much as it produces these as part of its argument. These elements of material facticity are co-constitutive of the spiraling introspectivity of his speculations.

Of course, Baudrillard's writings, along with all the other mnemotechnical recordings of individual human experience, are themselves part of this facticity. This means that recorded theories are part of the material practices and projected systems of coherence with which one must struggle to interpret one's chosen examples. That is, theories are themselves exterior actions that have an impact on the development of other technical objects. Consequently, I argue that computer games and the different things written, spoken, and otherwise recorded about them are continually in play in the ongoing concretization of computer games in and as contemporary technoculture. The habitual understanding of contemporary existence in and through this technocultural moment is therefore at stake at least in part in our habitual orientation to computer games.

And by all accounts this is an increasingly significant part. Industry lobbyists and commentators cite revenue statistics to indicate the comparability of scale and reach between Hollywood and the commercial games industry.[20] More astutely, other analysts are identifying the way in which computer games are becoming a central component in the transmedia diversification of the entertainment business. Films, video games, Web sites, television series, toys and merchandising, comics, magazines, and novels can all be envisaged outcomes of a contemporary commercial entertainment project.[21] Elsewhere, influential games theorists make predictions about the evolution of computer games into the predominant leisure-time pursuit of future generations. For Edward Castronova, the "synthetic worlds" of massively multiplayer online role-playing games will evolve into one of the main habitats of future populations.[22] Gonzalo Frasca calls simulation—having identified games as being essentially simulations—the "form of the future."[23] By this, he means that not only will games be more important in the future than narrative and dramatic cultural forms, but that this is in no small part because, as simulations, they concern themselves more essentially with the future than these traditional forms of recording and processing human experience. Narrative deals with the past, he argues, while drama is interested in the present moment of performance. Simulation is able to ask "what if?" questions from a grounding in a general situation, the elements of which are modeled in the construction of the simulation.

Place Your Bets: The Stakes of Computer Game Theory and Practice

I will give closer consideration to this manifesto-like articulation of the rightful destiny of simulational forms in chapter 7. For now, it serves as an index of a much broader current of the discursive concretization of computer games as a form destined to become the central component of entertainment and audiovisual culture. The future anticipated here is what is in play and what is at stake in this process. The game being played according to this metaphorics is gambling—that is, betting for stakes. Some game theorists will question whether gambling activities can be rightly thought of as games because they have real-world stakes that constantly threaten to destroy the nonserious, playful quality thought to be a core characteristic of genuine game-based activity. Jesper Juul, for instance, will relegate gambling to the no-man's-land between games and nongames in his diagrammatic depiction of concentric circles of games, gamelike activity, and nongame forms.[24] I would propose, however, that the way the concretization of computer games wagers the future leads us toward a view that all activities are in the zone between games and nongames. To play a computer game today—or to think and write about it—is to be part of this concretization, to adopt this facticity, to participate in its economic, logistical, technocultural becoming. Whether ignored, denied, sublated, or explicitly confronted, it is always a question of how to adopt this becoming. We are all betting on the future of computer games, with, against, or in some other orientation to their predominant becoming under the aegis of what Stiegler calls the "programming industries."[25]

The program industries are the media and communications industries—those that today tend to monopolize control of the mnemotechnical archive by which the material practices and experiences of the past are stored and passed down as culture, heritage, and tradition. This has become integrated with the technical system of modern industrial production in general, a situation that Stiegler identifies as the unique and critical factor in the contemporary technocultural milieu.[26] The outcome of this integration is that the program industries orient themselves principally to the needs of the technical system of production. The development of computer gaming as a proliferating commercial enterprise at the heart of the media and entertainment industries exemplifies in many respects the expansion of global media culture through integrative cross-media publishing, marketing, distribution, and exhibition systems. This is borne out by emerging studies of the global political economy of online game business and play, research on the legal status of game content created by end users, analysis of the potentials and problems of emerging online communities of international participants formed around particular commercial games, or game projects striving for alternatives to hegemonic Western political and technocultural value systems embedded in mainstream computer games, to mention some principal themes of the first decade of computer game studies.

Inasmuch as they are constituted out of the relations between war, simulation, and technoculture, computer games offer a privileged place from which to articulate this globalizing technocultural tendency with the logistical tendency informing military, industrial, entertainment, and technoscientific progress since World War II. The two, the global and the logistical, may be seen as alternative adumbrations of the one tendency. From an historical perspective, one might propose that this tendency has mutated in a fashion corresponding to the passage from the cold war to the post–cold war period, the transitional period in which computer games first became a significant mainstream entertainment form. This, at least, is the hypothesis that emerges from my reflection on the factical milieu given to me, one that would merit a far more substantial articulation and demonstration than this book on computer games alone can provide. What it can do, however, through examining the transitional phenomena of computer games, is search for the continuities between the current dynamics of global transformation and the earlier period, so crucial for its technoscientific and economic emergence. Discovering these is necessary in order to better understand the future globalization seeks to program for us.

For this is what the program industries ultimately seek to accomplish: the global programming of future patterns of consumption and related behavior supporting consumption cycles. Their overarching tendency is to promote what Stiegler calls the hypersynchronization of consciousnesses.[27] This would aim to achieve the economies of scale required to amortize the large investments not only in entertainment software and programming, but in the industrial production of commodities marketed through media and communication technologies. I would add that this tendency toward hypersynchronization perpetuates the impulses toward preemptive control and the virtual, remote regulation of contingency that I have already shown are core to the logistical development of the postwar computer age. In any event, as Stiegler and many other commentators on globalization have pointed out, this tendency toward hypersynchronization directly challenges the processes of cultural and ethnic differentiation and diversification enacted through local, idiosyncratic adoptions of the existing factical heritage.

One can see everywhere, however, evidence that globalization generates the uncertainty and contingency it bets on programming out of existence. From, for example, the increasingly uncertain trajectory of the U.S.-led war on terror in Iraq and Afghanistan, to the systemic failure of nation-states in Africa and Asia, to the unanticipated adoption of new technologies (computer viruses, hacking, identity theft, cyberterrorism, the vast Internet porn industry, and mobile phone use in radical political activism and criminal or subversive activities), to school massacres with military assault rifles, to the boom in human trafficking and forced labor, to increasing (as opposed to decreasing) world poverty and global disease pandemics, to global warming phenomena, to the perpetual stream of crises and catastrophes that constitutes the news—all testify to the inability of systems and practices for regulating eventuality to maintain the planned order of production, distribution, and consumption. This is the landscape of accidents that Paul Virilio takes to be the paradoxically necessary component of the tendency to order everything in advance for the purposes of the globalizing military-industrial-entertainment complex.[28]

In the arena of computer gaming, phenomena such as unauthorized modding, gold farming, and postindustrial gaming sweatshops in developing countries, grief play, independent commercialization of online game elements, and activist intervention in commercial game worlds represent different instances of the unexpected adoption of programmed game activities. As in other spheres of technocultural activity, the game-producing/distributing companies quickly react to such phenomena in an attempt to reinstitute the pathway toward their objectives. A dialectic—or game—of preemption and exception ensues, each move betting on a different outcome.

This is another sense in which, as I argued above, to play a computer game is always to make some kind of bet on the future of computer gaming. Like all bets, this bet is also a way of mediating the future—one's own future. All play, perhaps, however removed it seems to be from the sphere of real life, has this serious component as part of its engagement of the player: it bets on the future of the play activity itself, and therefore on the future of the player to play, to be a recognizable player of this recognizable, meaningful activity. This bet attempts to mediate an anxiety about an uncertain future eventuality. In the most general sense, this anxiety is about one's own future identity as an individual member of a collective community of practice and significance, one in which the player may take his or her place for a time in the place of play. This points toward perhaps the most philosophical or meta-anthropological way of responding to Johan Huizinga's discovery in *Homo Ludens* of the etymological precedence of terms for play over terms designating the serious in a range of early and "primitive" languages.[29] Huizinga's research led him to conclude that the concept of play predates the concept of the serious across diverse ethnic groups, which only appears subsequently, if at all, and forms its meaning in opposition to the always pre-existent set of related concepts of play. If, however, all play is always already constituted via this serious engagement of the player with the future of his or her individual existence in a signifying community, then play takes its place as a mode of human engagement in existence, a kind of bet on the future that cannot not be serious, whatever else it may be.

To play is always, in a way, a life-and-death matter.[30] No surprise, then, that so many computer games play out mortal contests and violent conflict in virtual worlds. The logistical trajectories influencing computer game evolution—namely, their initial emergence (as computer games) from military technoscience and their subsequent convergence with war-fighting research and development in the military-entertainment complex—could be seen as confirmation of the overdetermined, mortally serious nature of contemporary computer game forms. On the other hand, these game forms offer themselves as the means of spending some time at play aside from, at least temporarily, the concerns of the real world. It is this separation of gameplay from real consequence that Birgit Richard defends in her criticism of the (in)famous adoption by the U.S. Marine Corps of the first-person shooter classic *Doom II*. For Richard, this gesture of mobilizing commercial gameplay in the service of serious military training, a milestone in the emergence of the military-entertainment complex, blurred the distinction between the symbolic death available to experience in computer games and the biological death that is the business of war fighters.[31]

I argue that the separation of the symbolic and the literal, the virtual and the actual, the playful and the serious is always itself in play in computer games. *Marine Doom* only makes the stakes of this play strikingly explicit. Gameplay mode is always a modality of the serious, while the serious is always already constituted in the wake of an act(ivity) that plays a gambling game with the nature and meaning of existence. The scope and opportunity for play that computer games provide as forms of entertainment is nonetheless what makes them so valuable an object of inquiry into the contemporary technocultural moment.

As entertainment forms, computer games rely on providing at least the illusion of a suspension of the practices and routines that go with the implementation of technoscientifically produced and regulated productivity. The

French origin of the word *entertainment*—*entretenir*, "to hold between"—captures this sense of a suspension from the temporal regime of productive endeavor missing in English terms like *pastime, fun,* or *leisure-time activity*.[32] As theorists and historians of leisure in modern capitalist society have demonstrated, this suspension is no doubt always circumscribed in carefully regulated regimes of commodification by what Horkheimer and Adorno called the culture industries, which serve "to mark the meaning of men from their exit from the factory in the evening, until their arrival at the timeclock the next morning."[33] For his part, Lev Manovich will discuss how in the postindustrial era of new media, this separation of work and leisure time has become less and less distinct. The user, he argues, follows a rapidly alternating rhythm of "cognitive multi-tasking" where work and leisure use of the computer interface tends to converge in the frenetic daily routine of computer usage.[34]

However temporary and circumscribed is the suspension of the serious that the player lives as player, it opens the possibility for reflective, idiosyncratic, and inventive adoptions of the technocultural facticity that computer games reproduce in a ludic mode. Games provide at least minimal relief from the rule of technoscientific reason dominating the conduct and means of work, education, politics, and all serious endeavor today. In doing so, they allow for the possibility of replaying the interactions between war, simulation, and technoculture out of which computer games come to us. Computer games, as objects dedicated to this suspension of the serious, have greater potential to play with this factical milieu of contemporary technoculture than computer programs dedicated to serious instrumental objectives and activities. In a discussion of critical and experimental computer game projects, Shuen-shing Lee identifies their critical potential as arising from a distortion of conventional "gaming etiquettes and design principles."[35] These distortions all "display a bent towards suspending the player's in-gaming immersion in favor of augmenting his off-gaming engagement."[36] I would agree with such a proposition, but it is important to keep in mind that this suspension depends on the first suspension of the serious and, moreover, that this passage between in-gaming and off-gaming concerns is not the exclusive discovery of art games or their critics, however valuable their interventions and insights may be.

The potential to produce reflection on the technocultural moment in which they take place connects computer games to the other forms of entertainment media both alongside of and against which they have grown up in the last few decades. As forms resting from the outset on the platform of digital computer-based technologies, they offer a privileged avenue for speculation on the centrality of computer technology to contemporary entertainment and technoculture generally, even though digital processes of image and sound production have transformed the earlier analog forms of cinema, television, radio, and print media. The implications of this difference are a recurrent theme in this book. Computer games play with the playing out of the war on contingency that has been an animating force throughout the course of the development of computers as simulation platforms capable of modeling the future as virtually accessible to preemption. This play is the source of the critical potential of games as signal examples of this development.

3 Logistical Space

Flight Simulators and the Animation of Virtual Reality

The world flown over is a world produced by speed.
—PAUL VIRILIO, *Pure War*

James Cameron's *Avatar* (2009) opens with a sequence in which the viewer flies over a computer-generated landscape. The groundbreaking 3-D graphics approach, disappear out of the frame, and rock and sway to provide the fulfilling illusion that you inhabit a real flying vehicle in a real, exotically beautiful space. You are the warrior–protagonist whose voice-over accompanies these images in an introspective reflection on the circumstances that have brought him to this strange world. This film, oscillating between its simplistic allegory of the costs of the United States' aggressive pursuit of its post-9/11 military adventures and its box office–breaking presentation of the spectacle of colonial conquest and the inevitable combat and destruction that ensues, knew enough to pay tribute to flight simulation at the very outset of its display of the most sophisticated immersive digital imaging of space and movement that digital cinema had to offer. Indeed, arguably the most impressive sequences of this film's showcase of the best and latest are the extensive flight sequences featured throughout. *Avatar* knows its history—at least, that of digital imaging and virtual reality (VR) technology.

This chapter examines the role played by computer-based flight simulation in the virtualization of space that is a common characteristic not only of computer games but of computer imaging and interaction design more generally today. I will look at the history of the development of flight simulation technologies from the 1960s, a development that is a central thread in the wider history of digital computing, imaging, and virtualization. What I am calling flight simulation's "logistical space"—after Paul Virilio's identification of the powerful logistical dynamic influencing post–World War II technocultural and political transformations—is invented as a result of the enormous financial investment and technical effort to make flight simulation into an effective training and research technology for the U.S. Air Force. It is important to understand flight simulation's development because the world is increasingly viewed in and through the virtualizing windows of computer interfaces, in simulations and other modelings, in satellite, radar, and other surveillance system screens, in infographical media such as geographical information systems, in global positioning system (GPS) device mappings, in Google Earth, and in other derivatives of U.S. military–technoscientific efforts toward global information dominance.

Flight simulation was a major operational goal for digital computing development in the immediate postwar period. I examined in chapter 1 the Semi-Automated Ground Environment (SAGE) air defense project, which was critical in the 1950s and 1960s for digital computing generally and in particular for the technologies of realtime control via a virtualized environment. It is important to recall that SAGE started life as Project Whirlwind, a U.S. Navy flight simulation system. During Whirlwind's development, something critical was uncovered for its later reinvention as a tracking and targeting system. In the late 1940s, the Whirlwind developers accidentally found the possibilities of realtime interactivity with a digital computer through its visual display. To explore this, they devised what Benjamin Woolley suggests is a proto–computer game involving the manipulation of an image of a bouncing ball, fourteen years before what is more commonly identified as the first computer game, *Spacewar* (1962), devised by researchers similarly occupied with military-funded projects at MIT.[1] A vector toward both the expansion of virtualized realtime control technologies and their future as ludic entertainment can be drawn from this chance discovery of a graphical interface to the calculative machinations of the digital computer.

The difficulty of arranging an account of the development of flight simulation into the compartments of military use on the one hand and technocultural and commercial application on the other is manifest here in the importance of Whirlwind's discovery of the interactive potential of virtual space for both the military and entertainment futures of flight simulation. Video games and high-tech military training and weapon system controls are both indebted to this opening up of the virtual arena of action. The interpretative coherence of the conventional categories ordering such historical and critical accounts, like military and commercial, wartime and peacetime, is strained by these overlapping trajectories. This is an exemplary instance of the intrinsic connections between war, technoculture, and simulation with which I am concerned in this study. It is also, by the same token, a clear indication of the challenge this co-constitutivity of phenomena, military and nonmilitary, technocultural and logistical, fun and deadly serious, presents to critical analysis.

This is the question posed to critical analysis by the military-entertainment complex. Flight simulation is at the heart of this folded complicity of computer-based technical systems for the virtualization of space and its realtime regulation. Andy Darley calls the flight simulator the "progenitor and paradigm for work in the area of what is dubbed (oxymoronically) 'artificial realities.'"[2] The computer game industry amounts to an offspring of the development in the 1960s of realtime computer-based flight simulation for the U.S. military. But this offspring has grown up, and since the 1990s, gaming and other commercial developments in simulation and digital imaging technologies increasingly feed into and influence military research and development. They can no longer be understood as a mere inheritor of military technoscientific innovations.[3]

Perhaps they never could. Woolley and Erkki Huhtamo both discuss the connections between the earliest flight simulation devices and modern fairground attractions such as roller coasters. The first flight simulators emerged not long after the invention of mechanized flight itself and were sustained commercially both through military contracts in World War I and their appearance in the guise of fairground amusements.[4] Like flight itself, flight simulation, ostensibly a nonmilitary, commercial technical innovation, almost immediately became a preoccupation of military forces in the United States and elsewhere.

I could pursue this question of the "true" origins of flight simulation further—a task that would necessitate exploring the connection between amusement park technology (and the leisure time they both produced and assumed) and industrial modernity more generally, and from there to the relations between modernity and war. In relation to this, Huhtamo discusses the way the fairground ride was in effect a modal variation of the serious world of technological modernity: "The railway, like the elevator, or like (in its recreational form) the Ferris wheel, puts stilled bodies in motion. What these mobile technologies make possible, in different forms, are the thrill and panic of agency at once extended and suspended."[5] The fairground became a space in which the everyday routines of modern mechanized existence were ritually reenacted in modified form, more intensively but at the same time in a temporary suspension of the real "game of life." The real stakes of this game, in this case death and mutilation in the wreckage of an accident involving urban transportation technologies, are evoked and avoided as a momentary amusement.

I would claim that the military adoption of the project of developing flight simulation set itself the task of rededicating such a space of modified reenactment to the serious task of training for war. It set about this task by appropriating the particular characteristics of the recreational form of the extension and suspension of the thrill and panic of mechanized agency. It is precisely this ambiguous suspension of the serious business of real life that lies at the heart of both the exemplary nature of computer games as instances of contemporary technoculture and their potential to provide profound critical insight into its dynamics. The fact that they come to us in no small degree from the military project of flight simulation and have become the chief recreational form of virtualizing technologies means they offer special access to these dynamics of the computer age.

From this perspective, a pursuit of the true origins of flight simulation is less relevant for my purposes here than one that illuminates the key dynamics put in play by this development. As in the case of cinema, radio, and video, and indeed all major media and communications technologies of industrial modernity, the key role of war and the preparation for war in its development can be taken as a starting point in assessing the nature and significance of that development.[6] What must be considered is the mutuality in logical—or, rather, logistical—potential of flight simulation as both military and domestic entertainment technology, as key entertainment form of digital media culture and as essential component of the history of modern military training and weapons systems development.

Flight simulation is so significant for our concerns that I will dedicate two chapters to exploring it. In this chapter, I will concentrate on aspects of the history and development of flight simulation technology in order to characterize its logistical space. In the following chapter, I will look closely at a commercially released flight simulation computer game's gametime in order to consider the different temporal engagement implied in the dissemination of flight simulation technologies across military and nonmilitary spheres. It is, of course, arbitrary and ultimately unsustainable to compartmentalize discussion of the spatial and temporal elements of flight simulation in this way. The virtualization of space constructed and conceptualized in flight simulation technology emerges alongside the shift to realtime engagement in the training scenario. Together, they opened the way toward a new mode and model of computer use. Nonetheless, taking space and time one at a time allows us to lay out in a coherent form the key elements active in what I suggested above was a major reanimation of space and time well underway today.

Let me add one final introductory comment concerning the theme of (re)animation I just evoked. Animation is an important but neglected theme in the consideration of the computer generated images that are at the heart of the power of our virtual spaces. Inasmuch as the computer imaging techniques first devised for flight simulation systems are not only central to digital media but also have been incorporated into the standard recording and image production equipment of the traditional technologies of film, television, and video, the examination of flight simulation serves to illuminate a major basis of the literal reanimation of the world through these imaging technologies. The world seen through the digital and interactive media that come to us on the model of flight simulation technology is not the same as that seen otherwise. In the epigraph to this chapter, Virilio says something similar about the "dromoscopic" vision—a vision produced at speed (*dromos* is Greek for "racecourse" or "roadway")—made available by powered flight. Flight simulation draws upon this dromoscopic reimaging of the world—a reimaging that is necessarily also a reimagining of the world.[7] As Alan Cholodenko has shown, every animatic process, technique, and system (including cinema and classic animation, as well as all the technical ways of endowing with life, motion, or both that follow from these) must be thought not only for what it brings to life, but also for its relation to the opposite of life—that is, to death, not only for what it makes appear, but for what disappears in that appearance.[8] I will need to consider flight simulation's logistical reanimation of space from this dual perspective.

Constructing the Potential of the Virtual: Military-Industrial Developments in Flight Simulation's Virtual Reality

While flight simulator devices were in use in World War I, the deployment of these devices for pilot training (as opposed to their alternative use as fairground attractions) was, like the use of airpower itself, limited and experimental rather than systematic and widespread. From the time in 1934 when the U.S. Army Air Corps purchased six of Edwin A. Link's Blue Box flight trainers to train Army pilots for instrument flying in bad weather, however, the history of the development of flight simulation has been the history of a systematic military-driven development. It is one that absorbed and then set the standard for nonmilitary commercial applications of flight simulation.[9] Link's 1929 invention—the patent application describes it as both a "novel, profitable training device" and "an efficient aeronautical training aid"—was based on pneumatic organ and player piano technology.[10] It articulated flight controls with a motion simulator system without any visual display component. The use of the Link Corporation's Blue Box and other simulator training devices in its wake expanded massively during World War II, when huge numbers of pilots needed to be trained quickly. The war firmly established flight simulation as a central component of military pilot training.

With the advent of video cameras in the early 1950s, "real-time visual feedback" for simulated flight became possible.[11] Cameras on motion platforms controlled by the simulator pilot through the flight controls moved over "terrain boards" containing scale models of ground scenery. These terrain boards were, according to James L. Davis, "akin to those found in model railroading," indicating a further point of connection between leisure-time practices and the serious business of the preparation and prosecution of war.[12] The video images produced by this coupling of the latest audiovisual technology with toy models were projected onto a screen substituting for the pilot's forward view out of the cockpit. The scale reduction of reality involved here is an essential feature of the modeling process, the pleasure of which, like that enjoyed by toy railroad hobbyists and those engaged in play with dolls, has found its way back from the serious world into the little worlds available on the monitors of contemporary commercial game players. The goal of realtime audiovisual interactivity drove developments in flight simulation from this point, realtime tactile and proprioceptive interactivity having reached a successful level of fidelity through Link's pneumatic technics, later superseded by hydraulics-based feedback systems. Finding the balance between achieving a viable level of credibility for the (necessarily reductive) represented milieu and maintaining the operating speed of the simulation became an ongoing preoccupation.

This videographic miniaturization gave way in the 1960s to the animation of the space outside the simulated cockpit by the computer, the next leading-edge technology advantageous to the development of simulation training for military pilots. The scene generator software and hardware developed by Ivan Sutherland and David Evans in 1968 initiated both the movement toward the sophisticated digital flight simulators developed in the 1970s and 1980s and, equally significantly, the expansion of the flight simulation industry across military, commercial, and entertainment sectors.

The idea for the scene generator came out of Sutherland's work on the first head-mounted display units. Such pioneering work has made him a major figure in the history of computer-generated imaging (CGI) in general and VR in particular.[13] Sutherland's 1968 paper, "A Head-Mounted Three Dimensional Display," described the technical components required to produce a device capable of giving the user a convincing illusion of three-dimensional space in real time. The imagined device, familiar from the subsequent development of VR technology, was a wearable helmet combining a motion tracking sensor and mini video monitors for each eye, displaying a CGI-constructed virtual space.[14] As Woolley points out, while this paper is usually identified as a key moment in the development of CGI and VR technology, the potential of such a system of spatial simulation and virtualization for general application beyond flight simulation is articulated by Sutherland in a paper published three years earlier, "The Ultimate Display":

> The ultimate display . . . would . . . be a room within which the computer can control the existence of matter. A chair displayed in such a room would be

good enough to sit in. Handcuffs displayed in such a room would be confining, and a bullet displayed in such a room would be fatal. With appropriate programming such a display could literally be the Wonderland in which Alice walked.[15]

Sutherland described this space as being a "mathematical wonderland"—that is, one made out of the translatability of geometry into algebraic equations, the possibility of the quantification and simulation of analog experiences such as touch and hearing via the mathematically based symbolic languages of computer programming.[16] While Woolley notes in passing the "macabre" nature of Sutherland's examples of possible simulated experiences inside his ultimate display, I would add that the military context of his research is evident in his prop list for a controlling, potentially lethal virtual scenario—chair, handcuffs, gun.

In 1972, General Electric's Electronics Laboratory produced for the U.S. Navy the Advanced Development Model (ADM) to test the effectiveness of Sutherland's Computer Image Generation technology for flight training. The results were positive. Instead of the helmet-based stereographic video display, the ADM's setup of three screens placed in front and at either side of the cockpit meant that the simulator pilot's vision was now filled with close to 180 degrees of realtime visual feedback. Moreover, the possibility of simulating opponents within the virtual space of the mission greatly increased the combat training potential of flight simulation—and its subsequent potential as a model for computer games of various genres whose gameplay revolves around combat with an opponent (human or computer controlled) in a virtual environment.

The linking together of two or more simulators made virtual dogfighting and group mission simulation possible. As Lapiska et al. state: "Aircraft and weapon systems developers could now evaluate the performance of the aircrew, aircraft and weapons as a total system in a combat environment."[17] Digital simulation expanded the use of the technology to include the development and testing of new aircraft and weapons systems, as well as related applications such as air accident investigations. The ADM is the starting point for the visual display component of today's top-end dome simulators. Lenoir and Lowood have given a detailed account of the subsequent phase in flight and vehicle simulation developments in which the networking of remote simulators and locally networked simulator units became the predominant concern.[18] In the 1980s, the Defense Advanced Research Projects Agency (DARPA, which, as ARPA, had funded Sutherland's groundbreaking work) sponsored major projects toward this end, the most significant of which was SIMNET. The technical advances made in this effort have been instrumental in the proliferation of realtime online simulation-based activities in both military and commercial spheres, not the least of which is online gaming. I will have more to say in the last section of this chapter concerning the reorienting effects of the technics allowing the spatial and temporal synchronization of the virtual experience for its participants.

In relation to the balancing act between simulator speed and credibility that has been a constant theme in the development of flight simulation, the move away from stand-alone systems toward "distributed interactive simulation" necessitated a shift away from the goal of maximum illusionistic realism toward the goal of "selective functional fidelity."[19] This was to reduce the demands on the scene generator component of the visual display systems of remotely networked simulators to a level capable of maintaining realtime interactivity for participants in the shared space of the simulation. We could say that the computer simulator's virtual space is dromoscopic in the very mechanics of its simplification of the real. The greater the complexity of the scene being rendered—that is, the greater the amount of information it contains about terrain, fixed structures, and objects moving in the scene—the more the calculations required to generate the successive images needed to animate the virtual world. Flight simulation is a vision produced by a race: the algorithm against the clock. The stakes are realism and effectivity.

As more powerful and more rapid microprocessors became more affordable, the level of virtual world detail sustainable in real time increased. The history of the development of flight simulation reveals how significant economic considerations have been in advancing simulation technology's role in pilot training and aircraft/weapons testing. As mentioned above, Link's original Blue Box units played a crucial part in matching pilot production to the mass production of military aircraft during World War II. This motivation has sustained the military-industrial development of flight simulation for pilot training and the testing of experimental aircraft and weapons systems. In the commercial aeronautics industry, Lapiska et al. point out that the U.S. Federal Aviation Authority (FAA) has had sufficient confidence in simulation fidelity since the mid-1970s to equate time in the simulator with time in a real aircraft for the purposes of pilot certification: "A simulator and training program approved to the highest level allowed by the FAA permits a pilot to obtain the type rating for that vehicle *without ever flying the actual aircraft.*"[20] This utilization of the simulator has the principal advantage of freeing up aircraft for revenue-generating activities.

The extension of flight simulation's "*mise-en-scène* of war"—in which instructors could teach students "not just to pilot an aircraft with instruments but to pilot a startlingly realistic series of images"—took place, Virilio argues, largely unnoticed at around this time.[21] He links this expansion of the role and influence of simulation technology across the military and commercial sectors to the 1970s oil crisis and the associated threat to military/industrial energy reserves. The expansion of the logistics of perception underwent a decisive acceleration with this endorsement of the operational modeling of the real, one that supported the overflowing of military ways of seeing and organizing vision into other areas of visual culture.

In the 1990s, the drive to economize on military research and development spending led the Department of Defense under the Clinton administration to issue Directives 5000.1 and 5000.2, which redefined its policies and procedures of procurement. As part of this, Directive 5000.1 mandated "that models and simulations be required of all proposed systems" in order to reduce development and testing costs.[22] Funding priority was (and is) given to projects utilizing existing commercially available computer technology and software. The military-entertainment complex is, in effect, the result of this logisticoeconomic mutation of the military-industrial complex.

In the military arena, logistics is generally associated with the economic, supply, and transport considerations taken into account by military planning staff in their preparations for war or for maintaining standing armed forces. Manuel De Landa defines logistics as "the art of assembling war and the agricultural, economic and industrial resources that make it possible."[23] It has also gained a wider usage in describing labor and resource management and deployment more generally. This is already an indication of the diffusion of a military model to the domestic sphere. Moreover, according to De Landa, the interrelation between military logistical considerations and the development of modern mass production has a long history beginning with the interplay between the U.S. Department of Ordnance and private enterprise munitions producers from the 1830s onward.[24] The trajectory of computer games such as the military fighter simulator *Falcon 4.0* (Spectrum Holobyte, 1998) from the commercial arena back to specific military use as a training simulation is one of the most explicit illustrations of this general dynamic, one that Lenoir and Lowood identify as a signal example of the kinds of interactions constituting the aptly named military-entertainment complex.[25]

Virilio writes in *War and Cinema* about the process of "derealization" in train today under the influence of representational and simulational technologies such as flight simulation. "These devices," he states, "appropriate everyday images which as a consequence lose their ability to reflect reality."[26] If this corrupting appropriation of everyday images is at the heart of derealization, then to understand it we will need to consider what the uncorrupted realization or reflection of reality would look like. Further, we will need to consider whether this opposition of reflection and derealization is the most productive portrayal of the dynamic with which we are concerned. In other words, relating this question to that of the reanimation of space in VR, we will need to consider how and to what extent the derealization of reality reanimates an existent animation of the real. That is, how can it be seen to revivify or transform it—and to what degree is the animation of reality in everyday images always already its reanimation?

The Logistical Space of the Flight Simulator's Reanimation of the World as Virtual

If I call the world inside a flight simulation system a logistical space, what would the qualifier *logistical* represent, and how should we characterize it in relation to Virilio's claims about the process of derealization underway today? As noted above, logistics is about the assemblage of war and the collective's resources for making it. Virilio states that logistics first arose as an issue for military planning in the Napoleonic era, which was the beginning of the era of mass wars, and that the first person to use the term in this military sense was the nineteenth-century French military theorist Henri de

Jomini. For Jomini, logistics was not limited to the subsistence of the new national army mobilized by Napoleon:

> Logistics is not only food. It's also munitions and transportation. . . . The trucks bringing ammunition and the flying shells bringing death are coupled in a system of vectors, of production, transportation, execution. There we have a whole flow chart which is logistics itself. [27]

Logistics as the management of a system of vectors requires a translation of economic activity, transportation systems, and armed conflict into a flowchart, a diagrammatic representation of an incredibly complex and dynamic reality. This process of translation produces an informational space where logistical problems are anticipated, mapped, and resolved. Virilio describes the advent of logistics as revolutionary because of its potential to refigure economics, politics, and military strategy by subordinating them to the ever-increasing requirements of the logistical process. He sees in General Eisenhower's management of the D-day invasion the launching of an "a-national logistical revolution," subsequently formulated for general applicability in an early post–World War II definition of logistics that issued from the Pentagon: "Logistics is the procedure following which a nation's potential is transferred to its armed forces, in times of peace as in times of war."[28]

This definition raises a crucial point in Virilio's account of the postwar era. If the logistical tendency were to run its course to its "logistical" conclusion, the transfer of a nation's potential to its armed forces would be, before anything else, the transformation of a nation into logistical potential. This is why Virilio will recognize in this definition a key to understanding the "a-national logistical revolution." The nation as origin of identity and as the locus of political and sociocultural propriety disappears with the predominance of the logistical flowchart.

The decisive increase in importance and consequent proliferation of the logistical flowchart in the postwar period is the central element in the overflowing of the military sphere into all other spheres of human activity. The transformation of a nation into logistical potential leads to the transformation of the reality of the world of nations into a virtual reality. That is to say, the traditional elements and relationships of sociopolitical and cultural reality become increasingly virtualized. All walks of life and all institutions, while maintaining their conventional appearance, tend to be determined more and more by the dictates of the logistics of perception, communication, politics, strategy, economics, and so on. Accepted modes of reasoning, interpretation, and decision making in these fields are subordinated to logistical considerations—the anticipation of threat, coordination of resources toward the minimization of contingency, security (rather than defense)—and survive only to legitimate processes that they no longer govern.[29]

The space animated by the flight simulator is both a significant material instance of and contributor to this transformation of a politicostrategic real into a logistical diagram. As such, the virtual space of flight simulation is a descendant of two related representational traditions: the diagram and the map, which is itself a form of diagram. According to Michael Benedikt, both the diagram and the map exploit the power of René Descartes's insight into the translatability of algebra and geometry into each other. The Cartesian coordinate system for plotting mathematical equations in two-dimensional space has led to the notion that "*space itself* is not necessarily physical: rather it is a 'field of play' for all information."[30] Diagrams and charts are thus "hybrids, mixing physical, energic or spatiotemporal coordinates with abstract, mathematical ones, mixing histories with geographies, simple intervallic scales with exponential ones, and so on."[31]

For Benedikt, the proliferation of diagramming in the twentieth century—from "simple bar charts and organizational 'trees' through matrices, networks and 'spreadsheets' to elaborate, multidimensional, computer-generated visualizations of invisible physical processes"—raises questions about the "ontological status" of diagrammatic representation. The diagrammatic spatiality of these "entities," he argues, exceeds the geography of the two-dimensional "piece of paper or computer screen on which we see them. All have a reality that is no mere picture of the natural, phenomenal world, and all display a physics, as it were, from elsewhere."[32] This "reality" is, for Benedikt, writing in the early 1990s, the "first evidence" of the "materializing" of cyberspace and the precursor to cyberspace's "parallel universe created and sustained by the world's computers and communication lines."[33]

This derealizing of physical space in favor of the materialization of a "physics from elsewhere," so fundamental to the advent of cyberspace, is a necessary part of the virtualizing, logistical process.[34] The virtual space of flight simulation enacts this diagrammatical reanimation of the world as an informational field of play. The simulator does not simply represent a real space, even if it does so with ever-increasing verisimilitude. This is a re-animation because it brings to life the world in a new way, one in which logistical considerations dominate over all others. The virtual space of the simulation is designed with the parameters of its interactive affordances in mind. That is, it is a modeling of both the world and what can and needs to be done within it.

This new life of the world would be, in a sense, a living death because the possibility of nonlogistical modes of interpreting and acting (political, ethical, strategic) wither in this world. The dying away of these traditional modes of interpreting (and) existing in the new logistical world could even be considered to be an inevitable consequence of the process of reanimation at work in this transformation of the real. As Cholodenko has pointed out in a discussion of the "uncanny" nature of animation's "illusion of life," the generation of this illusion always has a relation to death. He argues that

> animation cannot be thought without thinking loss, disappearance and death, that one cannot think the endowing with life without thinking the other side of the life cycle—the transformation from the animate to the inanimate—at the same time, cannot think endowing with motion without thinking the other side of the cycle of movement—of metastasis, deceleration, inertia, suspended animation, etc.—at the same time, and cannot think the life cycle without thinking the movement cycle at the same time.[35]

F/A-18 Hornet Strike Fighter (Graphic Simulations, 1993) is a good illustration, in a commercial, ludic register, of how this logistical reanimation of the world tends toward a living death of the real. Working in the realistic rather than simplified, arcade-style field of flight simulator gaming, Graphic Simulations released this game in the wake of the first Gulf war as a part historical and part hypothetical mission simulator for current and potential post–cold war conflict scenarios. The simulated three-dimensional space over the Middle East in and through which I pilot my F/A-18 in the game is a projection of that most unstable of geopolitical regions into a logistical dimension. The politicostrategic dimension is reduced to a residual pretext displayed in the Mission Briefing window before I arm my plane for takeoff. This explains the strategic purpose of the mission, and provides its implicit legitimation in a schematic evocation of traditional ethicopolitical discourse. The briefing screen for the mission entitled "Hole in One" reads as follows:

LOCATION: Saudi Arabia: Omar Kiam Base near Iraqi border

TIME: 6.40 am

CONDITIONS: Clear

DESTINATION: Mt Shatrah

NOTES: Enemy forces are finishing construction of a giant cannon (waypoint 1) which they intend to use on a neighboring country's civilian population. Intelligence reports that a nuclear shell has been developed for this gun making its immediate destruction imperative. You have been authorized by the President to use the B-57 [a tactical nuclear bomb] to destroy this target.

The presidential authority to use a nuclear bomb in this briefing represents the vestiges of the strategicopolitical realm in the era of the logistical necessity of weapons testing and preparation.[36]

This game's generation of an animated real space for simulated play has an important linkage to a certain disappearance and death of an established illusion of cultural and geopolitical reality. The generative movement toward the new forms of computer animation—with the development of flight simulation constituting an initiatory factor in this movement—is a process inescapably entailing degeneration of existing conventional conceptualizations of reality. Flight simulation's reanimation of the world as what Virilio calls the "*mise-en-scène* of war"—of pure war—must be thought in relation to the multiple forms of degeneration that make up the loss of the conventional form of the real that is the other side of this animatic process. The endowing with life of the diagrammatic, informational world has this intrinsic link to the transformation of the hitherto animate real into a state of inanimation or of suspended animation.

The uncanny quality of flight simulation's reanimation of the world (and its suspension of another life of the world) can also be understood in terms of its strange familiarity. The virtualization of space in flight simulator visual systems continues the lengthy tradition of diagrammatical representation Benedikt discusses. Its addition of illusionistic verisimilitude at the speed of realtime interactivity is crucial to its making strange of established uses of diagrammatical traditions such as terrain maps, perspectival drawings, and diagrams of flight formations and aerial tactical maneuvers, as well as such things as schematic representations of rates of change of aircraft armament and fuel supply. We will return to the temporal dimension of this process below and in the following chapter. It is important to note in the context of our discussion of the space of flight simulation that the selective reduction of the real enabling this attainment of realtime operability draws on this long tradition of diagrammatical reduction and abstraction of more complex phenomena. Indeed, it relies on the very image of space itself that has come to us from the history of Western scientific and technological revolutions. That is, the logistical reanimation of the real is in this sense an uncanny reproduction of Western modernity's ongoing (re)animation of space as perspectival, planar, and, with Descartes, as susceptible to mathematical (re)formulation. The surprising "physics from elsewhere" that Benedikt sees emerging in the increasing proliferation and sophistication of diagramming—and I would say culminating in the VR technology inaugurated by flight simulation systems—comes back to us from this strangely familiar space.

Benedikt's notion of a physics from elsewhere captures the sense in which a rethinking of the principles and workings of space has emerged out of transformations in the techniques and technics of its recording, measuring, and representation. As Judith Roof has explained, it is precisely alongside the development of modern techniques and technologies of the measurement and representation of visual perception—beginning with the Renaissance rediscovery of Greek perspectival techniques and geometrical reasoning—that modern scientific theories of human spatial perception developed.[37] The perception of depth came to be understood as the extension of two-dimensional perception via several depth cues and via the "illusion of binocular parallax" produced as a synthesis of the two discrete (two-dimensional) images arriving in the brain from our two eyes.[38] Roof argues that the origins of the notion of spatial perception as essentially planar, and only extended into a "supplemental third dimension," cannot be disentangled from the invention of new techniques for the recording and representation of perspectival space.[39] She argues that the confusion is endemic between the theory and the technics of perception, between the constative science of (the perception of) space and the performative demonstration of the theory via the instruments of empirical measurement and representation. The theory and the technics of perception are coemergent rather than existing in a cause–effect or theory–demonstration relationship. Together, they have and continue to (re)animate the real as a factical milieu for human contemplation and involvement.[40]

The process through which flight simulation came to reanimate the real in and as a logistical space via breakthroughs in digital computing, communications, and CGI technologies continues and alters this longer-term dynamic of the technics and theories of the human imaging and imagining of the real. As Roof points out, the positing of perception as founded on a two-dimensional optical physiology—the rounded geometry of the retina being taken as a special case of the camera obscura's flat registration surface, rather than the obverse—meant that three-dimensionality would always depend on a mysterious restoration of reality to the image:

> If we agree that we exist in a three-dimensional world, and if we agree that our eyes work two-dimensionally, then the illusion produced through binocular parallax matches the conditions of the real world, making binocular parallax a kind of compensatory illusion machine that brings us up to speed with the "real" state of affairs. Given the limitations of our anatomy, truth is already an illusion, or so our conceptual reliance on two-dimensional models would suggest.[41]

Sutherland's visionary generalization of the possibilities of flight simulation systems, envisaged in the course of his efforts to achieve the breakthroughs in CGI and VR techniques for which he is credited, imagines the new physics of virtual space as an operational double of real-world space completely amenable to effective instrumentalization: mutable and flexibly equipped, with designable levels of interactivity and approximation to real-world physics. It is animated by specific technical developments that allowed Sutherland to pursue his breakthrough research, which in turn animated subsequent efforts by himself and others toward the generalization of VR technology. The realization of these efforts amounts to a major advance in the prosthetic of Roof's "compensatory illusion machine" of perception. This enhancement was always already a reanimating of perception. It drew upon the techniques and theories of stereoscopy (for example, in the head-mounted display), of the mathematical abstraction of space in the Cartesian system and the resultant facility of programming the construction of three-dimensional spatial cues on a two-dimensional screen—the foundation of three-dimensional computer animation.[42] It led to the contemporary simulational systems that brings us up to speed, in real time, in a virtual, logistical space.

In view of this, it is necessary to qualify Virilio's claims of the radical difference between the reflection of reality in everyday images and its derealization in modern vision machines. Everyday images have for a long time been constructed and theorized as perceptions on the basis of the "compensatory illusion machine" described by Roof. The opposition of reflection and derealization cannot be sustained unequivocally. If the real is being reanimated today, this is in part on the basis of an existent (re)animation of the real, one with a long tradition, and one that no doubt transformed a preceding animation of existence. It is critical to assess this in each technical/ theoretical, or imaged/imaginary, reanimation of the world. The challenge of making such a critical assessment in the complex situation mapped out here—one in which the perception not only of reality (considered as an objectively stable phenomenon) but also of what perception itself is when technical and theoretical developments seem to reciprocally determine each other in an ongoing dynamic—is one that Virilio has persistently tried to meet and thematize. This is the challenge to critical thought discussed at the outset of this chapter and posed by phenomena such as flight simulation. Virilio, despite being caught up in the critical complexities and paradoxes of this project, has nonetheless gone further than most in gesturing toward some of the key elements of the transformations underway in the logistical reanimation of space.[43]

Reorientation: Adjusting to the Foreseen Virtual Reality

What tends to die away in this bringing to life of logistical space is the space in which the geopolitical, economic, and cultural spheres of human existence can persist and develop. The selective reduction of the real privileged by realtime flight simulation systems is both a technical requirement and a mechanism of this logistical reanimation. The scene generator component of the flight simulator accesses a database of images and visual information that it uses to produce its animation of space. The database must be selectively accessed by the scene generator to enable a realistic but not overly complex virtual space to be generated. The sources of a flight simulator's database represent the major components of contemporary military topographical and territorial information gathering: satellite pictures, topographical maps, aerial photographs, highway maps, photographs of important objects, and on-site inspections.[44] In this regard, the scene generator's treatment of the database can be seen to offer a logistical solution corresponding to the problem the contemporary military commander confronts in processing all the available information in the increasingly diminishing time allowed by the speed of modern weapons systems and at the commander's increasing remove from the war zone. Here is Virilio from *War and Cinema*:

> The level of foresight required by the geopolitical dimensions of modern battlefields demanded a veritable meteorology of war. Already we can see here the video-idea that the military voyeur is handicapped by the slowness with which he scans a field of action overstretched by the dynamic revolution of weaponry and mass transport. Only the further development of technology could offset this tendency to which it had given rise. For the disappearance of the proximity effect in the prosthesis of accelerated travel made it necessary to create a *wholly simulated appearance* that would restore three-dimensionality to the message in full.[45]

This restoration of the message from the battlefield in its "wholly simulated appearance" was for Virilio a logistical necessity. Although it restored an illusion of depth to the complex and dynamic reality of modern war by animating the commander's illusion of the battlefield, it did not restore its strategicopolitical dimension. What it did do, however, was supplement the commander's unfavorable position through the provision of this operative simulation, one that made available new views, knowledges, and capacities:

> The macro-cinematography of aerial reconnaissance, the cable television of panoramic radar, the use of slow or accelerated motion in analysing the phases of an operation—all this converts the commander's plan into an animated cartoon or flow chart.[46]

Flight simulation development has been responsible for major breakthroughs in this conversion of military command systems into this logistical flowchart/ cartoon. For instance, Lenoir and Lowood give a detailed account of the development and application of the simulation of a significant armored vehicle action from the 1991 Iraq war, the Battle of 73 Easting, by key members of the SIMNET development team.[47] One of the major applications of this simulation was in Project Odin. The database of the 73 Easting simulation was incorporated in the Odin war game simulation engine. Odin

> was not designed to destroy targets, but to assist in visualizing the battle about to be entered, or ideally, even going on. SIMNET technology was at the core of Odin. . . . Odin combined a digital terrain database of any part of the world; intelligence feeds of friendly and enemy orders of battle (through another DARPA program called Fulcrum); an order of battle generator; a map display with a two dimensional as well as an out-the-window three dimensional display called the "flying carpet"; and a war gaming engine with semi-automated forces using AI [artificial intelligence] components.[48]

Flight simulation led the development of such systems, and the continuing significance of the dromoscopic vision produced by overflying the world is clear in this description of the dromoscopic supplement to the commander's capacity to envision the contingencies of battle.

Indeed, Odin's database of the world instantiates in simulated, virtual form the cyclopean ambition of the U.S. military's doctrine of global information dominance discussed at the outset of this chapter. It is nonetheless a form of this desired dominance that plays a key role alongside other instances of this doctrine in action, such as the almost complete reliance of commercial and military aircraft navigation today on the U.S. military's GPS, as well as the use of communications technologies for jamming designated enemy military and commercial communications networks and broadcast systems. A world database is a necessary correlate of the proliferation of networked simulation systems possessing the desired flexibility of deployment in the global disequilibrium of asymmetrical conflict with indistinct enemy combatants.

The distributed interactive simulation protocols devised to facilitate simulator networking operate on the principle of the coherence of time and space. For Project Odin and military simulation systems like it, the world database satisfies the principle of spatial coherence, while Greenwich mean time obtained from a GPS receiver accomplishes the time correlation.[49] In this global synchronization of space-time, the distributed interactive simulation standards follow the procedures of military operations that have long since shifted to this system of coordinating the operations of multiple units (often based in different time zones) engaged in a particular mission. The reanimation of the world in and as logistical space is thus also a reorientation of the world via this global repositioning technics. Just as each animation is also a reanimation, one could say here that this new orientation to the world as a global space of instrumental interventionist potential is also a kind of reorientation in relation to an earlier convention of geopolitical, cultural orientation. This reorientation is paired with a disorientation, just as reanimation is with a deanimation of what had come to life previously. Virilio's "a-national logistical revolution" takes place compellingly in and as this disorienting animation of logistical space first brought to life in flight simulation.

Bernard Stiegler characterizes disorientation as the undermining of the stability (and therefore the viability) of "calendarity" and "cardinality"—the temporal and spatial references to which individuals refer in situating themselves vis-à-vis others.[50] Stiegler argues that every orientation has an intrinsic relation to disorientation and is therefore always enacting a reorientation of a former stable (or metastable) situational matrix. From this perspective, disorientation is originary.[51] While the orientation of the individual is always a question of particular adoptions of the collective matrix, the scope and potential of what can be adopted is always conditioned by the technocultural facticity in and through which one engages with others.[52] Calendaric and cardinal references are always and only available through the technical heritage of a cultural grouping, through such things as writings, images, rituals, stories, games, art, monuments, clothing, tools, weapons, techniques of measurement, transport, navigation, calculation, and simulation. The characteristics of the logistical space we have examined here have had a decisive influence on the disorienting/reorienting processes of adoption in train today in the globalized milieu of technoculture. Just where in the world we picture ourselves to be today is to no small degree a consequence of flight simulation's reanimation of space and its widespread dissemination across our interactive screens.

4 Military Gametime

History, Narrative, and Temporality in Cinema and Games

The perpetrators of the 9/11 terrorist attack included commercial and game flight simulation software systems in their training regimen for their sui-cide missions.[1] As one of the many facts to have emerged via mainstream media reporting to the American (and worldwide) audience in the weeks after the attacks, this contributed to the shocking sense that the world was not what it had seemed to be for people living in advanced Western democracies before September 11, 2001. The news about the simulation training amounted to a disturbing defamiliarization of flight simulator tech-nology from useful or entertaining virtual reality system to dangerously accessible tool resting in the hands of opportunistic terrorists. From my perspective, however, it presents itself as an uncanny return home of flight simulation technics to a wartime context of training toward an effective execution of established mission objectives—albeit in the perverse form of a suicidal appropriation of commercial airliners. This uncanny homecom-ing all too clearly illustrates the debt that mainstream interactive systems owe to the key technical developments of military flight simulation dis-cussed in the previous chapter. These bring with them a particular (re)ori-entation to space and time that I characterized there as logistical in nature. Their redeployment for military purposes becomes yet another turn in the spiral of (re)adoption of entertainment systems for serious military uses and vice versa.

I raise the use of flight simulation technology by the 9/11 perpetrators here as an extreme instance of the dissemination of logistical character of flight simulation across the audiovisual forms of contemporary techno-culture. The terrorists in effect weaponized components of the West's audio-visual media (above all, the live television news services, but also flight sim games) that, from their perspective, had long been used as key elements in the continuation of global economic and cultural domination in the post-colonial world. The logistical reanimation of the world that we discussed in the previous chapter was a significant technical and aesthetic vehicle of the globalizing tendencies Islamic extremism seeks to counter. That this reanimation takes place in real time and not the deferred time of earlier time-based media is decisive in this regard. The terrorists could not have taken a movie or a novel, or even a conventional documentary or instruc-tional video about flying an aircraft, and gained the same training effect from its use. These modalities would all have to be used in conjunction with actual or simulated flight training. Flight simulation games incorporate instructional lessons—via a manual, training exercise briefings, and so on— about the theory and practice of flight along with realtime practice.

In the realm of audiovisual entertainment, computer games that mobilize realtime interactivity represent the major potential successor to narrative-based, deferred-time forms such as mainstream cinema, television drama, and literature.[2] Yet even these forms have undergone significant transforma-tion in the last few decades in response to their remediation by computer-based audiovisual forms. As Andy Darley points out, the traditional modes of image making in cinema, television, and print technologies have all been taken over and transformed by digital imaging techniques.[3] The time-based forms of cinema, television, and video have also been affected by the newer interactive mediation of experience in their configuration of the temporal engagement of the spectator within their duration.

This chapter will present a comparative analysis of two products of the military-entertainment complex—a combat-based flight simulator and a Hollywood war movie—that remediate narrative and interactive forms of temporal engagement in different but symptomatically related ways. While the film *Pearl Harbor* (Michael Bay, 2001) does not literally engage the viewer interactively in real time, it simulates aspects of a realtime aesthetic.

In a similar way, one could say that *Microsoft Combat Flight Simulator 2: WWII Pacific Theater* (Microsoft, 2000), a game that uses the *Microsoft Flight Simulator* game engine, simulates narrativity via its historical realtime recreation of the air war in the Pacific during World War II. Taken together, they are both readable as exemplary instances of the reorientation to historical temporality underway in and through the military-entertainment complex.

Microsoft Combat Flight Simulator 2's History of the Pacific War

Microsoft Combat Flight Simulator 2 was the second installment of a series of combat-based games rooted in air campaigns in the major theaters of conflict in World War II.[4] World War II is a popular military conflict for flight sim games, although more recently games based on air warfare in Korea, Vietnam, and Iraq have also proliferated. Of interest here is the way in which *Microsoft Combat Flight Simulator 2* mobilizes the historical events of the air war in the Pacific from 1942 to 1944 to simulate a reality for gameplay. My particular focus will be on the game's construction of an experience of historical time—or, rather, a matrix of experiences of time and the way that history functions as part of this matrix. In this construction of time out of both narrative and interactive solicitation of the gamer, one can see a central element of the logistical transformation of spatiotemporal orientation in play in flight sim games, and indeed in computer games more generally.

As Lev Manovich has argued, computer games perfectly manifest the logic of the algorithm that is a core component of what he calls the "ontology of the computer."[5] In this ontology, "the world is reduced to two kinds of software objects that are complementary to each other—data structures and algorithms."[6] In the way they set the player a well-defined task, computer games exemplify the logic informing the predominant modality of computer interaction, which is to master the algorithm's manipulation of the data structure. The algorithm provides the means for mobilizing the information held therein. Manovich says, "for better or worse, information access has become a key activity of the computer age," and he calls for the elaboration of an "info-aesthetics—a theoretical analysis of the aesthetics of information access as well as the creation of new media objects that 'aestheticize' information processing."[7] New media objects such as computer games innovate forms of information processing that have implications for understanding contemporary culture. My discussion of *Microsoft Combat Flight Simulator 2* examines the logistical nature of its aesthetic of information processing.

In this game, the simulator's information database is drawn from major historical events, namely, those arising from the Pacific war of 1941–1945. The Single Mission and Campaign modes of gameplay have as their temporal and geographical parameters major events in the air war in the Pacific theater from early 1942 to late 1944. The game's Single Missions are reconstructions of actual missions flown by Japanese and U.S. Navy aces in the Pacific war. For instance, "Aces—Iwamoto's Mission" is introduced in the Mission Briefing window as follows:

On November 17, 1943, IJN [Imperial Japanese Navy] ace Tetsuzo Iwamoto escorted dive-bombers from Rabaul on a strike against Cape Torokina on Bougainville. In the course of the mission he tangled with Navy Corsairs (of VF-17 squadron) for the first time, and claimed two of them shot down over Empress Augusta Bay. Now you will fly Iwamoto's mission.

Campaign mode involves playing an extended sequence of missions based on the major conflicts in the Pacific war after the commencement of hostilities at Pearl Harbor and up until late 1944, when U.S. forces took control of islands in the Marianas.[8] The first mission flown as a U.S. Navy pilot is on February 1, 1942, over the Marshall Islands, and the last is over the island of Tinian in the Marianas. The campaigns comprise sets of missions based on the major battles of the Pacific war, such as the Battle of the Coral Sea, the Battle of Midway, and the Guadalcanal and Solomon islands actions. These mission sets are separated by cut scenes, which are short predesigned animated sequences that introduce the next phase of the campaign. They take the form of a graphically illustrated journal of an anonymous pilot combatant who relates his personal experience of the war as it unfolded. Along with introductory, usually higher-resolution animated sequences known as cinematics, the interstitial cut scenes are a common convention in many computer game genres, including role-playing and adventure games as well as flight sims and other military campaign simulations where gameplay progresses from one scenario and locale to another, or from one level to the next.

The other modes of gameplay—Free Flight, Quick Combat, Training Missions, and Multiplayer—all occur somewhere over a map of the Pacific area, the spatial delimitation of which reflects the same sequence of historical events. This map and the menu of possible missions and aircraft available to fly may be modified by additional scenarios that can be either purchased from game design firms or downloaded as shareware from amateur programmers. Moreover, players who have the time to learn the complex Mission Builder program packaged with the game can design missions to add to the list of available single missions. The design of *Microsoft Combat Flight Simulator 2* to make it amenable to various modifications (or "mods") by players typifies a widespread feature of game software today. Some mods play with the historical consistencies of *Combat Flight Simulator 2*. For instance, in multiplayer mode, players can fly anachronistic aircraft models such as jets or biplanes from other Microsoft flight sim games, or they can use different icons or skins for the pilot figure visible in the objective ("spot") view of the action, such as the Osama Bin Laden skin that appeared in many forms for different games shortly after September 11, 2001.

Many modifications of the original game, however, supplement *Microsoft Combat Flight Simulator 2*'s coverage of significant air campaigns in the Pacific war. One such mod is "In Defense of Australia," a downloadable freeware campaign based on air actions involving Japanese and Australian forces over Papua New Guinea in 1942.[9] It was reviewed on the official Microsoft *Combat Flight Simulator 2* Web site, with the unnamed reviewer noting that "additional campaigns like this can also help to fill in the gaps in the [game's] historical representation of World War II."[10]

Microsoft's games division team set out to create a compelling game by envisaging gameplay as play in and with a reconstruction of history drawn from the narrative modes of more traditional media such as official histories, journals, archives, war films, and documentaries. Accordingly, the game's manual is packed with photos and reproductions of maps, as well as other documents such as illustrations from the period and quotations from diaries and flight instruction manuals. The manual also has a chapter with summaries of the major conflicts, another with biographies of the most famous aces and key players of the conflict, and extensive listings of aircraft specifications and details of other vehicles and equipment simulated in the game.

In the acknowledgements, the contributions of veteran naval aviators Bob Campbell and Mike Weide, as well as "two living legends of the air war in the Pacific, Saburo Sakai and Joe Foss," are noted under the heading "Historical Advisers."[11]

As a task-driven, interactive form, *Microsoft Combat Flight Simulator 2* redeploys narrative but does not therefore abandon it, something that is made most apparent by the structuring role that the cut scenes fulfill in providing a progression through the extended Campaign mode of gameplay. The postwar comic book aesthetic employed in these sequences of still images with moving transitions works to produce an analog of the historical recollection of the war by nostalgically evoking the childhood experience of encountering the war in the comic books of what Tom Engelhardt has called the "victory culture" of the postwar years in America.[12] As J. C. Herz has observed, flight sim games are generally marketed to older men.[13] *Microsoft Combat Flight Simulator 2* cleverly invokes the mediated memories of this target generation in an elegant, allusive aesthetic.

Manovich claims the employment of the gamer in a goal-directed task "makes the player experience the game as a narrative."[14] If this is so, there is nonetheless a crucial transformation effected in this refiguring of narrative experience, one especially apparent in *Microsoft Combat Flight Simulator 2*'s redesign of historical narrative. Whether the player's experience is indeed best described as narrative experience is a point to which we will return. In order to explore these questions further, I will compare the game to the 2001 film *Pearl Harbor,* a commercially successful but critically savaged film about the Japanese surprise air attack that brought the United States into World War II. This will allow us to consider the differences between the game's task-based representation of historical events and the spectacular cinematic representation of history in *Pearl Harbor.* While this comparison serves in part to contrast new media interactivity with old media narrativity, what we will see is that not only is interactivity bound up with reconstructing narrative in *Microsoft Combat Flight Simulator 2,* but also that *Pearl Harbor* evidences the "transcoding" (as Manovich would have it) of computer-based logics—or, rather, logistics—of imaging and simulation into contemporary filmic narrative forms.[15]

Comparing Filmic and Ludic War Entertainments

Like *Microsoft Combat Flight Simulator 2*, *Pearl Harbor* reconstructs historical events as a form of audiovisual entertainment. The marketing strategies that supported the film's release correspond closely to the packaging of *Microsoft Combat Flight Simulator 2* as an historical work. As is customary with major commercial film releases, a flood of publicity material from Touchstone Pictures and related video and television programming accompanied the film's release. These featured interviews with veterans from the December 1941 attack.[16] The film's Web site is an archive of this marketing material. It includes a section entitled "The Documentary" that amounts to an oral history project focusing on both the Pearl Harbor attack and the making of the film as a record of the event.[17] The user can download three- or four-minute clips of interviews with veterans of Pearl Harbor and the later Doolittle bombing raid on Tokyo, an event also featured in the film. Interviews with representatives of the U.S. Navy Office of Information and the Department of Defense are also available concerning the consultation process the film production company entered into with various military and veterans' organizations and the extensive support the U.S. Navy lent to the production.

As mainstream audiovisual cultural productions, both film and game invest a great deal in presenting themselves as authenticated reconstructions of major historical events. As entertainment forms that incorporate fictional elements with these reconstructions, they do not purport to be official or proper historical projects. Nevertheless, the stakes are high for any media work setting out to portray Pearl Harbor in an American cultural context, given that it occupies such a crucial position in the mainstream historical narrative explaining the United States' involvement in World War II and legitimating its conduct of that war. This is perhaps why *Microsoft Combat Flight Simulator 2*'s simulation of the Pacific theater conflict does not commence with the Pearl Harbor attack, leaving a significant gap in its historical representation. Another reason for this absence and for that of the air campaign's climactic nuclear conclusion—not to mention the incendiary bombing campaign resulting in the systematic destruction of most of Japan's cities that preceded it—might be that the game is better able to situate the player in the midst of the war in the Pacific. Without the reconstruction of its beginning or end, the Pacific theater conflict can be experienced in gameplay less as a predetermined history and more as a series of contingent moments.[18]

Pearl Harbor, on the other hand, does portray the attack as its central subject. By also narrating the story of the famed Doolittle raid over Tokyo of July 1942, it reaffirms what Tom Engelhardt calls the predominant "victory narrative" of American history. The film concludes by pointing ahead to the ultimate victory over the Japanese through airpower.[19] Indeed, *Pearl Harbor*'s production history of close cooperation with the U.S. military winds the clock back to the days of the early cold war that Engelhardt describes, when U.S. forces were tantamount to coproducers of many films and television programs. In this regard, it typifies the renewed influence of the U.S. military on commercial film production reliant on military hardware and personnel for a credible depiction of combat action of one kind or another.

While *Pearl Harbor,* the most expensive Hollywood film production at the time of its release, was overall a box office success domestically and internationally (including in Japan, where it reached number three in box office ratings during its release), it was largely panned by mainstream film reviewers.[20] Criticism of the film centered on its poor character development in the central narrative thread. This involves a contest between two U.S. Army Air Corps pilots for the affections of an Army nurse. The film was dismissed by most reviewers as a special effects movie that failed to rise above the presentation of its CGI-driven spectacle of airborne death and destruction. The relevance of this dismissal to our discussion is highlighted in a particularly scathing critique of the film by David Thomson, who pronounces the ultimate condemnation of *Pearl Harbor* when he likens it to a video game. The film is, he says, "not just a colossal bore, but a defamation of popular history that leaves you in despair for cinema." The defamatory nature of the film is identified with the loss of the "complexity of our history" that occurs when "the kids in the audience and the kids in charge have spent two decades playing video combat games."[21]

The comparison of *Pearl Harbor* to video games is a recurring motif in Thomson's broader attack on effects-dominated films for the deleterious effect they are having on cinema. Further on, Thomson identifies the "essential Bay shot" in *Pearl Harbor* as the

POV [point of view] of the bomb that falls on the [battleship] *Arizona;* it has all the gravitational zest, and the denial of damage or tragedy, that's built into the trigger-jerking spasms of video games. What that means is a *mise en scène* that concentrates on preparing charges, mixing the explosive brew to get the right blend of amber and scarlet in the fireball, and making sure that every extra knows the art of being lifted off his feet and brought down on some union-approved mattress.[22]

For Thomson, *Pearl Harbor,* along with other special effects films that are preoccupied with presenting combat sequences, signals the "defeat [that] narrative has yielded up to technology" in the terrain of the representation of the reality of armed conflict.[23] *Saving Private Ryan* (Stephen Spielberg, 1999) and *Pearl Harbor* are two recent World War II films he cites as part of this trend.

Thomson's characterization of computer games reiterates a widespread stereotype of computer games and gamers. In this view, video games induce an uncomplicated but addictive sensory-motor engagement that deemphasizes intellection in favor of a mode of interactivity typified by quasi-autonomous "trigger-jerking spasms." This is a simplistic and reductive view of computer games, as anyone who has spent many hours learning and then playing complicated flight sim games such as *Microsoft Combat Flight Simulator* 2 or adventure, role-playing, or strategy games like *The Legend of Zelda: Twilight Princess* (Nintendo, 2006), *Civilization* (Microprose, 1990), *Age of Empires* (Microsoft, 2000), and *Napoleon: Total War* (Sega, 2010) would immediately affirm. Playing *Combat Flight Simulator 2,* the game that corresponds most closely to the war films that Thomson concerns himself with, involves learning basic flying techniques and tactical combat maneuvers; it also requires management of communications and coordination with other pilots (player or computer controlled). This is in addition to the extensive amount of historical material and information provided for the gamer to learn and explore.

Thomson's employment of this stereotype of video gaming to condemn *Pearl Harbor* nevertheless provides an important parallel between special effects films and computer games. The shot he singles out in affirming the gamelike mise-en-scène of the film—the point-of-view shot of the falling bomb—could only have been achieved with the aid of computer-generated imaging. It does indeed resemble a virtual shot one could see in a computer game such as *Microsoft Combat Flight Simulator 2* (Figure 3). The Views options in flight and other simulation games include a variety of points of view from which action can be seen via the game's virtual camera, and a weapon's-eye view is usually one of these options (bomb/rocket view in *Microsoft Combat Flight Simulator 2*). In some flight sims, such as *Falcon 4.0* (Spectrum Holobyte, 1998) and *FA-18 Hornet Strikefighter* (Graphic Simulations Corporation, 1995), this weapon perspective duplicates that of the weapon itself, reproducing the now-famous automated vision of destruction celebrated in media coverage of "smart bomb vision" during the U.S.-led allied assault on Iraq in the 1991 Gulf war.[24] In other games, such as *Microsoft Combat Flight Simulator 2*, it is more like the shot in *Pearl Harbor,* a kind of over-the-shoulder shot of the weapon or a tightly framed, objective tracking shot of its trajectory.

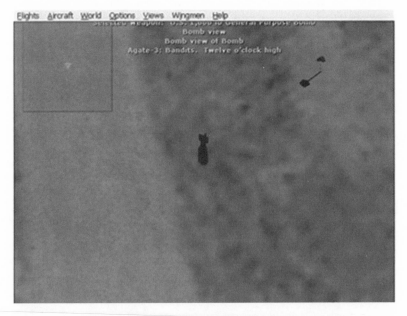

FIGURE 3 Bomb view from *Microsoft Combat Flight Simulator 2: WWII Pacific Theater,* 2000.

In any case, *Pearl Harbor*'s citation of this kind of vision is only achievable by means of digital visual effects. Bay's audiovisual combat spectacle presents extraordinary views of the action, such as the bomb POV and shots that portray aerial dogfighting maneuvers in a way that is not possible with a real camera. In doing so, it also stages the imaging power of contemporary digital visual effects as part of the film's spectacle. As Angela Ndalianis has observed, special effects films are highly reflexive films that foreground their effects as spectacles to be both enjoyed by the spectator as part of the film and marveled at as technical achievements. These films "perform for an audience, and the performance centers around special effects technology and its illusionistic potential."[25]

Thomson says that the bomb POV shot "has all the gravitational zest, and the denial of damage or tragedy, that's built into the trigger-jerking spasms of video games." Like video game gameplay, argues Thomson, the film is characterized by the weightlessness of its representation of grave human events. The impossibility of recording in live action the free fall of a bomb in this manner says something crucial to Thomson about Bay's digital aesthetic. For Thomson, the "essential Bay shot" is both literal proof of *Pearl Harbor*'s inauthenticity and an emblem of the constitutive lack of narrative gravitas in its addressing of such a significant historical subject as war.

Thomson's argument about the legitimacy of *Pearl Harbor*'s effects as a means of representing the events could be challenged. For instance, the Industrial Light and Magic team, who were responsible for the film's digital effects shots, state that their work was done in order to enhance the realism of the film's portrayal of the attack. In their view, this enhancement was in the service of fidelity to historical events. In an article about the film's effects, including the digital animation of many of the human figures seen in the battle scenes, Barbara Robertson states, "Although digital, each of those sailors on the *Oklahoma* and on the other ships represents a real person who was at Pearl Harbor nearly 60 years ago."[26] In a similar fashion, Thomson's view of what is a substantial and authentic narrative treatment of war—one that focuses on the psychological experiences and social relations of the people caught up in the fighting—is also open to debate. Other meanings, other critical and ethical accounts of the sequence of events being depicted, could be produced in a different narrative treatment that would also have claim to legitimacy. For instance, *Tora! Tora! Tora!* (Richard Fleischer and Kinji Fukasaku, 1970) covers the Pearl Harbor attack in a manner evoking an extended documentary reenactment. There is little emphasis placed on the emotional experiences or social interactions of the military personnel involved. It attempts to construct an objective portrayal of both Japanese and American activities leading up to and during the surprise attack, explaining how surprise was achieved and what diplomatic moves and military strategies and tactics were mobilized on both sides.

Leaving aside these points of contention concerning *Pearl Harbor*'s merit as a fictional account of war, what is most relevant to our examination of computer gaming is Thomson's assertion of the "defeat [that] narrative has yielded up to technology." I would argue that this assertion, while simplistic in opposing narrative to technology (as if narrative itself was not an elaborate technical tradition), points to a significant transformation of narrative function in special effects films, one due in no small part, as Thomson indicates, to the impact of digital imaging technology on film production. Thomson attributes this "defeat" in a characteristically mainstream and stereotypical fashion to the pernicious influence of video games on the younger generations now in control of filmmaking—and now also the principal audience for films. We would say, however, that what is in evidence here is the fact that the logistical principle informing computer games design manifests in a different but not unrelated way in digital visual effects cinema. In both, narrative has been transformed in a process conditioned by the impact of digital imaging and simulation on contemporary audiovisual culture.

How best to approach narrative in order to unpack this transformation? Christian Metz is pertinent when he states that a narrative produces an ordering of events into a closed temporal sequence.[27] This ordering "unrealizes" the events inasmuch as they are not experienced in or as this order in reality. The narrative structuring of events (real or fictional) into a temporal sequence is the ground of narrative significance for the semiologist Metz. Video games, with their configurable (that is, variable) ordering possibilities, do produce sequences, but not as pregiven structures.

The historiographer and narratologist Hayden White extends this view of narrational order by arguing that this structuring of events in time is an interpretative process. The significance of the events narrated arises from the connections that are constructed between them in the formation of the whole sequence.[28] In narrative, the significance of the work inheres in the structuring.

The phenomenologist Paul Ricoeur describes this process as a "configurational arrangement which makes the succession of events into significant wholes that are the correlate of the act of grouping together."[29] For Ricoeur, the nonchronological "configurational dimension" of narrativity combines with the chronological "episodic dimension" in the narrative, in which events are experienced successively. Through the configurational act of plotting, a pattern is elicited from succession. While it is through this plotting that the possibility arises for a judgment to be formed concerning the significance of the events narrated, Ricoeur insists on the importance of following the story in the episodic dimension for the constitution of this possibility. Indeed, he argues that "there is no story if our attention is not moved along by a thousand contingencies."[30] In *Time and Narrative,* Ricoeur refines this point by distinguishing between "followability" along the episodic axis and the sense that the end is foreseeable. The conclusion is expected to be "acceptable"— that is, "congruent with the episodes brought together by the story"—but this is "far from [being] foreseeable," logically speaking.[31] The difference from the way a video game like *Microsoft Combat Flight Simulator 2* provides gameplay can be seen as a function of this reciprocal dynamic of the resolved configurational structure and the episodic unfolding of the narrative.

For White, the significance produced by the arrangement of events is ultimately ethical in nature. A narrative would be acceptable to the extent that it had something to say about the value of human actions in the face of experience. "Could we ever narrativize without moralizing?" asks White.[32] The narrative produces time as a meaningful sequence of events that has ethical significance. Here, something crucial about the difference between narrative and simulation-based forms like video games is glimpsed—where does the ethical potential reside in the structural openness of the simulational work? I will return to this question in the conclusion to this chapter and in chapter 7.

While we have been focusing on the prominence of the visual effects in *Pearl Harbor,* the film can be viewed as a conventional narrative that produces a temporal ordering of events into a meaningful, ethical sequence in the manner I have just outlined. A typical period film scenario plots the character arcs of three individuals that are played out against the backdrop of larger historical events. The melodrama of romantic discord first provides a thematic reflection of the wider historical tale of treachery and destruction. This is then resolved by way of submission to the needs of the greater good. The personal competition between the two friends for the love of one woman dissolves in a consensus of cooperation between all three in the face of a fight for national survival that overwhelms their private lives.

Paralleling the function of the representation of history in *Microsoft Combat Flight Simulator 2*, the story line of *Pearl Harbor* operates in what I would call a secondary register: it functions as a supplement to the main operation of the film, namely, to stage the intense, extended battle scenes, chief of which is the Pearl Harbor attack sequence, which lasts for approximately forty minutes. It provides a narrative motivation for these digital and special effects spectacles and a way of punctuating their presentation. This is the central plank of most of the critical condemnations of the film—that the effects do not serve the narrative, but rather the reverse.[33] In this regard, Thomson's condemnation of *Pearl Harbor* represents a common accusation leveled against effects films, as well as the action movie genre more generally. While I have sketched out some counterclaims to Thomson's position above, these instantiate only part of what is a much larger discussion in film studies concerning mainstream cinema spectatorship and reception.[34] I am unable here to engage comprehensively with the debate about the ethical value of effects films and the legitimacy of Thomson's defense of conventional narrative cinema against other modes of filmmaking that privilege spectacle over narrative substance. It should be noted, however, that in a film like *Pearl Harbor,* the stakes of this debate are particularly high because of the cultural significance and value placed on the historical events it depicts. This is the case even if, as Thomas Doherty has pointed out, war and cinema have been closely intertwined since the inception of the latter because of the spectacular nature of the former.[35]

I would propose that the rise to prominence of effects films, and particularly digitally produced effects in Hollywood in the last couple of decades, is one manifestation in mainstream audiovisual culture of the logistical dynamic of the pure war tendency. What Thomas Schatz called the "New

Hollywood" of high-concept blockbuster production coemerged with the rejuvenation of special effects design through computer imaging technologies.[36] The "secondarization" of traditional narrative function is in no small part an adjustment of narrative form to the production pipelines of the computer-based imaging processes that dominate these films. *Pearl Harbor* is a signal film in this regard. Michael Bay said of his film that "our goal is to stage the event with utmost realism."[37] The digital and effects sequences are the key means of achieving this goal. Their planning and coordination were prioritized in the making of the film. Digital visual effects have to be combined with live-action sequences and conventional special effects (called practical effects). Shooting schedules have to be devised with this coordination in mind. Robertson details the major elements that had to be created digitally, namely the airplanes and their flight paths; smoke, fire, and related weapons effects; airplane crashes and ship explosions; and human figures.[38] Live-action shots must be planned and precisely executed to facilitate their contribution to the final digital–live-action image synthesis that is the goal of the production. The whole process of creating the effects and combining them with the live-action footage has to be conceived in advance to coordinate the different durations of various procedures with the sequential demands of image composition and sound production. Live-action material is taken up as just one pathway.

The logistical impulse is evident, I would argue, in the way the demands of the production pipeline take precedence over the live-action shooting, formerly the privileged moment of the film production process—conventionally described as a three-stage progression from preproduction to production to postproduction. Digital visual effects technology has, through the requirements it imposes on all aspects of a film's creation, effectively rendered this conventional understanding of mainstream filmmaking obsolete. The production of the effects demands that all other aspects of the production be treated as tasks whose execution must be planned in advance and managed in terms of preset priorities calculated to facilitate the creation of the digitally enhanced images.

The presentation of the resulting effects becomes the primary function of the film, and their staging celebrates this accomplishment. The bomb POV shot discussed above is one excellent example of this display of the unique power of digital imaging to obtain such a shot. Others include similar weapon's-eye views from a torpedo's perspective and aerial dogfighting scenes that show planes being hit by bullets in a way that has not been possible except by resorting to archival combat footage. Another occurs later on in the Pearl Harbor sequence during the air attack on the Haleiwa airfield. A U.S. P-40 aircraft attempts to take off when it is destroyed by enemy fire. The shot involves a low-angle point of view from the runway surface as the damaged plane advances toward the camera. In what is actually a practical effect, the plane explodes, and debris and smoke overwhelm the point of view. The shot includes a digital element: the addition of the trajectory of tracer bullets advancing right up to the fixed camera position. The shot of the destruction is held longer than usual, registering the impact of the debris on the screen—the eye of the spectator—and the ability of the film's production process to composite digital and practical effects into this overwhelming view of deadly destruction.

Pearl Harbor's conventional story line supports the film's staging of the sequence of effects. The resulting sequence may be called a form of narrative inasmuch as it evinces a temporal progression from event to event. Its primary purpose, however, is not the interpretative construction of temporality as outlined by narrative theorists such as Metz and White. This transformed narrative is no longer a mechanism for plotting events into ordered and significant relations—an interpretation machine—but another kind of operation. Narrative becomes the plotting of a trajectory of tasks to accomplish. The pattern produced out of the succession of events is the output envisaged in the charting of the film's production pipeline. The digital effects film theatricalizes the achievement of these tasks as its principal operation.

Gametime

I propose that computer games such as *Microsoft Combat Flight Simulator 2* manifest most clearly the transformed logic of the employment of narrative that is present in effects films like *Pearl Harbor.* This logic is logistical; that is, it answers to the pure war tendency Paul Virilio describes, the tendency according to which logistical processes increasingly determine the way things are today. As an entertainment form that has evolved out of military innovations in computer imaging and simulation, computer games evince important aspects of the pure war tendency's transformation of audio-visual media. In this regard, our chief focus here is on the mutation of narrative time in computer games, something that, as we have seen, also affects mainstream film in the era of computer imaging technology.

If in *Pearl Harbor* conventional narrative has become a supplement to the film's effects display, in games such as *Microsoft Combat Flight Simulator 2,* narrative is by design always already secondary to the interactive mode of user engagement. "Decentered" in Andy Darley's view by the prerogatives of interactive immersion in action games, narrative supports the presentation of a task or a whole sequence of tasks the user must undertake (instant combat, training missions, networked play against other users, or whole campaigns of twenty or so sequenced missions).[39] A computer game is designed to immerse the player in the fictive space of the game, and for that purpose, methods similar to those of conventional film and literary narratives are mobilized. To recall Manovich's point about the game's infoaesthetic of database manipulation, however, the primary object of playing the game involves learning the game's algorithm in order to win. Gameplay amounts to a form of zero-degree narrative experience realized by constructing a linear, teleological sequence of play in an illusionistic mise-en-scène. This narrative arranges the time the player spends in a feedback loop with the game's computer model into a story of sorts, one of personal discovery and achievement. The game's secondary narrative—in the case of *Microsoft Combat Flight Simulator 2,* the history of the air war in the World War II Pacific theater—provides a contextual frame that enhances the player's illusory immersion in the gameworld.

Whether narrative is the most appropriate term for this characterization of the user's experience of gameplay is debatable. Espen Aarseth prefers to characterize computer games as instances of "ergodic discourse." For Aarseth, the notion of the ergodic is a way of specifying the difference of various traditional and new media works from the conventional narrative form of temporalization. He explains the logic informing his appropriation of this term as follows:

> The word "ergodic" is appropriated from physics, and it is constituted by the two Greek words *Ergos,* "work," and *Hodos,* "path or road," and in this context

it is used to describe a type of discourse whose signs emerge as a path produced by a non-trivial element of work. Ergodic phenomena are produced
by some kind of cybernetic system, i.e., a machine (or a human) that operates
as an information feedback loop, which will generate a different semiotic
sequence each time it is engaged.[40]

The ergodic work is a form of interactive machinery that does not equate
with the narrative configuration of a predetermined linear order. The ergodic
work generates multiple sequences of events, so that what the interactor
experiences is "one actualization among many potential routes within what
we may call the event space of semio-logical possibility."[41] Aarseth states elsewhere that while ergodic discourse is constitutively different from narrative
discourse, ergodic forms will contain some elements of narrative.[42] Computer games such as *Microsoft Combat Flight Simulator 2* and the first-person
shooter, *Doom* (id Software, 1993), would be ergodic works in these terms.

The ergodic core of these games is the interactive, goal-oriented gameplay.
Each time play commences anew, the gamer actualizes one of many potential routes through the simulated event space. In *Doom*, the player takes on a
first-person perspective of the game's virtual world and attempts to survive
frequent deadly attacks by a variety of monsters while navigating labyrinth-
ine environments of increasing complexity and difficulty. Aarseth examines
Doom to articulate his theory of ergodic temporality. "It is *Doom*'s raw, min-
imalist event space," he says, "that makes it particularly relevant as an illustration in the analysis of ergodic time."[43] More so than in narrative forms,
which privilege the time of the tale and its telling, ergodic time concerns the
time of the audience—or, more accurately, the interactors who are producers as well as recipients of the work.

According to Aarseth, ergodic time unfolds on three levels. His insightful
analysis leads to a curiously ahistorical conclusion for an essay so concerned
with the cybernetic, computer-based specificities of the ergodic work. The
first level of ergodic time is the "event time" determined by the controlling
program in which the player reacts to the challenges put forward by the
game or acts to preempt those challenges. The next level is a time of knowledge acquisition and takes place on a level outside the game's event time. Its
form may vary structurally from game to game. Some games, like *Doom*,

See Aarseth.

explicitly acknowledge the need for a "negotiation time" level, by letting the user "save" their progress (i.e., start over from a certain state of affairs, instead of at the beginning), in order to repeat difficult actions. Other games [like *Microsoft Combat Flight Simulator 2*] must be played repeatedly to gain the necessary experience that will allow a successful progression.[44]

If the second level of negotiation comes to an end, the third level of temporalization can be experienced, one in which the game is perceived as a complete sequence from beginning to end. This level would correspond to the quasi-narrative of achievement Manovich identifies with the tasking function of computer games.

Aarseth argues that these different temporal engagements with the ergodic work can be thought of as aspects of a "single dynamic: the basic structure of any game, which is the dialectic between aporia and epiphany."[45] This dynamic is a problem-solving process. An aporia, literally a "nonroad," is thrown up by the game in order to be negotiated by the player. Reflection on the challenge posed by the aporia in the negotiation time outside of actual play alternates with experimental repetition of the aporetic encounter until a solution to the problem is found. The product of this alternation between the first two forms of gametime is an epiphany, that is, "a sudden, often unexpected solution to the impasse in the event space."[46] The third level of ergodic time, the quasi-narrative experience of a completed temporal sequence, is attained when all the game's aporias have been overcome. Aarseth calls this "ergodic closure," something that games typically require but that is not essential to the operation of ergodic discourse in other forms.[47]

For Aarseth, the way computer games conjure an event space of aporias and epiphanies evokes the prenarrative, fundamental structure of all experience "from which narratives are spun."[48] Leaving aside an examination of this formulation of the underlying structure of experience in its transcendent generality—a task I will take up in the following chapter—I would propose that the aporia/epiphany dynamic Aarseth identifies as the basis of computer gametime enacts the logistical principle Virilio has described as a driving force of the pure war tendency. Computer games model problems in anticipation of their solution by the player. If ergodic discourse requires the user to work, then gameplay is a form of training. Gametime is the process of learning the solution(s), as Manovich indicates when he says the player's goal is to master the game's algorithm. Attaining the third level of gametime, that of the experience of the game as a completed temporal sequence, is a function of successfully anticipating all the eventualities of the event space.

Training was and is the primary rationale driving the military development of simulation. This is the case even if in the era of the military-entertainment complex no clear distinction between battlefield and training ground can continue to be maintained.[49] In general terms, we can say that training is future directed to the extent that it is about developing proficiencies in order to better execute some task. Military training is about improving skills so that one may survive to attain an effective level of control over the event space. This control of the semiological possibility of the simulated event space allows one to prevail by destroying or otherwise negating the threat of the enemy. As a combat-based flight sim game, *Microsoft Combat Flight Simulator 2* draws directly on this tradition of developing a lethal anticipation of events in its gameplay. Events are encountered in order to be preempted—that is, literally acquired in advance in the manner in which one refers to target acquisition by smart bombs.

Logistics names for Virilio a process in which things are transformed into potential resources for military appropriation, but which in pure war has exceeded its conventional military framework of pertinence and comprehensibility. The mode of temporalization in *Microsoft Combat Flight Simulator 2* and other computer games is one avenue where this overflowing is apparent. Gametime is that of the transformation of events (in an event space) into potential resources for the execution of a controlling procedure or algorithm. Ergodic closure is reward for the foreclosure of eventuality.

The ergodic temporality of computer games as Aarseth characterizes it enacts the anticipatory function of computer simulation. The game design of closed or closable ergodic works amounts to a two-part process: staging a set or sequence of potential problems, and providing the player with the means for completing a flowchart of solutions. The event space in which these problems are situated is conceived in terms of this flowchart. In discussing what he calls the "navigable space form" so pervasive in computer media, Manovich cites the importance of Virilio's work in identifying its military origins. In this form, says Manovich, space becomes "something traversed by a subject, a trajectory, rather than an area."[50] It is a medium through which the gamer (as the model of the computer user) encounters a number of key elements that are constitutive of the problems being modeled and the work required to deal with them. In *Microsoft Combat Flight Simulator 2*, these include the player's aircraft, his or her weapons and fuel provisions, the aircraft carrier or airstrip where the mission may originate and conclude (depending on the gameplay mode being played), members of the player's flight, other aircraft and units such as ships and ground vehicles, damage effects on the player's aircraft and avatar, and elements of the milieu such as cloud, sun glare, and topography. The world amounts to a dynamic matrix in which the interaction of the player with configurations of these elements can be played out to advance the plotting of the flowchart of possible outcomes of the gametime.

The inclusion of DIY mission-building software with the game, now a common feature of flight and other simulation gaming, supplements the player's training in the processes involved in coordinating the interplay of all these elements in the design of gameplay. For Aarseth, this is an index of the "postindustrial culture" in which "game design becomes part of gameplay, and the distance between the makers and users becomes less."[51] I would add that it further indicates that audiovisual entertainment in contemporary postindustrial culture involves play with and around the increasingly central logistical impetus that orders that culture today. As Manovich has pointed out, computer gaming is a playful modality of computer use in the computer age. Computer usage involves "cognitive multitasking—rapidly alternating between different kinds of attention, problem solving and other cognitive skills."[52] This is a central aspect of computer culture in which one's interface with a computer is more or less the same for a variety of different functions: "At one moment, the user might be analyzing quantitative data; the next, using a search engine, then starting a new application, or navigating through space in a computer game; next perhaps, using a search engine again, and so on."[53] For Manovich, the temporal shifts between interactive gameplay and the experience of the noninteractive elements of gaming is best understood ultimately in the framework of this switching between mind-sets required in the multitasking milieu of computer culture. Gametime operationalizes the space-time of virtual worlds in order to play (with) multitasking.

For Virilio, the pure war tendency's logistical transformation of the world is more than anything else an accident of the speed race of modern technology, and in particular weapons technology. Anticipation is foresight—that is, it is a form of speed through which one sees into the future, so that one comes to be in advance of events. Virilio has analyzed the rigorous demands of modern technological war for this kind of foresight and its realization in the extension of total war into the pure war of permanent preparation. Gametime contributes in no small way to the realization of this logistical demand.

Here the distinction Ricoeur makes between the "followability" of a story and a foreseeable ending assumes its full significance. One could say that foreseeability has become paramount; in the task-based game and in the spectacle-based film, the outcomes are more or less clear from the beginning of one's commitment to spending time with(in) them. A predictable ending is a sign of a poorly constructed narrative, one that, as Ricoeur suggests, fails to successfully constitute a narrative inasmuch as it fails to keep the reader/ viewer engaged in following the episodic dimension of the story. As a hybrid form that combines interactive simulation with narrative-based historical orientation, *Microsoft Combat Flight Simulator 2* takes the dynamic structure of episodic contingency and configurational unity and remakes it as foreseeable objective and potential obstacle to its achievement. The expectation of a congruent, but precisely not logically predictable, conclusion—one capable of contributing a new, ethical perspective about the world from which it emerged and to which it returns in the person of its reader/viewer— mutates into the anticipation of a successful performance.[54] In *Pearl Harbor,* this amounts to the delivery of a successful audiovisual spectacle.

Paul Virilio describes the anticipatory function of electronic surveillance and satellite reconnaissance as leading to the reconstitution of a battlefield space-time "*in which events always unfolded in theoretical time.*"[55] This theoretical time amounts to a foreclosed, or rather foreclosable, chronology

where contingencies arise only in a negative form as more or less temporary delays of the foreseen victory. This victory is achieved through the plotting of vectors of repressive response through the milieu. Space is derealized in favor of its reappearance in and as the simulated relief of the flowchart of vectored movements. Flight simulation, and the computer games that have been modeled on its immensely influential example, extend and generalize this process of rendering events in theoretical time.

This theoretical time is coemergent with the logistical space discussed in the previous chapter. This simulated space is, I argued, an uncanny theoretical double of real space; it is a strangely familiar mutation of technological modernity's drive to instrumentalize the exterior milieu through predictive calculation, probabilistic and statistical extrapolation, cybernetic modeling of dynamic systems, and so forth. Similarly, realtime is a hypothetical double of the real time of human social, political, and cultural engagement, one dedicated to the development of a maximal reduction of contingency in the passage from the hypothetical to the actual, from theory to practice, and, ideally, from realtime to real time.

Gametime allows for the leisurely refinement of theoretical time in the ergodic iteration of the encounter with event problems until, in the end, the gamer prevails. As the reanimation in computer gametime of the air war in the Pacific—albeit one that modestly (or, perhaps, with false modesty or even shamelessly) avoids the ultimate acts in that theater of operations—*Microsoft Combat Flight Simulator 2* highlights the continuity between the deterrent impulse of pure war logistical processes and the ultimate expression of the theory of airpower. This was the nuclear bombing that ended the war in the Pacific. Nuclear deterrence was born out of the proof of the hypothesis that a war could be won through the use of strategic bombing alone if it were sufficiently devastating to the enemy. This hypothesis had developed out of reflection by several combatants on their experience in World War I. As Philip K. Lawrence has argued, it was especially embraced by the allied powers of the United Kingdom and the United States, who were most successful in putting its premises into practice in World War II. Lawrence's account of the reasons for this turns on the appeal airpower had for the instrumental discourses of modernity that dominated social and technological developments in these most advanced of Western liberal democracies. Lawrence states that "modernity seeks to colonise the future; its watchword is control."[56] Air war was enthusiastically promoted by its supporters as the most effective means for attaining that control in the context of armed conflict.

Air war answers to a dream of remote control, one that particularly suited the United States' and the United Kingdom's geographical positioning and their desire to prosecute war at a safe distance from home territory. Strategic bombing, even in a total war context, helped to distance citizens in the West from the moral consequences of war. The terrible killing and destruction of strategic bombardment were rationalized by proponents of the theory of airpower such as American World War I veteran William Mitchell. He saw it as the necessary means for bringing about a more rapid conclusion to hostilities.[57] Airpower could wreak destruction far more quickly, it was theorized by the Italian airman Giulio Douhet, obviating the need for a traditional, land-based military conflict by compelling surrender.[58] Its potential to foreclose on the eventuality of land-based military conflict was tested with the nuclear attack on Japan. Its success opened the nuclear arms race and the pure war trajectory toward a generalized logistical anticipation of every contingency in the permanent preparation for absolute war.[59]

Virilio discusses the post–cold war period in terms of a mutation of the doctrine of nuclear deterrence under the pressure of

a growing threat of nuclear, chemical and bacteriological proliferation in countries concerned to forearm themselves on a long-term basis against the effects of an attack involving weapons of mass destruction and yet not able to employ high-precision weapons remotely guided from space.[60]

This proliferation of weapons of mass destruction under the impetus of an anticipatory logic of forearming is the necessary accident in Virilio's terms of the legacy of the theory of airpower, carried forward by the pure war logistical tendency. The resultant "unbalance of terror" is something that the illusion of precision weapons and remotely controlled conflict "sadly caused us to forget," says Virilio, namely, "the fact that aero-spatial war goes hand in hand with extremes of destruction and *the imperative need for an absolute weapon,* whether it be an atomic or neutron device, or chemical/bacteriological agents."[61]

Flight sims, along with the other computer games that use three-dimensional graphics—and indeed all the interactive media forms based on the navigation of virtual space developed in flight simulation—disseminate this anticipatory impulse in and through mainstream audiovisual culture. Their mode of temporalization, characterized by Aarseth as an ergodic, pathfinding experience, is a function of their design as anticipation machines. Gametime of this kind is about training for the day when the whole sequence of challenges can be overcome and the player can prevail over the event space, anticipating the advent of the game's narrative of achievement. It answers a logistical demand for control in a contemporary milieu in which, as Virilio reminds us, the anticipatory deterrence of threatening contingency goes "hand in hand" with its proliferation.

Game Over: Prevalence Versus Closure

I have argued that narrative persists in digital technocultural forms like computer games and digital visual effects–driven films, but in a transformed supplementary mode. In a similar vein, Manovich suggests that the concept of narrative developed in relation to literary and traditional media works might be "too restrictive" for new media. Instead, he paraphrases Tzvetan Todorov's characterization of "minimal narrative" as the "passage from one equilibrium to another (or, in different words, from one state to another)."[62] This notion of a minimal narrative progression should not be taken as simply a neutral opening up of narrative possibility to a variety of alternative specifications. The history of its mutation of established narrative convention is in no small way a military technoscientific one. In the minimal, logistical narrative of gametime, the end state is one of pre-valence, literally, one of superiority, of effective dominance over the events encountered in the game. To win the game is to prevail in this sense—that is, by discovering and perfecting the means to control the events in advance of the encounter with them.

This minimal narrative does not function like the interpretation machine of conventional narrativity. The historical framing of *Microsoft Combat Flight Simulator 2* functions to support the logistical emplotment of event problems by providing a coherent, significant story line that facilitates the player's engagement with the fictional gameworld. Like the secondary character of *Pearl Harbor*'s conventional period film story line, to its project of staging a sequence of spectacular audiovisual effects, the story of the gamer's involvement in larger historical events is only a supplement to the prerogatives of gametime. If computer gaming encourages the temporal oscillation Manovich associates with multitasking, however, *Pearl Harbor* could perhaps be seen as producing a similar oscillation between narrative time and the intensive experience of the spectacular effect. The supplementarity of the narrative might be best understood in terms of a transcoding of multitasking from computer usage into the experience of the filmic medium.

This is to say that, as Jacques Derrida has shown, the supplement is never only a supplement. Its exteriority to the thing it supplements is never simply in the manner of a pure surplus. It also replaces something, namely, the identity of the supposedly self-sufficient entity to which it is added as an optional extra. This means the supplement "insinuates itself *in-the-place-of*; if it fills, it is as if one fills a void."[63] In doing so, it alters the ensemble of which it forms part and is therefore never purely extraneous or inessential. Historical narrative, in filling the interpretative void of computer game and digital effects film, replaces what is lacking in their minimal narratives of the execution of a controlled sequence of events, whether these are game challenges or effects displays. The resultant form is not simply a minimal narrative devoid of higher-level significance. It is a mutated temporalization that is perhaps best perceived in the way it refigures the classic task given to historical discourse: the prevention of history repeating itself.

According to this task, historical discourse is meant to produce a significant and ethical recounting of the destructive or negative events of history so that they themselves will not be repeated in the same way (or, conversely, it should render a comprehensive understanding of the great achievements of the past so that they become instructive models for the present). Clearly, an anticipatory logic is operative in this characterization of the historian's task of uncovering the "lessons of history."[64] The historian's recollection of the past in the "configurational dimension" of narrative temporality—to recall Paul Ricoeur's term for the way the narrative "construes significant wholes out of scattered events"—is a repetition of the events that is ultimately future directed. This posture is crystallized in the ethical project that history (and all narrative) serves.[65] The reader is, in a material way, the future destination of this project. Indeed, as a technique, narrative is comparable to simulation training inasmuch as a narrative designs its reader as what Ricoeur describes as an "operator" of its reconfiguring of events, one who responds to a "set of instructions" laid out in and by the tradition informing the reception of narrative works and instantiated in the narrative form.[66]

The logistical gametime I have analyzed here deemphasizes the ethical positioning of the user/audience in favor of the demands of training for control. For fun, gamers repeat history in order to develop their control over events. They experience them ergodically—that is, as so many challenges modeled in the event space. Ergodic time prevails over the arrival of the event so that it always arrives in the familiar form of a recognizable and surmountable aporia to be negotiated in play, even when it is encountered for the first time. Inside a story, however, in the episodic dimension of the time of its telling, events happen as contingent, uncontrolled, and as yet lacking in their ultimate comprehensibility or resolution. As Ricoeur has argued, this experience of the uncontrolled alterity of events is inseparable from and co-constitutive—with the nonchronological configurational dimension— of the ethical potential of narrativity. This is because there is no story without the encounter with contingency at each moment of the story's unfolding in time. In gametime, the unrealized potential of preemptive control over the event is the predominant (but not necessarily sole) configurational horizon of the episodic dimension. The tendency is toward a minimal ethics of prevalence over the event's contingency in the ergodic foreclosure of the "game over," a time anticipated in the closing of each feedback loop between aporia and epiphany.

5 The Game of Life

Experiences of the First-Person Shooter

A certain kind of targeting defines "opportunity" strictly in terms of the present in order to bring the future, and with it *tuchë* [happenstance], under control.

—SAMUEL WEBER, *Targets of Opportunity: On the Militarization of Thinking*

This chapter examines the experience of information in first-person shooter computer games. At first glance, this might seem to refer to the rich layerings of textual and graphically presented information that accompany the perspectival animation of virtual space in these games. Elements of the screen interface, such as a compass heading graphic, a mini map, or a radar screen giving extra information about the player's surrounds, avatar health level, and weapons selection indicators, are common informational supplements to the visual field of perception provided to the player. These elements are included as characteristic of the experience of first-person shooter play, but as the acronyms IT (information technology) and ICT (information and communications technology) indicate, information is more fundamental to this experience than the provision of these supplements. Information processing is what the computer does to make the experience of the game, of its world of interactive possibility, via a dynamically updated, perspectivally illusionistic interface, available to the player.

Both the player's experience of information at work in the game screens and the experience that information makes possible are objects of my inquiry. To envisage these is to seek to articulate perspectives concerning what are best understood not as two separate phenomena, but as two adumbrations of the first-person shooter game-player object, or, in a term more appropriate to this dynamic entity, the game-player system. The components of this system exist in relationship to each other. Indeed, this system instantiates one of the most pervasive interconnections between war and technoculture that is of central relevance to this study. This is the logistical expansion of the military technoscience of cybernetics into and across technoculture. The notion of a game-player system evokes this cybernetic frame of reference for contemporary mediatized engagements.

To play a first-person shooter is to adopt a view of information that emerges from this quite particular and historically conditioned cybernetic frame of reference. In the dynamic, interactive view of the game's challenges the player envisages or, as Samuel Weber would say, "targets" the other as a particular and particularly generalizable kind of enemy.[1] This is what Peter Galison calls the "cultural meaning" of the cybernetic legacy, an "ontology of the enemy" that emerged out of Norbert Wiener's 1940s wartime research on improving antiaircraft weapons technology. This legacy, argues Galison convincingly, dies hard, and serious attempts to understand the contemporary technocultural moment downplay it at their peril.[2] My approach to first-person shooters in this chapter proceeds from this cautionary perspective.

As I discussed in the previous chapter, Espen Aarseth proposes that works like the first-person shooter *Doom* (id Software, 1993) make their interlocutors work by functioning as "some kind of cybernetic system, i.e., a machine (or a human) that operates as an information feedback loop, which will generate a different semiotic sequence each time it is engaged."[3] Computer games such as *Doom* embody a fundamental modality of human experience, namely, one in which life seems to play itself out as a dialectic of "aporia and epiphany," that is, obstacle to and discovery of the forward

progress of experience conceived as a journey along a pathway of learning, development, and growth.[4] This pair of "master tropes" constitutes, Aarseth says elsewhere, "the dynamic of hypertext discourse: the dialectic between searching and finding typical of games in general."[5] Having discovered the workings of this dialectic in the classic first-person shooter, Aarseth claims that the constant struggle against aporia to achieve epiphany so evident in *Doom* gameplay models one of the "prenarrative master-figures of experience."[6]

Aarseth's notion of the aporia–epiphany master tropes couches experience in terms of an anticipatory, problem-solving process that corresponds perfectly with the expansion of military technoscientific modes of technological research and development across the military-industrial and military-entertainment complexes. His explicit identification of the ergodic work as a cybernetic system only confirms the historical technical origins of ergodic phenomena as a major element of the logistical tendency. In responding to the transcendental scope of Aarseth's formulation, it is not enough to identify it as historically determined and therefore faulty in its metaphysical conception. Galison is right in insisting on the significance of the historical context of the emergence of cybernetics for an understanding of the computer-based technoculture that developed in the postwar period. Yet it is important to pay attention to the general, universal dimension of these technocultural developments of the war and postwar years of the 1940s–1960s.

As Galison points out, the father of cybernetics, Norbert Wiener, was aware of the more transcendental, universal implications of his work. He argued that a new conceptualization of the human in relation to the exterior milieu in general (organic and technological) is inaugurated with cybernetics.[7] As we will see, Aarseth's speculation on the universal resonance of pathbreaking in the first-person shooter can be understood as a later echo of Wiener's generalization of his war research on weapons systems. The success and influence of Wiener's project, or, rather, projection of military technoscience, is due in no small part precisely to its ability to reorient thinking in general around themes of information processing and management.

What has always been at stake in this projection of cybernetics is the universal validity of the experience of information as that which provides a credible, meaningful experience of the world. We will explore the significance of the coemergence of the cybernetic information age, in its projective universalism, with technical advances based on an expanding application of cybernetic systematization. In a sense, we will follow Aarseth's path in reverse, from life back to game, to replay the parallelism between the two. We will see that the classic first-person shooter form is in many respects a ludic tribute to the primal scene of cybernetics situated in Wiener's wartime experiments. And if the legitimacy of the information age's worldview is reiterated in the model of experience the player adopts in playing a first-person shooter, it is also reproduced in a ludic register that has the potential of all reproductions to alter, undermine, and qualify the model. The possibility of the reinvention of the transcendental master figures of experience is contained in this reproductive potential, something that we will envisage in aspects of gameplay as well as in the generic evolution of the first-person shooter genre. As an arena of experimentation in interface design and information processing aesthetics generally, computer games are privileged sites of this potential rethinking of the experience of information.

At the same time, however, redoubled efforts at confirming what Weber calls "a certain kind of targeting" are made in this era in which the stakes of controlling and managing information seem ever more urgent as a consequence of the return of enduring wartime to the United States and the Western industrialized nations caught up in the war on terror.[8] What is more, in isolated instances, the target practice that is the ground of the first-person shooter and other game forms developed in its wake plays a part in bringing the human carnage of armed assault to bear inside the Western homelands struggling to secure themselves from threats they project as external. Simon Penny has scrutinized the first-person shooter's role in these exceptional events as part of his critical and ethical meditation on what he identifies as the behaviorist, programmatic anti-intellectualism implicit in this popular form of computer-mediated interactivity. In this context, we will examine the first-person shooter's potential for critical encounter with the ontology of the enemy—a potential that would seem to lie in the possibility of opening up its own aporia in the theoretical journey toward the aporia–epiphany master figure of experience, that is, one that counters the reduction of aporia to mere roadblock on a predictable trajectory.

The Military Information Society

If, as Aarseth claims, *Doom* tells us something fundamental about living today, then this is because of the programmatic nature of the prevailing cybernetic worldview of which *Doom* is an elegant illustration. The phrase that perhaps best evokes the origin of this worldview, "military information society," was coined by Les Levidow and Kevin Robins in their 1989 anthology, *Cyborg Worlds: The Military Information Society*. It characterizes their prognosis for contemporary society and culture under the ever-increasing influence of infotech.[9] As such, it represents their strategic response to 1980s debates about cultural transformations typically identified in terms of postmodernism as well as the postindustrial and/or the information age. This military information society is one in which the military plays a pervasive role via the spread of computer culture and the resultant dissemination of a military-inspired cybernetic envisaging of existence in all areas of human activity. It is worth citing their introduction of this term in *Cyborg Worlds*. They argue that the kind of discipline promoted in contemporary society

> involves disavowing human qualities not so easily reducible—or, rather, redefining them according to computer metaphors. Through infotech, military models of reality appeal to widespread illusions of omnipotence, of overcoming human limitations, even as they conceal our relative impotence. Computer-based models of war, work and learning can promote military values, even when they apparently encourage the operator to "think." In all those ways, we are presently heading towards a military information society, which encompasses much more of our lives than we would like to acknowledge.[10]

Levidow and Robins emphasize the centrality of computer simulation practices in infotech's promotion of "military models of reality" that are designed to attain "total control over a world reduced to calculable, mechanical operations."[11] The "military values" thus promoted concern the control of complex situations, the anticipation of contingencies, and the development of reliable problem-solving techniques and technics.

As I discussed in chapter 1, Wiener's protocybernetic efforts to develop the AA predictor, a sophisticated antiaircraft system capable of anticipating the flight path of a targeted aircraft, emerges as a key progenitor of the military information society. The first-person perspective on the virtual world has its technological and conceptual origins in this project. Work on the AA predictor in 1941 incorporated flight simulation technics in a modeling of reality for the purposes of automating lethal control over it. The flight simulator setup was used in a series of experiments by Wiener and his collaborators to "simulate the data input of an enemy plane that would enter the AA predictor."[12] It is instructive to examine this process more closely because it indicates something critical concerning the goal of the AA predictor system, the methods devised to attain the goal, and what became generalizable in the abstraction of this methodology in Wiener's subsequent invention of the new science of cybernetics.

The flight simulator apparatus consisted of a joystick controlling the aiming of a light beam that shone onto a wall in front of the apparatus. A mechanical lag was built into the joystick so that movement and response differed in an analog of actual aircraft controls. The operator had the task of flying his light beam to match another light spot as it zigzagged on a wall in front of him (it was always a him), simulating the ideal flight path of a plane flying evasively while on a mission to a predetermined objective. Recordings of the position of the operator's light spot in relation to the guiding light spot provided the data for the programming of the AA predictor. The programming was based on statistical prediction techniques for the minimization of erroneous predictions using the data from a number of simulated flight paths to calculate the minimum error over the entire series of flights.[13]

The operator–flight simulator–guiding light spot ensemble amounts to a cybernetic system avant la lettre, designed to provide the mathematical data for the modeling of the system devised to control its real-world counterpart via incorporation in a more comprehensive cybernetic system: AA gunner—AA weapon—aircraft—pilot. Comprising elements interacting with each other in various ways, a cybernetic system models these interactions as the communication of messages back and forth between the nodes. The messages incite responses from the elements in the form of messages effecting the events or actions of the system and affecting its status as a whole. Feedback is a crucial aspect of the communications from the point of view of the primary goal of the cybernetic analysis and modeling of systems, namely, the regulation of the system's operation through controlling communications.

The feedback loop of most interest to Wiener's team in this setup was between the guiding light spot and the pilot-controlled light spot. Galison points out that they were most interested in modeling the "feedback difficulties" experienced by pilots trying to fly an evasive course under combat conditions. To this end, they resorted to "racing the target across the wall at high speed" as well as inserting the mechanical lag delaying the responsiveness of the operator's light spot to joystick manipulation.[14] The disjunction between "kinaesthetic sense and visual information" was the source of the feedback difficulties affecting the operator's control of the flight path.[15] In other words, his struggle to reduce the gap between the "'intended' position and the actual position of the operator's light dot" in a simulated hostile environment was the target of this data collection exercise.[16] Galison puts quotation marks around "intended" here to alert the reader to a key move in the subsequent inflation of this specific war-fighting research into a theory of human action (on its way to becoming a general theory of natural, mechanical, or human action). This move involved a redefinition of intention that stripped away any reference to psychological or other nonobservable interiority and focused on the identification of observed behavior as goal directed or not. The equivalence, from this perspective, of the human with the mechanical or natural phenomena was expressed in the "black box" vision of the human nervous system adopted by Wiener in the "servo-mechanical theory" of the human that emerged as cybernetics in the wake of the AA predictor project.[17]

Galison's main contention is that this vision never amounted to a pure abstraction from wartime concerns and could not fail to carry over to the general science of cybernetics the implicit "ontology of the enemy" as a wily, calculating, threatening, "Manichean" complex of human and weapons technology.[18] The object of cybernetic analysis is always an avatar of this enemy or "his" opponent, the "mechanical analogue" set in place to control the threat. One of the classic problems extensively discussed in the first phase of postwar cybernetics was that of the human being as such an analog, sandwiched between weapons technology capable of performance speeds superior to those of its operator. This was the question of the man in the middle, a formula for considering the human machine generalized from the situation of the AA gunner sitting between his radar tracking, targeting, and firing systems.[19]

In Wiener's experimental, prototypical model of this agonistic milieu, the operator, simulating an enemy bomber—"bomber" here as complex of pilot and aircraft—struggled against the disjunction of present and future, between actual and intended position, between immediate kinaesthetic sensations and vision of what lay ahead. The information exchange that would be central to the new science of control mechanisms envisaged in Wiener's 1948 book, *Cybernetics; or, Control and Communication in the Animal and the Machine,* took its place here between the actual and the virtual, the present and the future. It is also at the heart of the playful experience of a "disassociated" kinaesthetic embodiment that Andy Darley identifies as the key characteristic of the action gamer's "immersion" in first-person shooter and similar game forms.[20] The capacity to model and then program the dynamics of the operator's feedback difficulties into a system of information exchange is what made these exchanges between time and space possible, between war projects and postwar technoscientific developments in information systems, computing, cybernetic-influenced social sciences, and cognitive science, between serious and entertainment technologies, between 1940s wartime, the cold war, and the time of the war on terror.

Information and Speed: Playing with Time in the Medium of Digital Experience

Information, as Bernard Stiegler says, is not immaterial but "a transitory material state."[21] In a sense, we could think of the passage of the "feedback difficulties" of the operator of Wiener's enemy bomber simulator into the programmed electronic calculator of his AA predictor system as a becoming-informational of kinaesthetic and perceptual experience, that is, of lived material–technical existence. This is so even if it is lived inside a virtual modeling of actual flight. This points to the dependence of this becoming-informational on the possibility of a technical and conceptual reduction of the full complexity of technical being-in-the-world in a virtual modeling of the world that facilitates given operational objectives of the cybernetic process. This passage from the material to the informational with a view to a decisive return to the material (enemy object) became a privileged methodology of technoscientific development. Wiener's successful cross-disciplinary promotional endeavors in the wake of the termination of the failed AA predictor project did much to establish this privilege. The emergence of the programmable digital computer, operating through variable signal communications and processing—itself generalized largely from specific

targeting and code breaking calculators—overlapped and dovetailed with
the cybernetic effort to model and regulate dynamic systems of all kinds.

Understood in terms of this passing out of and back to material factical
existence in a directed, active, transformational trajectory, "information processing" would be one of the most important of the "computer metaphors"
mentioned by Levidow and Robins that redefine "human qualities" of intelligence, thinking, and decision making. Douglas D. Noble argues that information processing was first conceptualized as a field of inquiry in early
1950s research conducted by the United States Air Force–sponsored Rand
Corporation as "part of the military endeavour to understand 'the human
factor' within a complex man/machine weapon system."[22] This research
included the simulation of human decision making in experimental computer programs and was thus also instrumental in the birth of the science of
artificial intelligence, initially known as cognitive simulation.[23] Information
processing, decision making, and problem solving—these 1950s synonyms
for a cybernetic notion of mental functioning, in concert with complex
weapons systems under battle conditions, dominate mainstream conceptions of efficient mental labor in today's computerized society. It is no surprise, then, that its native entertainment form, the computer game, will
reflect these conceptions in a ludic register.

In the first-person shooter, information is the medium through which the
gamer strives for control over the system—measured via achievement of
the game goals—in which he or she is involved. This involvement in the
game can be described in relation to the computer devices that form the
other components of the system. The gamer is between the output devices
of screen and audio reproduction and the input devices of keyboard, mouse,
joystick, and game pad. Henry Jenkins and Kurt Squire note that one engages in a kind of virtual primal struggle in the space of a first-person shooter.
I would say, however, that this sense of an archaic, archetypal human conflict—their sharper figuration of Aarseth's prenarrative master tropes of
experience—is provided by the way this form recalls the "primal scene" of
computer-mediated interactivity, namely, Wiener's AA predictor research.[24]
In this contested space, the player plays at mastering the communication
network in which he or she is a key node. Information concerning variables
such as player avatar location, enemy threats and actions (whether human

or computer controlled), weapon selection, ammunition stocks, secrets discovered, and health levels are received via the output devices. The player processes this information under the pressure of realtime updating of the dynamic situation and responds with messages sent back along the communication network via the input devices, perpetuating the mutual feedback of player and gameworld. This gameworld is what in 1980s artificial intelligence research parlance would be termed a microworld or toy world—what Tom Athanasiou describes as an "artificially tidy world" programmed through collections of "statements in formal computer languages" that are not about the "real open-ended world."[25] Programming such a microworld is precisely about making possible controlling communications with predictable outcomes.

Realtime flow of information, then, is the engine driving the generation of possible outcomes in virtual microworlds. It is central to first-person shooters and to the simulation industry more generally. Paul Virilio calls the computer an "inference engine" to highlight its efficacy for the modeling and simulation of alternative scenarios, indicating its deep affinity with the "logistical" dynamic of anticipatory virtualization that in his analysis prevails over technocultural becoming.[26] The crucial point for our discussion of the experience of information is that speed is central to information processing.

Information, in its cybernetic ur-form as a mathematical expression of the probability that a given message will be transmitted in a communications network, calculates the future for the cybernetic purpose of better controlling it. As such, information aspires to the absolute speed of being in advance of events. As theorized by Wiener and Claude Shannon, the quantity of information is not static in complex cybernetic systems, but rather is recalculated after the receipt of each message at a control node.[27] At the level of the human user, information processing may be thought of as the translation of this military–cybernetic mathematical venture in generalized preemption, that is, acquisition in advance of the encounter with whatever is to be encountered.

In *The Information Bomb*, Virilio states that "whether it be speed of acquisition, transmission or computation, *information is inseparable from its acceleration in energy terms*—slowed up information being no longer even worthy of the name, but mere background noise."[28] Anyone whose avatar has been killed by a rapidly passing blur while standing around waiting for his or her screen to update in a multiplayer first-person shooter such as *Call of Duty: Modern Warfare 2* (Activision, 2009) knows the truth of this. Connection lag and ping rates become as critical as one's skills in the successful execution of the game goals. Information's ephemeral quality speaks of the relation between it and the present moment, a relation that is inherently virtual inasmuch as the function of information is to anticipate the future so as to render it already past, that is, already under control, already squared away in the present moment of the controlling instance.

This is the contribution the cybernetic approach to information makes to that form of targeting Weber speaks of as increasingly prevalent today, one in which the future is brought "under control" by being determined "strictly in terms of the present."[29] In this scenario, there is no need for a delay between perception and action; it is precisely this delay that is the danger motivating Wiener's founding research. "Knowledge must constitute action," says visionary cyberneticist Stafford Beer, dreaming of a computer model of the social system based on the U.S. Air Force's Semi-Automated Ground Environment (SAGE) air defense system.[30] As with Aarseth's master figure of experience, knowledge here is conceivable as a product of information processing that maps out goal-directed pathways requiring decisions about how to proceed. Information enables the user to extrapolate the twists and turns of those pathways as if they had already been traversed.

The functional effectiveness of this as if is exactly what becomes imperative in the nuclear age. If, as Galison recounts, "humans acting under stress" was the scenario in which Wiener worked toward the AA predictor and imagined the future of cybernetics (and the cybernetic future), the arrival of the atom bomb "multiplied one hundredfold" Wiener's hopes and fears for cybernetic technology.[31] If Wiener himself was profoundly affected by news of the bombings of Hiroshima and Nagasaki in August 1945, causing him to reevaluate his active involvement in military technoscientific research and development, the cybernetic paradigm nonetheless became a key methodology for the cold war buildup in response to the implications of nuclear conflict. As Virilio has shown, the immediately grasped potential for the absolute intensification of total war into the duration of nuclear detonation had an accidental impact on peacetime, refiguring it under the imperative of complete and permanent preparation for this potential future moment. Systems promising the preemptive regulation of this absolute contingency at the speed of electronic, computerized calculation and response proliferated, along with the desire and the anxiety concerning their functioning.

Extensions of and Generic Reflections on the First-Person Shooter Game of Life (and Death)

The first-person shooter game serves better than most other technocultural media forms as an illustration of this dominant tendency of contemporary technoculture in the age of information. Speed is of the essence in executing a successful sequence of controlling communications in a first-person shooter game. The first-person shooter provides an experience by which one comes over time to achieve this realtime performative success by means of frequent repetition and review of the challenges the game presents. Aarseth provides an apt characterization of the classic first-person shooter game experience with his notion of ergodic time. This he characterizes via a tripartite schema of the interlaced temporalities in which one becomes involved when playing *Doom*—the realtime interaction of gameplay, the negotiation time during which one reviews failures and hypothesizes solutions to game aporias, and the experience of the game as completed pathway.[32] The aporia–epiphany dialectic Aarseth identifies at the heart of this temporal complex is the dynamic struggle between game challenges and their overcoming or circumvention. Playing is training—training for the performances that overcome particular game challenges within one level, stage, or mission, and ultimately for the performance that one day will end the game. Of course, a game may still be fun even after this performance is achieved, such may be the variety of possible successful performances and eventualities in the fullness of its ergodic temporality. Nonetheless, the essence of the mechanism is this problem-solving dynamic of modeling solutions via experimental repetition of the challenging scenario.

While the first-person shooter is not one of those "computer-based models of war, work and learning" that Levidow and Robins list as influential in the promotion of military values of control, it is not difficult to see that it has drawn on the development of these models in its design of an enjoyable training routine in an imaginary microworld of one kind or another. The 3-D rendering engines at the heart of the first-person shooter and its variants, such as the third-person shooter and the tactical or team shooter, including id Software's groundbreaking *Wolfenstein 3D* and *Doom* systems, the influential "id Tech 3" engine used first for *Quake III Arena* (id Software, 1999) and more recently by the highly successful *Call of Duty* franchise (Activision, from 2003), Epic's *Unreal* engine (Epic, 1998), powering such games as *America's Army* (U.S. Department of Defense, 2002), *Gears of War* (Microsoft Games Studio, 2006), *Bioshock* (2K Games, 2007), and *Tom Clancy's Splinter Cell* (Ubisoft, 2002), and Bungie's engine for the Xbox launch of arguably the most influential shooter game series of the last decade, *Halo* (Microsoft Game Studios, 2001), are commercial innovations. They are nonetheless very much part of the military-entertainment complex discussed in chapter 1. This is all too evident in the profound debt they owe to the military-driven development (in flight and vehicle simulation) of an interface based on an embedded perspective, not to mention the breakthroughs in remote computer networking in DARPA's development of SIMNET that make online multiplayer gaming possible.

In many respects, then, the first-person shooter can answer to Aarseth's evocation of it as the "game of life"—albeit life (re)conceived less metaphysically and more as life in the contemporary logistical milieu of information processing. As a game form, however, it always retains the potential for play with the elements that make it a game. This is part of the fun of any game— for instance, the play between the intent of the designers of gameplay and the useless pleasures that can be had of the game. For example, in the first-person shooter and other shooter games that have developed in its wake, the desire of players to shoot things such as background scenery items for the fun of it has gradually been incorporated in the interface of many games. This was a notable innovation in games such as *Metal Gear Solid 2* (Konami, 2002) and *Return to Castle Wolfenstein* (id Software, 2001). Today this is fairly routine, and indeed has been recuperated into the experience design of the more open scope of play in games such as the *Grand Theft Auto* series (Rockstar Games, from 1997) and adventure and cross-genre game deployments of the first-person perspective mode of play.

In the case of the genre of the first-person shooter, what is also evident is an evolving generic awareness or reflexivity about how the game is played and evaluated as a cultural form. After the groundbreaking success of early first-person shooter games such as *Wolfenstein 3D, Doom,* and *Quake,* the genre was initially dominated by science fiction/horror fantasy scenarios. What has emerged as a trend within the genre from the late 1990s is a hybridization with battle strategy simulations and realtime strategy games, so that games like the *Medal of Honor* series (Electronic Arts, from 2002), the *Battlefield* series (Electronic Arts, from 2002) and *Battlefield 2* series (Electronic Arts, from 2005), and the *Tom Clancy* (Red Storm Entertainment and Ubisoft, from 1998) and *Brothers in Arms* series (Ubisoft, from 2005) of tactical shooters draw on actual historical military conflicts or on realistic near-future scenarios for the design of levels and mission maps. In these games, the military roots of the logistical ethic of training for preemptive control seems especially marked in the cut scenes, the attention to weapon authenticity, and the training missions. It is as if the fantastic monsters of *Doom* and its progeny have been unmasked retrospectively as discarded disguises for enemy soldiers.[33]

The U.S. Army's own game, *America's Army* (U.S. Department of Defense, 2002), and projects developed for both military and commercial applications such as *Full Spectrum Warrior* (Pandemic Studio, 2004) would seem to be the logistical end point of this trajectory. But this unmasking needs to be understood as itself an element of the genre's playing out and playing with its own history and with perceptions of the first-person shooter game, a point well illustrated by the French game *Ironstorm* (Wanadoo, 2002). *Ironstorm* represents the genre's ironic counterpoint to the military recruitment of the first-person shooter as another training simulation modality. This game, which in one of its opening credit screens describes itself as an "anticipation fiction," proposes an alternative world history for its setting, one in which World War I never ended. It extrapolates a decades-long European conflict and stages the action in 1964. Weapons and communication technology designed for the game function as quirky and imaginative products of this alternate historical trajectory and are an important component of its novelty.

Like the counterfactual speculation at the margins of historical discourse upon which the game draws, *Ironstorm* plays a double game with the real (historical) world. On the one hand, it depends for its realization of the alternate world on conventional notions of historical development and the belief that present reality is a product of history. On the other hand, it foregrounds its own reflexive play with these conventional historical notions and beliefs by mobilizing them to produce a virtual reality from hypothetical premises. As such, *Ironstorm* comments ironically on the recent inflation of the first-person shooter genre from fantasy game to historical reality simulator. It provides something of a critical counterpoint to numerous titles that stage their combat-based gameplay on hypothetical conflicts drawn from recent and current military campaigns and zones of global political instability such as the Middle East, the former Soviet bloc countries, the Korean peninsula, and Central America. In doing so, it has some fun with those accounts—including in some ways my own—that adopt their critical perspective in response to the famous Ronald Reagan comment that computer games are training tomorrow's warriors.[34]

The *Time Splitters* series (Eidos and Electronic Arts, 2000–2005) also plays around reflexively in the space between fantasy and realism. Players jump between different time periods to play on maps that reference the gamut of generic fictional gunfighting milieus from film and video games such as the Wild West, jungle temple ruins, Chicago in the Roaring Twenties, and so on. The games have numerous references to other games from *Lara Croft* to *Gears of War.* In the related genre of the driving simulator, games like the *Grand Theft Auto* series have been successful in offering an ironically excessive incorporation of violent combat and killing routines in civic, urban social spaces and urban organized crime scenarios. The games play on the difference between the credible representation of real-world spaces and their ludic function as the arena for virtual lethal violence.

Resonances with *Ironstorm's* reflexively ironic commentary on virtual realism can, to a greater or lesser degree, be found in all first-person shooter games. This was more apparent in the early releases before the conventions of the interface became established. In *Wolfenstein 3D* (Apogee Software, 1992), for instance, the bar at the bottom of the screen featured readouts of player score, location, ammunition, and weapon selection. One of these was an image of the avatar's face, which was animated to look from side to side as the player made corresponding moves in the virtual space, and to

s commensurate with the player's health level as it changed
n play. This impossible and amusing perspective on the avatar
was dropped from the later stabilization of the first-person shooter screen
elements. Other common aspects of the first-person shooter game universe
play a similar role in perturbing the correspondence between the game and
Information Processing 101. For instance, the Health component of gameplay constantly undercuts the parallel between game and real. In most first-
person shooter games, the acquisition of a first aid kit or the audible swig of
a drink bottle with a red cross on it boosts one's health meter reading, constantly reminding the player precisely of the impossibility of such an instant
fix outside the game. Perhaps the very aspect of the first-person shooter that
Aarseth identified as essential to its ergodic temporality—the capacity to
experiment repeatedly with different solutions to a given aporia until a way
forward is found—also provides the most enduring challenge to the assim-
ilation of the first-person shooter genre to a paradigm of logistical discipline.
If the game form is a tonal variation on the training simulation model of
war, work, and learning so prevalent today, it also amounts to a metamodel-
ing of this model in a space suspended, however provisionally, from utilitar-
ian frameworks of productivity. That is to say, in its very mode of constant
repetition and starting over, the game provides a restaging of this routine
of information processing. The closure implicit in this microworldview of
experience as the progression from predefined problem through experiment to solution is opened to speculation in this restaging. The exclusion of
the unforeseen is made evident by the first-person shooter game in the very
achievement of that winning performance where each enemy attack is dealt
with exactly as if it is seen before it arrives because it has been seen exactly
like this, eliminating any latent contingency in the "as if."

The Stakes in Play: Ethical Debates around Violent Routines

In the view of Simon Penny, the critical potential of the speculative doubling
of the cybernetic worldview provided by the first-person shooter would be
relatively insignificant in comparison with its capacity to program quasi-
automated behaviors. For him, its capacity to game life by playing out the
encounter with the other in a scenario of aggressivity and compulsive repetition is its most important and influential aspect. Penny criticizes the

sidestepping of its military behaviorist characteristics in accounts of the first-person shooter such as Frank Lantz and Eric Zimmerman's discussion of *Quake*.[35] In Penny's view, Lantz and Zimmerman downplay the explicitly violent iconography of armed conflict in the game in favor of a characterization of it that compares it to the more cerebral athletics of tennis, a game with a highly sublimated and historically distant relation to mortal combat.[36] Drawing on the work of noted antiviolent video game activist David Grossman, a "retired Lieutenant-Colonel and expert in desensitizing soldiers to increase their kill efficiency," Penny describes the first-person shooter as a form that "conditions the young in exactly the same way as the military does: they hardwire young people for shooting at humans."[37] Penny cites Grossman's analysis of the contribution made by shooter games in several infamous mass shootings perpetrated by children in the United States. The shooters appeared to exhibit a quasi-automatic passage from a single killing to multiple shootings, with an accuracy of fire better than the average scores of law enforcement officers.[38]

These events, and the questions they pose about the first-person shooter and similar video game forms, animate Penny's "academic and activist" reflections on the "ethics of simulation" and his call for a "theoretical and aesthetic study of embodied interactivity" that would lead to less ominous models of user engagement in the world than those that "actively contribute to gun violence among kids."[39] While my approach concurs in part with Penny's suggestion that computer games are the "product" of "two generations of Cold War mentality, of the militarization of education and entertainment, or possibly as an enactment, in the most graphic way, of the reigning dog-eat-dog ethic of the business world," I cannot follow him to the same conclusions concerning the inevitable consequences of the behaviorist, classically cybernetic mechanism replayed by the first-person shooter and similar games.[40] If Penny is justified in drawing on Grossman's work as a tragic confirmation of the effectiveness of the first-person shooter game as a training technology indebted to military training systems and their dissemination across technoculture, these terrible killings must nonetheless be understood as extremely isolated instances of a "passage to the act," in comparison to the millions of players of first-person shooter and similar games in the United States and elsewhere over the last two or three decades.[41]

Questions concerning the other factors leading to such passages to murderous violence in these particular instances necessarily assume critical importance in understanding these events.

Despite his avoidance of the more social and cognitive learning–based psychological opinion on the effects of violent video games (as a continuation and intensification of violent film, television, and video), Penny finds himself here entering the murky terrain of media effects discourse through his appeal to the behaviorism of Grossman. Jeffrey Goldstein has provided a comprehensive overview of media effects research on computer games.[42] He cites Anderson and Dill's paradigmatic articulation of the view that violent computer games affect, or even effect, violent behavior. They "claim that violent video games are the ideal means by which to learn aggression, with exposure to aggressive models, reinforcement, and behaviour rehearsal."[43] Goldstein demonstrates, however, the endemic inconclusiveness of claims made in effects research for the violent effects of violent video games, given the dubious and inconsistent methodologies, the conflicting interpretations of the same experiments, and the conceptual shortcomings of research design faced with the complex and diverse phenomena of computer game-play as situated individual and social activity. Goldstein concludes:

> Of course the media affect emotions and behaviour. That is why people use them. However, there is no evidence that media shape behaviour in ways that override a person's own desires and motivations. Can a violent video game make a person violent? It can if he wants it to.[44]

I concur with this response: media effects research seeks to isolate violent media as a major cause of violent behavior and attitudes. However, Goldstein's opposition between media and a "person's own desires and motivations" should be treated with some caution. To the extent that the various media have assumed an increasingly central role in providing access to recorded experience in the form of images, text, stories, simulations, information, and advertising, it becomes increasingly difficult to maintain an unequivocal distinction between the individual's own experiences—those that come to shape his or her desires and motivations—and the media's provision of so much of that experience. My account of what is given to game players in and through the technics of computer games rests on a general claim about the co-constitutive relationship between the media and the individual today. Individual context and choice is no doubt critical to the adoption of media technologies and what they provide. Goldstein is absolutely correct to point out the fatal absence of consideration of this from the methodologies of the social psychologists running the anti–media violence campaign. But what is given is also of critical interest in the evaluation of individual desires and motivations and their manifestation in the social and political spheres of the expanding technoculture of the digital computer.

Penny argues, contrary to the position that games are just play and not serious activities with serious implications and entailments, that "the truth is the opposite: play is a powerful training tool."[45] While I have also asserted the connection between computer gameplay and training, the key difference between Penny's account and my own lies in the relative marginalization of the context of gameplay in Penny's insistence on the conditioning effect of first-person shooter use. "We are drawn to the conclusion," says Penny, "that what separates the first person shooter from the high-end battle simulator is the location of one in an adolescent bedroom and the other in a military base."[46] Leaving aside a challenge to this claim on its face value—in fact, most commercial games differ considerably in representational fidelity, interface technologies, and the context in which one plays with such high-end battle simulators—the implicit claim here is that context changes nothing about the use and effect of the simulation experience. On the contrary, I argue that it is essential to keep in view the diversionary, idiosyncratic, and even critical potential of the adoption of these technoscientific givens of the military technoscientific legacy of World War II and its aftermath. While they have undoubtedly played a key role in determining the emergence and evolution of contemporary technoculture, they cannot negate the potential for their reinvention that comes with their reproduction in different contexts.[47] To restate Penny's claim, I would say that computer games are the reproduction rather than simply the "product" of "two generations of Cold War mentality, of the militarization of education and entertainment."

The tensions that David Nieborg discusses between the gamer cultures that have grown up around first-person shooters such as *Doom* and the more

tions sponsored by the military developers of *America's*
tance of the differences between the serious and entertain-
of use of different first-person shooter games.[48] Nieborg discusses the attempt of the managers of the *America's Army* servers to channel
the user community's activities into play that respects the official rules of
engagement, into organized player and team competitions and away from
various modding activities such as designing new skins for players and modifying game maps or creating new ones. The notion of a participatory or
co-creative culture of computer gameplay proposed by writers such as Joost
Raessens and Sue Morris on the model of cultural studies notions of participatory media culture elaborate, in a similar vein, the adoptive reinvention
by player communities of given game technologies.[49] Beyond—but not to
deny or dismiss—the question of the contribution the first-person shooter
has arguably made to the carnage wreaked by a number of individuals in
specific, extreme circumstances, I would argue that ultimately the critical
questions to be posed about the effect of shooter games as inheritors of the
massively influential targeting ventures of cybernetic technoscience concern
the part they play in reinforcing, reexamining, or otherwise reproducing
these ventures in and as the ongoing diversity and complexity of the contemporary technocultural moment.

Energetic Undertakings: The First-Person Shooter
Versus Second Wave Cybernetics

As Virilio has argued for a long time now, it is necessary to pay close attention
to the accident of any given technology and of technological developments
as larger transformational forces. Cybernetics, arising from the military
project of designing and programming accidents, has as its raison d'être the
control of events via the anticipation of all the vicissitudes of their possible
coming to pass.[50] In replaying for fun the process of elimination operative in
the informational experience of events—inaugurated in the AA predictor's
statistical programming to isolate the target's future position by means of
the exclusion of erroneous predictions—the first-person shooter enacts a
powerful technocultural desire to encounter the future in the form of anticipated, controllable contingencies. To target the future in this way is, as
Samuel Weber has argued in *Targets of Opportunity,* to attempt to bring the

YES!

boutique weapons (available) are the problem — AbC —

future under control by representing it in terms of the present. That is, it attempts to think of it as a present problem or goal in terms of a technical system for addressing it. The future as other, as other than anticipated, as the unfolding of other configurations of associated elements and pathways of emergence, is what tends to be excluded in this isolation of the target. In this wider perspective, we could see the cybernetic discovery of information processing and its post–World War II proliferation as both the response to (and the postmodern exacerbation of) the Western modernist dynamic that oscillates between projected, planned development and the institution of permanent innovation and destabilization. The cold war, pure war, and now the permanent war on terror are marked by this general adoption of an infor- *yes* mational solution to the challenge to maintain the program against the imminent, and immanent, threat of its undoing.

When N. Katherine Hayles argues that in the information age the pat-tern–randomness relation replaces presence–absence as the key concep-tual pairing orienting one's engagement in the technocultural milieu, she elegantly expresses the eventual result of Wiener's efforts to abstract and generalize his conclusions concerning the outcome of his work on the AA predictor.[51] With the threatening remoteness of the enemy taken as a given, the AA predictor sought to preempt the enemy's becoming-present. *yes.* The predictor's technics were designed to exercise the regulatory power of patterning the seemingly chaotic (but intentionally lethal) movements of his approach. The relevance of this context of the birth of cybernetics to the postwar nuclear age cannot be overstated. It explains Wiener's subsequent *?* equating of disorder and entropic decay with evil—that is, with the identifi-able enemy other—in his postwar texts. As Hayles points out, Wiener was a key proponent of this battlefield cosmology of cybernetic systems (of pattern regulation) and disorder where "life struggles against entropy and noise."[52]

Hayles shows in her history of the development of cybernetic theory that later theorists working in the cybernetic tradition—what she calls the second wave of cybernetics—came to question this agonistic, moralistic cosmology and to complicate the picture of noise/pattern relations. They sought to rethink information processing in less agonistic and controll-ing frames. Theorists working in different fields, such as Gregory Bateson,

Humberto Maturana, and Francisco Varela, developed more reflexive cybernetic positions, exploring concepts such as autopoesis, complexity, and emergence to complicate the picture of a pure opposition between system and disorder, between cybernetic model and its object, and between information and noise.[53] The success of the first-person shooter however, gives us cause to reflect on the persistence and pervasiveness of the early cybernetic vision of information exchange as the medium of preemptive problem solving. In view of later efforts to rethink the interchanges between pattern and randomness, informational exchange and noise, we can understand the first wave cybernetic project as the ongoing in its anticipation of the emergence of the second wave and the implicit loss of controlling redundancy that it implies.

Mark C. Taylor, another writer interested to examine the creative, critical potential of what he calls the "emerging network culture," has some acute insights into the nature of this desired redundancy.[54] Exploring the relations between information theory and the history of thermodynamics, Taylor looks at how the notion of entropy assumed a central place in the classic cybernetic opposition of order (pattern) and disorder (noise). It emerged in the cutting-edge discipline of thermodynamics in the nineteenth century in the wake of the steam engine's transformation of the European industrial system. Taylor recounts how the implicit reversibility of the classic Newtonian conception of the mechanistic clockwork universe was perceived as no longer viable with the discovery of the second law of thermodynamics, and with the incorporation of statistical uncertainty into particle theories of light.[55] Complex, dynamic processes come to be modeled scientifically as irreversible passages toward the entropic undoing of the order regulating their operation. The organizing effects of natural or human systems exercise their negentropic force against the backdrop of this ultimately inevitable passage to entropy for any closed system. Taylor gestures at the creative potential of this interaction between order and its undoing, where what constitutes information can slide between what regulates the existing system and the noise that presages the birth of another ordering.[56] The classic cybernetic theory and technics of information processing, however, set out if not to annul, then at least to manage the threat of irreversibility, anticipating the outcome so that it is virtually reversible. The designed information exchange targets the modeled event so that it is over before it has begun and consequently unable to impinge irreversibly on the present orderly homeostasis. A really great first-person shooter player is a still point amid a seeming frenzy of energetic interactions, neutralizing opponents before they have the opportunity to disturb this equilibrium.

6 Other Players in Other Spaces

War and Online Games

One cannot say outright: this is play, this is a project, but only: the play, the project dominates in a given activity.

—GEORGES BATAILLE, cited in Jean-Luc Nancy,
The Inoperative Community

The American new media artist/activist Joseph DeLappe is waging an interventionist campaign in the U.S. military's own multiplayer online game, *America's Army* (U.S. Department of Defense, from 2002). Having qualified for entry to the multiplayer mode of the game by completing the basic training (or "boot camp") missions, he joins a game on one of the official game servers as a member of one of two teams involved in the squad-based tactical combat. This allows him to stage his intervention into the normal routines of gameplay. He does not participate actively in the combat play—a refusal to act that soon results in his avatar's demise—but uses the multiplayer text chat channel to list the name, rank, and date of death of American armed services personnel who have been killed in Iraq during the invasion and ongoing occupation of that country by the armed forces of the U.S. and its allies in the "Coalition of the Willing."

Unlike most commercial first-person shooter–based games, if your avatar is killed during a mission in *America's Army*, there is no respawning to rejoin the game while the current mission lasts. Instead, players return to the action as a kind of revenant, capable of observing and communicating but not interacting through their now-inert avatar. Players can observe the rest of the contest by selecting and switching between the points of view of their own avatar and those of the other players on the mission map. They can also continue to use the online text messaging system of the interface. As "dead_in_iraq," DeLappe takes advantage of this spectral, textual "presence" to perform his intervention. He includes some screenshots of his practice on his Web site with some instances of the responses of other players to his chat messages, ranging from incomprehension to questions about his relation to the people listed to player identification of their own relation to real armed conflict—one player states that he or she is a soldier in real life (Figure 4).[1]

DeLappe's work is an elegant attempt to interrupt the smooth workings of the online multiplayer entertainment form that *America's Army* has set out, with considerable success, to become for the purposes of marketing and recruitment propaganda.[2] I have opened the consideration in this chapter of the online multiplayer gaming community with dead_in_iraq because what I see as key themes of concern in this book are at the heart of DeLappe's poignant unworking of networked group play in *America's Army*. One of

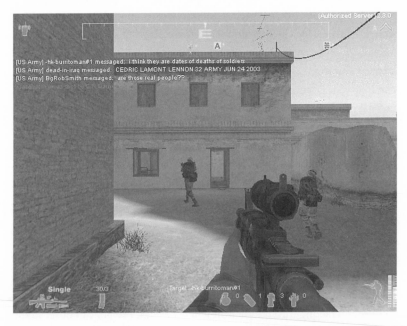

FIGURE 4 Joseph DeLappe, dead_in_iraq, 2006, courtesy of the artist.

these is the relation between the work and its interruption. That is, we will examine the complex interactions between the way the net of individual user–computer–communication systems works together to enable the shared space of common interaction and how community arises both within that working and, as with DeLappe's practice, in its suspension. The fact that DeLappe accesses the community of users in and through his technical competence both in computer use and in the game's basic skill sets, so that the community his intervention targets is indeed a part of the technical affordance of the computer game system, also signals something crucial for our discussion. Third, dead_in_iraq's introduction of death—not only actual military deaths as a nonvirtual, social-political context of gameplay, but the individual deaths of specific, recently existent individuals—into the usual ephemeral flow of in-game dialogue is a key to its power to illuminate the routine, realtime operation of these exemplary technocultural, virtual community forms. DeLappe's is a decisive defamiliarizing gesture.[3]

This chapter will set out some hypotheses about the nature of the engagement with others in online gaming in virtual spaces. Its examples will be in the main chosen from war and conflict-based games, which include first-person shooters, fantasy role-playing games (massively multiplayer online role-playing games, or MMORPGs), combat-based flight simulation, and strategy games involving war and conflict scenarios. While these represent the largest proportion of the games played online in multiplayer mode, I acknowledge that these are not by any means the totality of game genres played online by multiple players. Sport simulations such as the *FIFA* series (Electronic Arts, from 1993) are a significant exception. And well-subscribed games such as *The Sims Online* (Electronic Arts, 2002) and *Second Life* (Linden Lab, 2003) do not revolve around virtual violent conflict. Indeed, many writers will question the designation of *game* for such salable online activities, given their structural lack of specific goal-oriented contests such as those provided by the missions and death matches of first-person shooters or the quest structure that organizes the persistent, emergent forms of online fantasy worlds such as *Everquest* (Sony Online Entertainment, from 1999) and *World of Warcraft* (Blizzard, from 2004).[4] The *Sims Online, Second Life,* and similar virtual world systems have a somewhat different pedigree from these war-focused forms, and the precision of their classification occupies the minds of game studies researchers seeking to define the object of the discipline.[5] At a technical level of the provision of simulated realtime inter-action—that is, of a coherent virtual space in which to be here together—these forms all share important features. My hypotheses about online gaming will proceed from a phenomenological approach to the encounter with(in) that simulated coherence. It will then seek to develop a postphenomenolog-ical approach aimed at a thinking of the community made possible in and as this virtual "co-herence" of sociotechnical equipment and communication.

As I have demonstrated in the opening chapters of this study, this equip-ment emerges out of the interrelated developmental dynamics between war, simulation, and technoculture that I have characterized in this book through Virilio's notion of pure war and the analysis of the military-entertainment complex. Georges Bataille's observation about the continuum between play and (serious) project is relevant here. Because of the way the project is always implicated in the play, games and their players' involvements are an immensely valuable means of better understanding the project of contem-porary Western technoculture. The project, if it can have a singular desig-nation, that has driven technoculture for the last sixty years—the age of the digital computer—has had war and the preparation for war at its core. Virilio's running commentary on the century of industrialized total war, its logistical mutation in the cold war period, and its more recent transforma-tion in the twenty-first century's age of terror has sought to trace the permu-tations of this overarching tendency of technocultural and sociopolitical developments.[6] The conflict-centered gaming worlds are, in this light and not only because of their preponderance in the sphere of commercial online gaming, the best place to look for the characteristics and the possibilities of community given in the virtual spaces of online spatial simulations.

Player and/as Space: A Heideggerian Approach to Online Gaming

In most research on the online gaming phenomena, the player is taken to be an individual subject who utilizes a technical system to play and com-municate in a designed interactive environment with other player-subjects. As Martin Heidegger would say, this is no doubt a correct representation, but one that limits understanding of the gameplay phenomenon to conven-tional interpretative frameworks. The goal of phenomenology, as developed by Heidegger's mentor, Edmund Husserl, was precisely to avoid the assumption of a conventional relation to the object under consideration implicit in the notion of the knowing subject. The growing body of social science–based research on online gaming sociality assumes this conventional subject position when developing accounts of player interactions with other players, and the dynamics of online and off-line social relations. Consequently, I will detour around it in this first stage, with a promise to engage in subsequent sections with some of the more significant claims emerging out of this research.

The information technology and architectural theorist Richard Coyne has argued convincingly for the ability of a Heideggerian approach to information technology to do something different from what he characterizes as the predominant "Romantic/Enlightenment emphasis dominant in popular IT commentary," including that exhibited in the mainstream formulation of such notions as identity, proximity, and community.[7] He sees Heidegger's insistence on the radical "non-determinacy" of the human as a key factor in this rethinking of the IT revolution. This nondeterminacy is indicated in Heidegger's alternative designation of the human entity by the term *Dasein* (literally, "being-there") in his major study, *Being and Time*.[8] *Dasein* exists in the world and "is engaged before it is reflective."[9] These engagements are dynamic and constantly evolving, and thus the character of *Dasein* is primordially "fluid, situated and non-determinate."[10]

I would support this account of Heidegger's existential analytic in *Being and Time* to the extent to which it captures the sense of its effort toward establishing a different basis for the experience of space (and time) than that handed down to Western thought from a Kantian conceptualization of them as innate, transcendental forms of perception. I will draw on this work in trying to rethink the player's relation to the space of gameplay. Whether Heidegger's project remained resolutely or unequivocally in a thinking of human existence as essentially nondeterminate is the subject of much philosophical and critical theoretical debate, focused on and magnified by the controversy around the facts and the significance of Heidegger's notorious involvement with the Nazi Party while rector of Freiburg University in the 1930s.[11] Our movement toward a postphenomenological articulation of online gaming will need to address elements of this debate.

For Heidegger, *Dasein* is primordially spatial; that is, the human entity always finds itself in places. This means that at the phenomenological level of Heidegger's inquiry, space is always encountered as a place, or what he calls a "region" *(Raum)*, before it is conceived of as the objective space conceptualized by geometry or physics (or metaphysics). Heidegger states that "a three dimensional multiplicity of possible positions which gets filled up with Things present-at-hand is never proximally given."[12] It is precisely a question here of what is given, what precedes *Dasein* and enables its subsequent reflections and abstractions. Normal "reflective" conceptions of distance and proximity are not determinative of the region's definition or qualities. Rather, the region is where the things exist with which *Dasein* is occupied in its everyday activity. The orientation, or "directionality," of *Dasein* in regard to these things that are "ready-to-hand" is what constitutes the region.[13] Heidegger calls this everyday orientation to things "equipmentality."[14]

The fact that geometrical and hence geographical distance is only a secondary level of consideration for *Dasein* is a critical point in Heidegger's elaboration of a different notion of spatial orientation. Moreover, it is one of fundamental relevance to our considerations. To accept it is to affirm the reality of online involvements against the positions that deny the authenticity of social or communal engagements not founded on geographical collocation, and those that in a similar vein insist on a sharp demarcation between online and off-line sociality. A virtual gamespace can be understood in terms of the notion of region as Heidegger elaborates it in *Being and Time*, that is, as a primordial realm among others of *Dasein*'s everyday concernful dealings with(in) the world. The implications of adopting this position, however, raise further questions about both online and off-line sociality. Other players are encountered in the region of gameplay and are also encountered as part of the region, along with the virtual gamespace and the other entities with which one is occupied while playing. If this is a no less authentic encounter between human beings than those based on physical proximity, we need to consider both the equipmental basis of sociality in general and of online community in particular. Virtual community forms may be the leading edge of what Bernard Stiegler will describe as the social-cultural response to the disadjustment between the social and the technical systems initiated by the latest technical innovations in communication and simulation.[15]

The region is the primordial experience of space for *Dasein,* in which those things with which it is concerned are located as proximate to or "in their place" vis-à-vis *Dasein* (or not, as a possible variation of the structure). *Dasein's* state of being includes this structure in which things exist as distanced from it. But this does not mean they are identified at this or that measured spatial remove. Heidegger's term for this distancing in German is *Ent-fernung,* a modification of *Entfernung* ("removal," "remoteness," "distance") and is translated as "de-severance."[16] "De-severing," says Heidegger, "amounts to making the farness vanish—that is, making the remoteness of something disappear, bringing it close."[17] *Dasein* de-severs the things with which it concerns itself. The relative spatial remoteness of things is only a secondary consideration in this regard. Heidegger illustrates this with an example of the spectacles worn on the nose of a man. These are extremely close spatially but are "environmentally more remote from him than the picture on the opposite wall" to which he turns his attention.[18]

We can add a further example here of the computer or game console devices one employs to see and hear and interact with the virtual gamespace. They are part of the equipment ready at hand in the region of the game player's activity, although "environmentally more remote" than the gamespace with which the gamer is currently concerned. At least, that is the designed effect of the complex of technical systems given to the player in the region of gameplay. Time delays, or lags, that affect the synchronization of the player's interface with the server running the simulation, queues to join a game server, frequent patching downloads, server crashes, and so on all too frequently push the gamespace of a multiplayer online game away and bring its technical setup environmentally closer. A faulty instrumentality—whether it be the crashed game server or cracked spectacles—impedes a routine regional involvement and reveals by its failure to work the broader, primordial, existential character of *Dasein's* technical objects.

As noted above, in online multiplayer gameplay, other players are encountered both within the region and as elements of the region as Heidegger characterizes it. That is, other players are de-severed as ready-to-hand entities of the environment. Playing *Battlefield: Bad Company 2* (Electronic Arts, 2010) online via my Xbox Live account, other players appear as their avatars—soldiers or the vehicles they inhabit—in my avatar's field of vision (in several alternative states, including normal, aiming a handheld weapon, or sitting at the controls of a vehicle or stationary weapon), as well as on my radar window that indicates the position and direction of enemy and friendly units firing their weapons. Their relative closeness to me is a critical factor in my oriented involvement in the game. My fellow squad members, other friendly avatars, and the enemy constitute and maintain my involvement in gameplay. Their comings and goings from the game map are critical from the phenomenological perspective; their continued presence is necessary for the persistence of the gamespace in the region of *Dasein*'s concern.

To put it another way, they indicate a minimal condition in determining whether the particular online game (and game map) is still close to the player in the region of gameplay. Players may of course choose another map, another server, or another game to maintain their involvement in gameplay. The continued presence of other players' avatars is a precondition of the virtual gamespace being encountered in and as a particular region of de-severing by the player. Anyone who has explored an otherwise unpopulated map on a game server will recognize the difference between the experience of virtual space as the place of potential or completed gameplay and as a place encountered in the context of play. The difference between "space" and "region" in Heidegger's phenomenology is perceivable here. Play with other entities is a precondition of the region as gameplay region, as opposed to some other mode of concernful dealings with online virtual spaces such as exploration, or map design and modification.

This is a fairly obvious point, but it serves to establish that at this level of the analysis, the other players perform the same role as the computer-generated entities one encounters in single-player modes of gameplay. They are engaged as operative (interactive) elements of the game region that are also constitutive entities, on which the continued integrity of gamespace as region depends. As such, they are a key part of the equipment that belongs together in the region of gameplay, constituting it in this belonging together. Games such as *The Elder Scrolls IV: Oblivion* (Bathesda Softworks, 2006) and *Grand Theft Auto IV* (Rockstar Games, 2008) bear this point out. They are single-player adventure/role-playing games with enormous and complex virtual gameworlds populated by large numbers of computer-controlled characters with which players interact through their avatars. They deliver lengthy, sustained immersive experiences for players of the more emergent, open-ended type usually associated with multiplayer role-playing games.

Heidegger states that *Dasein's* primordial sense of location comes to it with reference to the de-severed entities in its region. That is, its "here" is a function of the relative closeness of the entities "there" in its region of everyday concern.[19] In *America's Army,* the Squad Assignment screens present me with basic choices through which I orient myself in relation to the other players on the basis of friendly or opposing team membership. Interactive involvement in the mission objectives is thereby structured in relation to this entry condition into gameplay. Without the other players' avatars (as an essential part of the mode of multiplayer gaming), the player will not be in the region of online gameplay.

Like the other players, the player commits him- or herself to play in and through the technical equipment supporting online gameplay—computer input–output devices, avatar and environmental representation, realtime distributed interactive simulation, and communication networks. That is, the players play in the gamespace by contributing to the technical constitution of that region of elements belonging together in play. What, then, of the nature of the interplay between players who play together online? In discussions of the forms of online community that have developed around online gaming, many writers have described a large range of activities extending beyond actual game-focused interaction.[20] The Heideggerian-based analysis developed thus far has necessarily excluded these from its phenomenological focus on the player that was aimed at avoiding the routine assumptions about his or her identity as a stable and preexistent individual subject using a technology. We have glimpsed, however, the horizon of the questions concerning the nature of online sociality through our approach. This horizon of the relations between the individual and other players is technical. Just after his example of the equipmental role of spectacles in making possible a certain orientation to space, Heidegger adds a now-famous observation—or, rather, question—about radio's potential role (among other modern technics of speed) in transforming the regions in which contemporary *Dasein* concerns itself:

In Dasein there lies an essential tendency toward closeness. All the ways in which we speed things up, as we are more or less compelled to do today, push us towards the conquest of remoteness. With the "radio," for example, *Dasein* has so expanded its everyday environment that it has accomplished a de-severance of the "world"—a de-severance which, in its meaning for *Dasein,* cannot yet be visualized.[21]

This observation looks forward to Heidegger's later formulations concerning the essence of modern technology as a "driving-forth" of the world as a "standing reserve" of resources for deployment in technological systems.[22] Similarly, Jeff Malpas extends Heidegger's thinking of technology in assessing the modern mass media's contribution to a covering over and "misunderstanding of the character of our own being-in-the-world."[23] This is achieved, he argues, through a total substitution of representation for the grounded, embodied, and situated encounter with things and others. Such an account would position online gaming in virtual spaces at the forefront today of such technics of misunderstanding and covering over.

We will develop a position in the following sections that draws on but also distinguishes itself from this more strictly Heideggerian take on online gaming. I will examine online gaming as a technics enabling a certain kind of opening of space and social interaction, one that operates through a confirmation and even intensification of an individual de-severing that privileges distant, affective, some would say quasi-tribal engagements over local, national, or existing political regions of situated sociality. We see these engagements emerging out of the logistically marked relations between war, technoculture, and simulation. In another post–World War II essay, "Overcoming Metaphysics," Heidegger notes the exemplary status of the logistical marshalling of all society in wartime total mobilization in his characterization of the accomplishment of Western metaphysics achieved by the trajectory of modern technology. This makes evident the correspondence between the postwar crystallization of Heidegger's account of technology and Virilio's notion of the logistical pure war tendency.[24]

My departure from this Heideggerian approach to online gaming, however, is calculated to avoid the assumption sustaining Heidegger's work— before and after the war in the view of some commentators, Stiegler and

Derrida among them—of some nontechnical, unmediated, poetical, potential being-together of human beings beneath the coverings and misunderstandings of technological being-in-the-world.[25] As many have noted in their analyses, Heidegger's turn toward language as the center of his concerns, his focus on poetry and poetic, nonphilosophical modes of writing, was dedicated to looking for a nonmetaphysical language untainted by technicity in which an alternative becoming for the human could be sought amid the totalizing of the "enframing" tendency of modern technical existence.[26] Following Stiegler, I adopt the position that there is no nontechnical, pure region of human concern with human social existence. The sociotechnical milieu is today undergoing significant transformations, and these demand careful theoretical elaboration and critical evaluation. Not the least of these is the emerging crystallization of networked sociality in online gaming phenomena. But it is only through engagement of, in, and with the technical that both these transformations and the possibilities for alternative communal possibilities can be thought and invented.

While the Heidegger of *Being and Time* cannot be the primary source for exploring this question, he does provide a valuable point of departure for this venture. He observes that "because *Dasein* is essentially spatial in the way of de-severance, its dealings always keep within an 'environment' which is de-severed from it with a certain 'leeway' *[Spielraum]*; accordingly our seeing and hearing always go proximally beyond what is distantly 'closest.'"[27] While this "leeway" is explained here as what allows *Dasein* to bring remote elements close within its region (such as the remote virtual space of gameplay with other players), let us also read *Spielraum*—playroom—as an invitation to speculate on *Dasein*'s leeway in engaging with others in the playroom of online gaming.[28]

Endless War: The Networking of Individual Players

Coyne, in his Heideggerian recasting of the information technology theme of community, argues that "digital communities are not to be understood primarily as formed from isolated selves communicating through networks, but there is already a solidarity, a being-with that is the human condition, into which we introduce various technologies, such as meeting rooms, transportation systems, telephones and computer networks."[29] From this perspective, online communities are modifications of existing communal structures rather than (re)inventions of new kinds of community in a new electronic milieu. This argument is a not inconsistent extrapolation from Heidegger's position in *Being and Time*. While I would support it in part against a simplistic positing of the complete reinvention of community online, I have two important points of disagreement, or one disagreement and one significant qualification, which I will address as a way of moving toward a postphenomenological account of online gaming community.

First, the qualification. With Coyne, I have argued that the engagement of the player with others in online gameplay is inherently communal inasmuch as the players co-constitute for each other the region of gameplay through their involved use of technical equipment. It is important to note, however, that the predominant expression of this involvement in online gaming reproduces the prevailing conception and practice of technologically supported activity. In this conception, the players operate through their communication and simulation technologies as "isolated selves" in a mediated, remote environment. As players of a game, their goal is pursued by seeking preemptive mastery of that environment. Of course, the situation of the player varies in different contexts of multiplayer play, such as local area network–based gaming, networked arcade machines, or home game console team play, where players come together in one space to play together. These each have different potentials for combinations of online and off-line social interaction, but all are premised on being enabled by a similar technological isolation via the networking of individual interface devices.[30]

T. L. Taylor is correct in proposing that not only MMORPG gamers in general but power gamers in particular—those players focused on maximizing their achievement as measured against the game's quest goals and other status markers—typify online sociability inasmuch as they "inhabit" not only "the functional and instrumental orientations to the game" but also its "affiliations, networks and engagements."[31] I would add to this account that war is never far away from this prevailing habitat for human action and interaction in contemporary online technoculture.

Players in the contemporary technospace provided by computerized simulation are in play in a logistical space. I examined in chapter 3 how this space of trajectories, objectives, and tasks has a widely acknowledged pedigree in military research and development. As the work of Timothy Lenoir and Henry Lowood has documented, the distributed interactive simulation protocols employed in online multiplayer gaming are adaptations of systems first developed to link military vehicular simulators together in real time.[32] Julian Holland Oliver succinctly characterizes this system that underlies all remotely networked simulation systems, including multiplayer gameplay.[33] Each player's computer loads and runs that part of the simulated environment relevant to the particular player's position and activity. Data concerning the player's interactions and movements are communicated from each player's computer on the fly to the server, which updates the simulation and communicates the new information concerning the changing position and status of other player avatars, nonplayer characters, and other nonstatic elements of the environment to each player's computer on a need-to-know basis. At this level of technical implementation, gameplay in realtime collaborative spaces such as MMORPGs, first-person shooters, flight simulation, and other online games is for each player a fragmented particularization of the simulated milieu directed toward progressively coordinating, controlling, dominating, or otherwise influencing the nature and distribution of the other fragments as a whole.

The whole here refers not to the entirety of the gamespace conceived as predesigned virtual environment, but to the whole made up of the aggregate of fragments of the simulated milieu belonging together in and through the interactions of the player with other players in his or her region of gameplay.[34] This relation of the part(icular) and the whole is repeated in the larger scale of the relation of game servers to the game as a whole. A MMORPG is played not in a single version of the virtual world but in numerous duplicates of it. These are called "Realms" in the log-on screens for *World of Warcraft*. Each Realm provides the gameworld, its artificial intelligence–driven characters, sets of quests, and other elements of the MMORPG experience for a maximum of several thousand players. *World of Warcraft* has approximately 230 Realms available at the time of this writing, each a partial whole enabling the players to develop their individual and grouped particularization strategies. In turn, each Realm is a composite of partial wholes and game functions that connect between and extend beyond particular Realms—the various maps on which one actually plays, instances of the gameworld made available for stand-alone missions for particular groups of players, the boat transportation, the banking and auction facilities, and so on. These are made available and managed in real time by Blizzard server farms, the number and location of which are kept secret by the corporation.

Taylor will insist on the communal aspect of MMORPGs, citing as evidence the fact that designers of games like *Everquest* make cooperation among players compulsory through both the provision of communication channels and other in-game facilities, and the grading of game challenges (computer-controlled monsters called *mobs*) that exceed the capacities of individual player avatars to defeat on their own. These design elements are from my perspective further illustration of the way gameplay is built on the base of the isolated input/output node.[35] Group play involves the coordination of fragments toward a higher order of particularization of the whole. Through the technically enabled group strategy, the player advances his or her individual fragment's success in influencing the simulation. Experience points, loot gained from kills, advances in talent and skill points, and so forth are quantified gains from each kill or other success divided up among group members according to a game (or, in some circumstances, player-derived) calculus.

In "player versus player" mode realms, the rewards of combat against enemy player characters may not be as readily calculated but are no less based on this assembling of a higher level of particularization of the region. While playing on a "PvP" realm on *World of Warcraft*, I joined an informal group of Alliance character avatars that spontaneously formed around the task of killing a high-level Horde character, who had appeared in our village in Alliance territory. Our shared pleasure in repeatedly defeating the level 40 orc on our home territory and celebrating with an impromptu postbattle dance (executed by entering the "/dance" command in the chat dialogue window) was a part of the sociotechnical outcome designed by the game developers.

The technical implementation of a realtime multiplayer simulation results in the appearance of a Cartesian homogeneous three-dimensional space existing in real time and occupied in common by a plurality of players. It is a fairly obvious point to make that a virtual, realtime gameworld is an illusion, even if this illusion is one that supports the constitution of real online sociality. In its very obviousness, however, the dynamics of the fragment and the whole supporting this playable illusion reveal something fundamental about Western technoculture.[36] This technical system is one designed to network individual players together. It is obviously supportive of and supported by the common conception of the human subject as individual, and of the individual as the basic minimum unit of human community.

As Jean-Luc Nancy argues in *The Inoperative Community*, however, community conceived on the basis of the individual human subject is always marked by war. The fantasy quest adventure games of archaic, mythical wars and magical weapons, such as *World of Warcraft*, would seem, in this light, to be well suited to our advanced democracies built on conceptions of the supreme value of individual liberty. Nancy, drawing on Georges Bataille's critique of the modern political sovereignty advanced by Enlightenment philosophy and its Romantic successors, pushes the logic of the individual to its extreme end point. The "metaphysics of the subject" rests ultimately on an atomistic conception of an "absolute for-itself." This conception necessarily separates the subject from other entities in order to constitute the minimum identifiable entity—the in-dividual—at the basis of identity.[37] Nancy articulates the internal contradiction of this conception when he states that "the ab-solute, as perfectly detached, distinct and closed" must, in its absolute realization, be totally separate, totally isolated, totally detached; this implies it must be totally alone. "In other words: to be absolutely alone, it is not enough that I be so; I must also be alone being alone—and this of course is contradictory."[38]

War arises from this contradiction: "Excluded by the logic of the absolute-subject of metaphysics (Self, Will, Life, Spirit, etc.) community comes perforce *to cut into* this subject by virtue of the same logic."[39] Nancy cites Bataille's evocation of "an unappeasable combat" that is the inevitable destiny of this modern conception of the individual.[40] Nancy calls the kind of contradictory sociality of the modern aggregation of individual subjects "immanence."[41] The immanent community—such as Taylor's exemplary clan of "power gamers"—works together to effectuate itself, that is, to make itself exist as a form of reassurance and denial of the intrinsically unviable nature of such a project. The identity of its individuals is immanent to this self-effectuation.

The sociality of online multiplayer gaming bears in large part the characteristics of this immanence. It is a sociality born of a common work to produce and sustain a gamespace. Individual players actualize their online self-identity through this work. The clans that formed around the multiplayer first-person shooter games of the early 1990s such as *Quake* (id Software, 1996) and, later, *Counter-Strike* (Valve Software, 2000), and the group mechanisms and formal Guild structures built into MMORPGs all evince this heavy investment in communal self-effectuation.[42] Gameplay routinely involves contest with and the playful extinction of other players (as other online individuals) alone or in cooperation with others in team play. As discussed above, the shared space of this community is itself a contingent, particularized appearing of being-in-common shaped by a permanent combat between the separate worlds of each player's fragment of the whole.

In this regard Holin Lin, Chuen-Tsai Sun, and Hong-Hong Tinn's discussion of game clan culture in a Taiwanese context is instructive.[43] From ethnographic research into players of *Lineage* (Ncsoft, 2000) and *Ragnarok Online* (Gravity, 2002), the authors discover online social formation emerging "not for social purposes but for character survival and game success."[44] Gameplay has been molded by game design, game managers, and player cultures "to create a 'law-of-the-jungle' atmosphere in the online gaming world, in which single characters are bound to confront dangerous and frustrating situations."[45] While it is apparent from their research that the player group profile and the sociocultural context of play differs somewhat from Western contexts such as those studies by researchers like Taylor, Morris, Kolo and Baur, and Wright, Boria, and Breidenbach, their account of the "primary reason" behind group formation in these games nonetheless indicates the basis on which other kinds of social interchange in gamer communities is built.[46]

Much of the extraludic activities of participants in online game communities can contribute to this kind of sociality tending toward immanence. For instance, the work of *Doom* gamers discussed by Sue Morris in producing home-built game mods, additional level maps, and individual avatar designs is indicative of a culture of the productive extension of gameplay.[47] Morris' influential argument is that such end-user-driven game development invites redefinition of commercial entertainment forms and their creation.

From our perspective, this widespread phenomenon in online gaming circles signals an attenuation of the contradictory impulse to work at community under the impetus of contemporary technocultural forms of individuation. It exemplifies a characteristic of postmodern cultural production—the invocation of consumers as coproducers—and obeys the positivist imperative to produce a common identity as digitally literate, online "prosumers" out of the distributed, isolating telecommunication components of contemporary global technology.[48]

Let us recap, then, the trajectory leading to this analysis from the phenomenological account of the player in play together with the other players in the region of gameplay. Nancy, like Heidegger, argues that the contemporary positioning of the individual in technoculture presents a particular way in which the human is determined as subject today. As noted earlier, Heidegger makes a similar argument in his famous postwar essay "The Question Concerning Technology," where the technical "way of revealing" the world, including the human and the other entities in the world, is as resources standing in reserve for deployment. According to Heidegger, this "way of revealing" increasingly dominates Western thought, precluding other possible "revealings" of other entities.[49] The phenomenological analysis of other players as equipmental elements accords with this technical way of being-with-others today. The implication of this analysis, however, is that other determinations of the human's relation to others are possible, and the account in *Being and Time* of *Dasein*'s involvement in particular activities is also premised on the leeway in which resides the potential for other determinations of the human in other configurations of concernful interaction. Our postphenomenological approach seeks to emphasize this potential for other determinations of human being and being-with, but without imagining a flight from the technical horizon of human activity into some pure, poetic region of nontechnical linguistic community.

For Nancy, genuine community is one potentiality among these other configurations, but it would arise in the undoing of the human subject's individualistic involvement with other beings in the permanent, but futile, work of self-effectuation. What Nancy points to is a kind of aberrant or counterproductive involvement in the labor of self-effectuation. I argue that the potential for such an undoing is available both thanks to and despite the system of online gameplay itself. This possibility of a nonimmanent dynamic of community emerging from the modern technics of enframing is what the postphenomenological approach of online game sociality seeks in the final part of this chapter.

Other Projects: Unworking the Networking

I have claimed that the project of contemporary technoculture is given us to think in the *Spielraum* of online multiplayer gameplay. As our discussion of Heidegger and Nancy has shown, however, the project is never assured, that is, a certain amount of play always remains in the system. From Nancy's perspective, something like true community can emerge from this play, through what he calls the "undoing" of immanent communal forms. In order to explore the nature of this undoing of the predominant form of technocommunity—something that is always occurring—I must now make explicit my second objection to Coyne's formulation about online community. To recap, in his Heideggerian reframing of the experience of online community, Coyne claimed that "there is already a solidarity, a being-with that is the human condition, into which we introduce various technologies." The implication of this formulation is that the "human condition" precedes "various technologies." Bernard Stiegler challenges this assumption, arguing that such a definitive separation of technology from the essence of human being is a pervasive, originary gesture of Western thought. Stiegler argues on the contrary that the human is always "in default," that is, lacking a self-sufficient essential nature. The human kind of being is essentially lacking. Technology has always already compensated for this lack of essence. The human cannot, therefore, be understood without considering the technologies with which it constitutes its existence. There is no "before" technology because the human is never fully and finally constituted apart from its technical supports.

In relation to our discussion of online gaming, this means that the "being-with" involved in networked gameplay is not simply a modulation of an essential human condition of community underlying that instantiated in the history of all communication technologies. Instead, the specific modalities of technical engagement with others are essential to the communal relations constituted via this social activity. I have characterized the experience and technical implementation of multiplayer online gaming as productive of an immanent sociality of individuated subject-players that extends the logistical tendency of contemporary Western technoculture. In terms of Manovich's work on computer-mediated interactivity, we could see this as a kind of hyperstandardization of sociality through its designed implementation in and as a simulated milieu of shared experience.[50] One could think of this game design process in relation to the envisioned social engineering of the utopian architectural design movements of modernity such as the early Bauhaus school and L'Esprit Nouveau of Le Corbusier and his associates. Traces of this prospective, utopian approach to online multiplayer game and virtual world design can be found in the works of game studies writers such as Edward Castronova and Espen Aarseth.[51] In relation to Stiegler's account of the originary default of human being, this hyperstandardization of community forms seems to heighten awareness of the intrinsic dependence of human subjective, interior experience (of self and self–other relations) on exterior, technical givens.

While other players are encountered in and through the technological apparatus that concretizes this sociality, there yet remains some ambiguity in the encounter. This ambiguity can be found in the idiosyncratic variation of the system of gameplay by its human components. The human should be understood here in the context of the technical system and not as some pre-existing discrete, integral entity outside of any (history of) technological systematicity. What would count as such a mutational idiosyncrasy in multiplayer online gaming? Do the kinds of "creative player actions" discussed by Talmadge Wright, Eric Boria, and Paul Breidenbach have such a potential to alter the gameplay system? They report on their ethnographic research into gamer expression in *Counter-Strike* (Vivendi Universal, 2003), one of the most popular multiplayer first-person shooter games. They examine such forms of communication as in-game chat channels, online name authoring, avatar and logo design, mapmaking, and avatar behavior. Their major claim is that significant social interaction and individual expression is evident in these communication channels evidencing considerable creativity. This social activity resembles, in their view, the kinds of appropriation of received commercial cultural forms seen in youth subcultures. The armed combat scenarios of the game (terrorist team versus counterterrorist team) are not addressed in their study—although it is acknowledged that the "most frequent type of discourse was talk related to *game performance or conflict*."[52]

Such activities and social interchanges around gameplay as they describe it would need to be considered on their particular merits for their potential to open a space of community other than that built substantially on the war of individual players. In the terms of subcultural appropriation advanced by Wright et al., however, these "creative player actions" appear as a consistent elaboration of the immanent gamespace of individuals working to effectuate a group identity out of the atomistic subjectivity of contemporary technoculture. The work of creating a memorable online ID or of designing a unique skin for an avatar are effortful gestures of self-effectuation that coproduce the community of players solicited to witness, respond, and participate in these gestures. As such, they correspond to the production of communities of players in MMORPGs examined by Taylor in *Play between Worlds*. She discusses the player-authored Web sites generated around *Everquest*, noting the way this "fan-produced culture" needs to be considered as not simply a community, but also a social hierarchy where status claims of individual players are negotiated and established through "gift, status and reputation economies."[53]

The dynamic, metastable, spatially scattered complex of off-line and online associations Taylor describes recalls Scott Lash's notion of a "nonorganizational," "chaotic" form of sociation arising amid the decline of conventional territorial, institutional, and ideological forms of organized community.[54] For Lash, shared values and affective attachment are at the core of these social networks, as opposed to rationally or ideologically motivated identification. The affect-based fan production of player community would seem to fit Lash's broad characterization of the rise of "disorganizations."[55] As indicated by Lash's preliminary listing of such affective communities, a list that includes the "tribes of gangster capitalism," ghetto youth gangs, as well as the "flexibly networked work sociations in the new sectors—bio-tech, software, multimedia," the war that haunts the becoming of individuals in the global expansion of Western technoculture remains, and remains largely unthought, in such accounts of online game community.[56]

My intention here is not to condemn or belittle such player activities, nor to deny the sociality of online gamer communities as merely a false, technologically supplemented appearance of a genuine communal experience only available off line. I reject the assumption of some technology-free, pre-existing human sociality. Instead, I seek here to characterize the form of technical gesture—there is no other kind according to Stiegler—that would move toward another kind of community of other players. For Stiegler, all technologies have a profound relation to death because death is at the heart of the human effort to survive and adapt to the challenges of the exterior world. It is to death, which is the future in its most challenging form of indeterminate inevitability, that technology responds.[57] The idiosyncratic modulation of existing technological regimes arises under the impetus of this permanently renewed challenge of the future.

Death, as the ultimate singularity and (the proof of) the limit of immanent individuality, is also central to Nancy's proposition of what constitutes a less conflictual form of community. The community of others is grounded only on a consciousness of the different, singular end of the other(s).[58] It is, he says, a "groundless 'ground,' less in the sense that it opens up the gaping chasm of an abyss than that it is made up only of the network, the interweaving, and the sharing of singularities."[59] The potential for another sense of community arises from the experience of the singular difference of the other with which one is in relation, rather than from the basis of a common, shared identity or the fusion of individuals together into a larger group identity. The encounter with the end of the other opens up the relation to one's own singularity, that is, one's own indeterminate but inevitable death, and the life that can precede it.

If the "groundless 'ground'" of this other community is the "network" of "shared singularities," then it would have to be sought through an unworking of the sociotechnical networking that produces immanent, self-effectuating communal identity. In *Targets of Opportunity,* Samuel Weber notes the curious confluence of concepts in the conjoining of "net" and "work," identifying there the effort of transforming a loose, open indeterminacy (the net) into a bounded, directed, productive structure (the network). This effort he characterizes as a kind of targeting, an inevitably violent, ambivalent, and unstable effort to limit the indeterminate complexity of the net. It always produces, along with the network, a guiltiness:

> Guilt is what results from the impossible attempt to clear, occupy, and secure the place that would turn the *net* into a *work,* the *network* into a *people, nodes* into *great men.* Guilt, marking the *unacknowledged* debt to the other, to the *net*

without work, appears in Freud's text *[Moses and Monotheism]* to serve as the glue that ultimately "holds together" the network, but only by dividing and deferring it through a "latency" period that endows it with an irreducible virtuality.[60]

To return to multiplayer online gaming, how or where would such an experience of this indebtedness to the other, that is, to the other who is other than the other player, arise in the activities of gameplay? Stiegler directs us to look for it in idiosyncratic variations of the existing technical regime enabling play. These are undoubtedly legion, and each of these has the potential to alter the quality of the community formed around the game. Aside from Joseph DeLappe's pointed, powerful performance as dead_in_ iraq with which I opened this chapter—a practice whose significance is, in the wake of our discussion of the death that unceasingly challenges the community of individuals, more fully comprehensible—I can only offer here a few examples. The first plays on the latency that Weber mentions and arises thanks to an artifact of the technical limitations haunting the promise of online game systems to deliver a fully immersive virtual world experience. Adrian Mackenzie speculates on the effect and the significance of the lag experienced by Australian-situated players of the multiplayer shooter game *Avara* (Ambrosia Software, 1997), hosted on a server situated in the United States.[61] The delay, argues Mackenzie, disturbs the codified and capitalized realtime flow of information between computers that founds the illusion of Cartesian spatial coherence. This opens the possibility of the experience of what he calls, after Giorgio Agamben, the "whatever body" that haunts the space between the individual player and his or her virtual, instrumental avatar, a kind of momentary in-between that opens the possibility— undoubtedly "slender" in Mackenzie's view—to "think how to belong to impropriety, or how to singularly inhabit indifference."[62]

My second example of a potentially unworking variation of the routines of sociotechnical networking in multiplayer gaming is the interventionist practice of Chinese artist, Feng Mengbo. In *Quake4U,* Feng inserted himself into the gamespace of *Quake* as an avatar that resembled his off-line appearance—it is constructed from a photograph—rather than one modeled after the conventional in-game character of high-tech future soldier (Figure 5).[63] Rather than contributing to the work of player self-expression that consolidates the community of gamers immanent to the project of gameplay, Feng posits his own cultural and ethnic specificity within the gamespace that is constituted by a suspension of such singularity in the standard technical procedures of creating a game id and avatar. That is to say, he displays in the gamespace his own Chinese ethnic and technocultural givens, what Stiegler would call the epiphylogenetic heritage of technical–human becoming in which his scope for individuation has been constituted, one that is under threat in the global expansion of Western technoculture. This gesture elicits a consciousness of both the limits of this suspension of singularity and the potential for idiosyncratic use of these standardizing procedures. To recall our discussion of Heidegger, Feng leads the player to reflection on the *Spielraum* that is exercised in the constitution of the region of gameplay, a leeway to bring the other players close as component elements of the region, but that, as leeway, can play out differently.

My final example comes from playing *America's Army*. The chat channel on one mission mediated an interchange between two players, one writing

FIGURE 5 Feng Mengbo, *Quake 4U*, 2002; courtesy of the artist.

in Spanish and the other responding in English. After a few comments apparently about game performance (judging from the English communications about the slow reflexes of the other player), the English-writing player insists that his or her interlocutor "speak f***** english!!" The other responded in English with inquiries about the identity of the other and whether they had played together before. The aggressive invocation of the norm of English-language communication points to a fundamental component of the immanent subjectivity fostered by *America's Army* (in particular, but not exclusively in this U.S. military–produced game). At the same time, however, this "other," Spanish-speaking player communicates his or her "end" in relation to the game's production of uniformly trained and functioning (including communicating) squad members. The community of witnesses to this chat interchange is constituted in a consciousness of their shared otherness to this production; at least it has such a potential ungrounding of the network of online players.

The Spanish-writing player continued to play, and the game went on. Feng's interventions suspended for a time on a particular, dedicated server, the usual forms of multiplayer *Quake* play. Server lag is usually borne (or avoided if possible) as a temporary frustration of the desired online game experience. DeLappe's haunting of *America's Army* through his chat window invocation of America's army dead may give pause to some players, bringing the usual sociotechnical region of gameplay into a different relation with the other sociotechnical regions of his or her existence. While it may seem that such minor moments and gestures do little to alter the character of gaming communities as they continue to expand and proliferate, I would insist that technoculture changes via the dynamic of systems in constant idiosyncratic iteration. The instances of play in/with multiplayer game system parameters I have mentioned here are only indicative of this permanent dynamic.

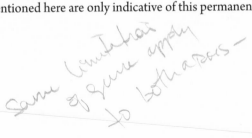

7 Playing Through

The Future of Alternative and Critical Game Practices

In this chapter, I will examine several alternative and critical new media projects taking computer game systems or practices as their major medium and/or theme. This will enable me to explore some instances of aesthetic and critical reproduction of mainstream computer game forms and technocultural practices for what they say about these, and for what they indicate of the future of aesthetically experimental and critical computer game projects. My examination of these works will initiate consideration of the question of critical simulation raised by several theorists, most notably in the arena of computer games by Gonzalo Frasca, who has called simulation the "form of the future."[1] There is certainly a need for critical and practical work to engage simulation as a key form and technic today and into the future. It is important, however, to attend to the full complexities of embracing simulation as a critical cultural practice. These have not always been adequately articulated in discussions of the critical potential of computer game forms. Many of the experimental projects we will examine—including Frasca's own—demand a more rigorous elaboration of the criticality they both perform and gesture toward as the future of such engagements in mainstream technocultural becoming.

Theaters of Cruelty

Two experimental game projects, C-level's *Tekken Torture Tournament* and //////////fur//// art entertainment interfaces' *Painstation 1* and *Painstation*

135

2 mount a critical interrogation of gaming culture by raising the stakes of playing the game. *Tekken Torture Tournament* is described on the C-level Web site as follows:

> *Tekken Torture Tournament* is a one-night event combining the latest video game technology, untapped public aggression and painful electric shock. Willing participants are wired into a custom fighting system—a modified Playstation (running *Tekken 3*) which converts virtual on screen damage into bracing, non-lethal, electric shocks.[2]

The *Tournament* was run at a number of venues from 2001 to 2004 while C-level remained active.

The *Painstation 1* and *Painstation 2* consoles allow for single or two-player contests in a table tennis game modeled on the early console classic *Pong* (Figure 6).[3] Pain is administered through both electric shocks and a small whip that is mechanically activated to strike the player's hand when the player loses a point. *Painstation 2* boasts increased flexibility in pain administration, whip varieties, and the inclusion of "different bonus symbols [that] appear on screen and result in multiplied pain, multiballs, shrunk bars [paddles], reversed directions etc."[4] The *Painstations* have been exhibited and played at a range of events, conferences, and exhibitions since 2002. In 2008 it was included in the Museum of Modern Arts' Design and the Elastic Mind exhibition and interactive Web site.[5]

Both of these projects involve the technical modification of game consoles so that individuals have an altered encounter with gameplay. They are what Shuen-shing Lee would call "re-calibrations [that] challenge the supposition that games equal fun." Lee considers a number of projects that perform this recalibration, "often by way of pain, rather than pleasure."[6] Lee focuses in particular on game-based projects that undermine the usual routines of goal achievement and competition. We will examine some similar projects later in this chapter. It is, however, the theatrical nature of the *Painstation* and *Tekken Torture Tournament* projects that I want to initially focus on, inasmuch as it is central to their impact and their engagement with the contemporary audiovisual and technocultural milieu in which computer games have an increasingly prominent place. The exhibition of players playing with a game console makes the volunteer players part of a witnessed performance. This staged performance draws on the practices of body performance work, and in particular those that include painful experiences for the performer or performers.[7] These gameplay performances involve the audience in a dynamic of participatory spectatorship in events and actions that challenge conventional frameworks for understanding and responding to gameplay. C-level's citing of "untapped public aggression" as one of the elements combined in the creation of *Tekken Torture Tournament* indicates the importance they place on this theatrical dimension to the work. My own viewing of the *Painstation 2* at *Level Up* (Digital Games Research

FIGURE 6 /////////fur//// art entertainment interfaces, *Painstation 2*, 2005; courtesy of the artists.

Association Conference, University of Utrecht, 2003) confirmed the theatrical nature of the game project. Arguably the single most popular item in an exhibition/dance party event at the game studies conference, *Painstation 2* was permanently surrounded by a crowd of people (including myself) delighted by the spectacle of two players submitting to the rigors of the *Painstation* game.

On the one hand—and literally, on the hand connected to the console—these experimental game projects work via a modification to the technical equipment providing the game experience. This modification increases the real-world consequences of losing the contest. On the other hand, this physical extension and intensification of the stakes of the game enables a theatricalization of the gaming situation. It allows a major transformation of the already performative social element of competitive console gameplay. This performance is usually dedicated to the creation of an affirmative spectacle of personal skill and the victorious execution of gameplay. It is replayed and complicated by these works in a staging of painful physical interaction including sadistically (and/or masochistically) motivated gestures and affects circulating between players and spectators. In this respect, these art projects also connect to the popular culture tradition of arcade amusements involving moderately painful or humiliating challenges that are ludic variants of real-world encounters with technology. Erkki Huhtamo has noted, for instance, the "curious parallel between the electric chair . . . , medical treatment with electricity, and popular arcade machines in which the subject's endurance is tested by leading electricity through his body."[8]

While it would be legitimate and valuable to explore and interpret the dynamics of this restaged gaming situation from sociological and psychoanalytic perspectives on spectatorship and group interaction, what is of most interest to our concerns here is the complex nature of the gesture that both of these game projects make toward the real-world context of computer gameplay. The bodily commitment each project demands from the volunteer players is an explicit response to the widely perceived virtual character of computer gaming. The amusement arcade—or in its more recent, sanitized reappearance as the entertainment zone of shopping centers and cinema complexes—has long been an arena of bodily performance, from the fairground-style amusements (hitting the hammer, shooting the ducks) to mini sport games (shooting hoops, passing the football), to the more recent performance games like *Dance Dance Revolution* (Konami, 1998) and drumming games. The virtual nature of the games modified by the *Painstation* and *Tekken Torture Tournament* is nevertheless defined as the absence of real-world consequences directly programmed into the computerized gameplay.

Through this modification the gaming situation is itself virtualized, or, rather, to use Samuel Weber's term, theatricalized: it is removed from the usual real-world context in which competitive computer gameplay is taken as a familiar and recognized aspect of contemporary audiovisual, techno-cultural experience.[9] It is not allowed to take its usual place in the real. Its habitual occurrence is suspended, and gameplay is put under a spotlight temporarily, in the time of its theatrical staging by each work.

For Weber, theatricality is a process of turning a general space into a particular place that subtends and enables theater as such to exist. While it occurs in the theater as traditionally understood, theatricality is not limited to the space of conventional theater but is also to be found in other processes where theaters are created, such as the military theater of operations. As this comparison suggests, this taking place is understood by Weber to always be caught up in the difficulty of finding the "proper limits" to this place. The importance attached in military operations to "defining, delimiting, and controlling the space of conflict" is an extreme case of the general situation in which theatricality works with a space that is intrinsically unstable.[10] This is because theatricalized space is always the space in which a certain scene is staged, that is, actualized as both a determinate, local space and one that is other than what, where, and when it is. In the case of a military theater of operations, the commander who prescribes and implements the boundaries of the operational milieu stages a scene of conflict—its motivations, the rules of engagement, the juridicolegal status of persons within the space, and so forth—that are, at the least from the standpoint of the opponents, other than what, where, and when they think they are.

The relation between theatricality and military operations is not irrelevant to our consideration of these game projects. As "cruel theaters," they stage a military theater of operations playfully, inasmuch as the object of war, as Paul Virilio points out, is to create an environment for your opponent that is uninhabitable.[11] This is the principal winning strategy in the *Painstation* contests I witnessed: to make your opponent leave the table. The games within these performance artworks are either staging a scene of violent conflict—the *Tekken* fighting game as model for *Tekken Torture Tournament*—or, in the case of *Painstation's* evocation of virtual tennis, a theatrical rematerialization of a more sublimated form of what game theory calls a zero-sum contest.

What do these specific performance works give us to think about gameplay as we usually perceive it outside their theaters of cruelty? For one, they gesture reflexively toward a computer game's virtual suspension of the real. As forms that simulate a space and a context of competitive conflict, the computer games that are the subject of these experimental works render an experience of contestation in the register of entertainment supposedly distant from the serious business and high stakes of real-life conflict. The separation of entertainment and leisure activities from the sphere of the serious is, however, by no means unproblematic. These projects play their part in undermining the legitimacy of this separation. They each rework the space of electronically mediated competition, either against real-world or computer-provided opposition. While the game exhibitions typically involve two-player contests, the systems provide the option of single player against the computer, making one volunteer a minimum condition of gameplay. To play against an opponent is to take up an option within the technically determined milieu of computer-generated gameplay. It is play in and through a virtual information space, a space negotiated via the characteristic bodily disposition of personal computing/console play. This requires engagement in a cybernetic circuit as a key node in feedback loops of rapid decision making executed via a physical regime of local immobilization enabling continuous micromovements of hand–eye coordination. This modality of interpellation into/as a key communications node between the input and output devices of a computing system reproduces the "primal scene" of cybernetics: the "man in the middle" of a mechanically enhanced weapons system.[12]

To reproduce a scene is not necessarily to repeat it identically. Moreover, as Bernard Stiegler points out (after Walter Benjamin), the act of reproduction always carries the possibility of change, differentiation, and invention. There is, in fact, no other possibility of change.[13] The milieu of technical facticity—what is already preserved, given, and produced before the individual arrives on the scene to take up, reject, or modify this heritage—is the condition for human history and development. Stiegler thinks the implications of this position at their most radical. He insists that human memory, and therefore human thought, is nothing without the external memory provided by the technical milieu, from tool, to agricultural techniques, to building, to the explicitly "mnemotechnical" technologies. These include writing, graphic and plastic arts, photography, cinema, television, and computing technics of database construction, information processing, interaction design, and networked communications.

Computer simulation is a mnemotechnical form combining elements from these technologies. Computer games assume their full significance in this light. They reproduce playfully cybernetic principles derived from cybernetic techniques for improved control of systems and events through the mnemotechnical power of computing and audiovisual technologies. Their critical, reflexive potential, as well as their entertainment value, depends on this capacity to both reproduce and modify the technoscientific heritage.

The *Painstation* and *Tekken Torture Tournament* reproduce the Playstation entertainment system theatrically to invoke reflection on the ludic adoption of military technoscience in contemporary audiovisual culture. This reflection is made possible by the playing out of these theaters of cruelty each time they are staged at a particular location. That is to say, design of the modified Playstations and the staging of the game event tournaments incites participants to think about gameplay and game consoles and their historical relation to warfare and the history of computing. This does not mean, however, that the content of the game projects can be described and stabilized as a set of propositions about these histories. In this regard, Weber points out something crucial: "theatricality is defined as a *problematic process of placing, framing, situating* rather than as a process of representation."[14] As such, it works toward achieving a certain effect rather than taking that effect as given. Theatrical taking place is principally projective rather than reflective, aesthetic, or representational—processes that can only commence in the security of a stabilized space of representation. This is in the future of the critical, theatrical projects that solicit one to participate in their forceful determination.

The future of the theatrical representation of the shared past of computer games, audiovisual culture, and military technoscience in these two game projects depends on the speculations and imaginary projections they elicit from their future participants. These speculations will be about a past that has always already come before the participant in the work, inasmuch as he or she is an inheritor of the technocultural history it represents. That is to say, the past involvements of military technoscience and technoculture are, paradoxically but necessarily, before the participant's adoption of them in his or her particular manner; they will have been (in) his or her future.[15] This is why reflection on the past runs always and inevitably into speculation on the future possibilities arising from this curious future of the pre-existing past. As Weber has argued, the theatrical taking place sets to work this paradoxical, speculative reflection as constitutive of the potential formal, conceptual, and aesthetic significance of events in their occurrence. The makers of the *Painstations* have indicated the speculative nature of their project on the Concept page of the old *Painstation* Web site: "Yes, the painstation does exist. And it's not only a construction, a machine, an automaton. No, it's rather the prophet of a future, not necessarily peaceful, but more-efficiency-civilization [*sic*]."[16] The precise contours of this "more-efficiency-civilization" that the makers of the *Painstations* envisage (ironically, no doubt) in and through their creation could be the subject of much speculation. But this is the point of this theatrical game project: it creatively reproduces a game technology and culture of use—influential within today's audiovisual entertainment culture—in order to speculate on the future of contemporary technoculture and civilization generally.

To speculate on the future is first to make the means of speculation possible. This is something that Gonzalo Frasca describes as a key element of the promise of experimentation with computer game design and form. In his view, this promise is intricately bound up with the nature of computer games as instances of the simulational mode of cultural production that is becoming central to contemporary technocultural forms. I will next examine this claim carefully because it seeks to identify the critical potential of computer gaming as simulational form. The theatrical game projects I have discussed so far stage the distance between gameplay and real life in gestures that destabilize the habitual place computer gaming occupies in contemporary life. They do so precisely in response to the phenomenon of computer games as a predominantly simulation-based form that has come to pose its own questions about life now and in the future. Frasca sets out to show how games could activate a critical force for change by modifying simulation's questions from within.

Gaming and Theorizing Simulation's Future

Gonzalo Frasca puts forward an argument about the future of media forms based on the interactive simulation model underlying the exemplary new media form, the computer game. He states that their future is tied to the fact that simulation deals in a futural temporal mode of user (player) engagement; a simulation, unlike narrative and drama, "is the form of the future. It does not deal with what happened [narrative] or is happening [drama] but what may happen. Unlike narrative and drama, its essence lies on a basic assumption: change is possible."[17] Frasca argues we are only beginning to explore the rhetorical possibilities of the simulation form. In this vision, the future-directed modality of simulation opens up its own aesthetic development as a key element of the possible change it promises.

In Frasca's view, this projected pathway of aesthetic development would ride on the coattails of the simulational form of generating representations of event sequences, a form that has an inbuilt, structural relationship to speculation. The computer-based simulational form represents for Frasca a significant increase in the projective potential of aesthetic innovations in cultural productions utilizing its platform. It is in effect a kind of force multiplier—a military concept describing factors that increase the capacity or effectiveness of weapons systems, expressed in ratios of friendliness to enemy forces (for example, in the coordination of use of weapons). The force multiplication of narrative in its adoption of and by the cinema could be thought of as the major precursor of the nature and scale envisaged in Frasca's invocation of a future for simulational artistic and critical practice.

Frasca argues elsewhere that a key difference between traditional representational forms (such as the narrative representation of events) and simulation is that traditional representation typically operates from the bottom up so that from the recounting of a specific situation from which general reflections are drawn.[18] In a simulation, however, a top-down process operates in which the general features of a system are modeled so that various specific hypothetical situations can be deduced or examined. This projective or experimental characteristic of the functioning of simulation is what makes it in Frasca's view the form of the future.

Frasca's is a provocative gesture toward possible other futures for games and gaming as cultural activity beyond the already well-established parameters of commercial entertainment gaming. He focuses on simulation as key to this possibility, responding to the widespread perception that simulation technologies are the decisively new element in contemporary technoculture.[19] This is an entirely justified and even essential move for any attempt to characterize the wider situation making itself evident in a range of phenomena associated with new media. Espen Aarseth neatly sums up the importance of simulation for thinking computer games in this wider context: "The question is what is the essence of computing? If there is such an essence we could say it is simulation: that is the essence from Turing onwards. Games of course are simulations and computers are a prime platform for doing simulations."[20]

Frasca's insight concerning the future-facing orientation of simulation is, however, and perhaps necessarily so—and this question of necessity is something to which we will return—limited by its naive apprehension of what simulation has to offer critical responses to contemporary mainstream technoculture. This limitation can be articulated as two significant and related aspects of his approach to simulation. First, the history of computer simulation is, as I have shown throughout this book, a history influenced substantially by military technoscientific prerogatives that are reproduced in gaming and experimental adoptions of simulation. While it is important to remember that any reproduction is also the possible mutation or innovation of what is reproduced, it is no less important to understand the nature and conditions that impose themselves on the invention of the new as reproduction of a given heritage.

In other words, if simulation is generally the form of the future for audiovisual, computer-based culture, this is in large part because of a history of specific, enchained, military-industrial technoscientific developments occurring in and as a particular technocultural history. The nature and legacy of this history of computer simulation technics must not be discounted in assessing the significance and potential of simulation in general.[21] The defining moment of this history would be the development of the digital computer across a number of military technoscientific projects in the 1940s. Other key links in the chain would be the rise of cybernetics, the birth of cognitive simulation research (later to become the discipline of artificial intelligence), the introduction of computer graphics and interactivity in military flight simulation, and the development of distributed interactive simulation networking software and protocols for multiuser, realtime simulation training. The very gesture of taking simulation as a form capable of being simply abstracted or extracted from this history already performs this discounting.

This gesture opens the space for Frasca's theoretical engagement with simulation, one substantiated by the claim (supported by reference to Aarseth's *Cybertext: Perspectives on Ergodic Literature*) that "it is necessary to study games through a cybernetic approach."[22] It has been in no small part the project of this book to counteract this discounting gesture by reconnecting it with the material and sociotechnical dynamics that make it possible, and in a way inevitable, in the context of the tenacious forgetting of war's co-constitutive relation to technoculture. This would be one dimension of the necessity of Frasca's rhetoric of simulation, which we can circumvent by describing and evaluating the legacy and the possibilities given to contemporary audiovisual technoculture by this cybernetic lineage of simulation.

Second, this forgetting of the past of simulation technology is echoed in the schematization of narrative, drama, and simulation as forms whose predominant temporal user engagement can be assigned as past, present, and future. We have already examined how Weber's notion of theatricality would disturb the placement of drama in the middle of this schema. A theatrical taking place is fraught with an oscillating, reflective, speculative solicitation of the participant in and as the present moment of the theatrical presentation. In Weber's terms, the *"problematic process of placing, framing, situating"* is always part of the theatrical event, however conventional the nature of the dramatic staging and performance.[23]

Frasca indicates an awareness of the simplistic nature of this schematic conceptualization of the temporality of different cultural forms elsewhere in his writings. In "Videogames of the Oppressed," citing Sherry Turkle, he criticizes the overly Aristotelian dramatic orientation of the commercial gaming industry, which he argues reproduces the "immersive" tendency of conventional entertainment forms. He calls for a more Brechtian theatrical engagement of the gamer in a more critically active process of game design and gameplay.[24] More precisely, he cites as a major influence on his approach to simulation the work of Brecht-inspired Brazilian playwright and theorist Augusto Boal, developer of the theater of the oppressed. This alternative theatrical solicitation of the gamer would promote a reflexive gaming experience focused on real sociopolitical issues or questions. It would do so by means of gameplay that encouraged reflection and intervention in the models underlying the game as a simulation system. This would alienate the player from an uncomplicated, passive acceptance of the game's simulation of some real or imaginary world and return him or her to the less assured process of "theatrical" taking-place (in Weber's terms). The goal of such a Brechtian game design would be to produce critical reflections and speculations on the game's construction of the world—real and imagined, existing and potential.

In relation to the first term in this schema—narrative, drama, simulation—the viability of the conventional description of narrative as a form dedicated to the past also requires careful interrogation, inasmuch as it serves to contrast with simulation as the form of the future. No complication or qualification of the placement of narrative in the schema is apparent elsewhere in Frasca's work. In order to elucidate the problems of preserving the future for simulation, we will examine some experimental and noncommercial serious game projects that answer (or fail to answer) to Frasca's call for exploration of the critical or transformative potential of simulation. This will enable us to identify how simulation engages the future and where the past is in its experimentations. It will also open up perspectives on other avenues to rethinking the future than that mapped out in Frasca's schema.

September 12th: A Toy World (Newsgaming, 2002), created by Frasca in conjunction with other members of the Newsgaming team, provides a powerful critique of the U.S.-led war on terror. It achieves this by means of a parodic evocation of the legion of shoot-'em-up, Web-based games that populated the Internet in the period after the September 11, 2001, attacks and during the ongoing U.S.-led war on terror in Afghanistan and Iraq.[25] Users have a mouse point-and-click interface to target and shoot missiles at terrorist icons moving among civilians in a Middle Eastern–styled urban landscape. The overhead point of view of the user elegantly evokes the remote control intervention of high-tech weaponry in its distantiation of the enemy from the space of the user/missile fire controller (Figure 7). Terrorist icons carry guns, and civilian icons do not. Identify the terrorist, put the crosshairs on him (always "him"), and fire and forget. The designers have put a time lag between the firing and delivery of the missile so that it is difficult to hit the target. In all cases, civilians and urban structures are also hit. In the countdown to the next missile becoming available, it becomes evident that more terrorist icons are generated out of the rubble produced by the missile strikes. If one does not fire (the only alternative to using the available interface), the number of terrorists seems to remain stable.

September 12th announces itself with a screen that states, "This is not a game. You can't win and you can't lose. . . . This is a simple model you can use to explore some aspects of the war on terror."[26] It answers the numerous antiterrorist JavaScript games that mobilize the shoot-'em-up form in a less

FIGURE 7 Newsgaming.com, *September 12th: A Toy World*, 2002; courtesy of the artists.

parodic or reflective fashion, generating a political critique principally by means of its interruption of the expected routines of the target-and-shoot form of game interface. In Shuen-shing Lee's terms, its unwinnable form undoes the trial-and-error pattern of gameplay by making it a fruitless exercise that amounts to a critique of conventional game design.[27]

As a gesture to the future of gaming and simulation rhetoric, *September 12th* proposes a modulation of established game modeling of war in order to open up reflection on strategic, political, and cultural assumptions latent in mainstream shoot-'em-up forms. In this, it lives up to Frasca's call for critical gaming that goes beyond a simple parodic appropriation of existing games. By contrast, this would be an apt characterization of the project of *Donkey John* (Boughton-Dent, 2004).[28] *Donkey John* is an advocacy game in support of East Timorese efforts to negotiate a better deal with Australia for sharing the revenue from oil and gas reserves situated in the Timor Sea.[29] It cites the classic Nintendo arcade game, *Donkey Kong* (Nintendo, 1981), substituting then–Australian prime minister John Howard for Kong and Timorese president Xanana Gusmão for the player avatar. In this game, the force of the political critique is carried by an appropriation of a familiar cultural work, the Nintendo game and character, that substitutes the political figures as the monster (game challenge) and as the player avatar. No modification of the game model exists in this political game, and consequently, the game functions as an amusing, ironic reference to the real situation as a game of geopolitics and economic competition between unequal opponents.[30]

In a similar vein, *Under Ash* and *Under Siege* (Akfarmedia, 2001–2005) rely for their critical polemical impact on an appropriation of the existing commercial game format of the first-person shooter.[31] These games invert the expected scenario of a commercial contemporary counterterrorist shooter by making the player avatar in these single-player games a member of the Palestinian intifada battling against Israeli occupation forces. The impact of this reorientation in the brutal space of urban warfare is undoubtedly significant. The game developers state on their Web site that they wanted to provide an alternative leisure activity for Palestinians over the age of thirteen to one "previously filled with foreign games distorting the facts and history and planting the motto of 'Sovereignty is for power and violence according to the American style.'"[32] They pursue this explicitly counterpropagandistic

goal in what is basically a reproduction—in a much less forgiving register and with no ultimate winning condition for the player—of the generic
spaces, game challenges, and nonplayer characters produced in the standard
game engines of commercial first-person shooters.

Conversely, *September 12th* realizes a situation imagined by Sherry Turkle
(and cited by Frasca in "Videogames of the Oppressed") in which a new
critical practice would "take as its goal the development of simulations that
actually help players challenge the model's built-in assumptions. This new
criticism would try to use simulation as a means of consciousness-raising."[33]
This is an apt and concise summary of the project Frasca outlines in his
discussions of the future possibilities of experimentation with the existent
forms of computer simulation, the project Newsgaming.com has set in train
through its first experiments in simulation/games.[34] In this projected and
partly instantiated future of critical game production, simulation is seen as
a tool for promoting critical thinking about the differences between the
modeling of a situation or phenomenon and the real thing in all its social
and political complexity. In Frasca's terms, it imitates the way Augusto Boal
"uses theater as a tool, not as a goal per se."[35]

In order to retain focus on the specific question here—namely, the question concerning the nature and potential of simulation in relation to theater
and narrative—let us leave aside a rigorous critique of the metaphysical concept of technology as tool mobilized in this formulation and pursue it by
other means closer to our immediate task.[36] If simulation is a tool of sorts,
like theater is in Boal's conception, then so is narrative. From this perspective, narrative could be thought of as a technology for selecting, arranging,
and understanding experience—an "interpretation machine."[37] Whether by
means of the production of imagined or actual historical event sequences,
characters, and worlds, what is decisive for our argument is the capacity of
narrative works—mythical/religious or historical/realist, theatrical or nov-
elistic or cinematic or televisual—to function as mnemotechnical, exterior
forms of the remembering and archiving of human experience. Narrative
works are dedicated to the retention of the experience of phenomena by living humans so that it is available to those who did not have that experience.

The crucial point for our discussion here is that, as a mnemotechnical
form, narrative is consequently always already futural in temporal orientation.

In other words, precisely as a technics of orientation, narrative forms are ultimately future directed; the recording, arranging, and interpretation of past experience produced and archived in narrative works is always accomplished with a view to the future. First of all, a narrative is produced to be read, watched, or witnessed in the future by a prospective audience or readership. The narrative work has the function of recounting to this audience-to-come what happened before them. Alternatively, it explains what happened in their own past, before they came to be the audience/readers on the day of the narration's taking place. This orientating function links what has happened before to where I—as always part of a "we"—am today. Orientation is a reflective and interpretative, but also and therefore ultimately projective, process: "Where to go from here? What to do next? What to become?" are the questions orientation is ultimately dedicated to answering. Stiegler explains the "ancient" human desire for stories by observing that it is the story that links generation to generation: "Insatiable, they [stories] hold out the promise, to generations to come, of the writing of new episodes of future life, yet to be invented, to be fictionalized."[38]

Consequently, simulation cannot maintain a monopoly over other cultural forms with regard to its capacity to engage people in their future. On the contrary, as a form that depends on the narratival mnemotechnical heritage, it is best understood to be reproducing narrative's dedication to anticipating the future as change, as potential, as the not yet determined. When Frasca describes the process of Boal's forum theater, one of the techniques of the theater of the oppressed, the dependence of simulation on historical narrative becomes evident. "Forum Theater is nothing but a game," argues Frasca, in which a particular scenario is first devised by the participants and then replayed several times in an experimental fashion in order to stimulate debate about the social and political dynamics animating both the real-world scenario and its modeling as a theatrical representation. The starting point is a process of narrative construction:

Forums are created around a short play (five to ten minutes long), usually scripted on-site, and based on the suggestions of the participants. The scene always enacts an oppressive situation, where the protagonist has to deal with powerful characters that do not let her achieve her goals.[39]

Protagonist, goal, antagonist, character arcs; the game begins from a classic narrative point of departure.

A certain circularity can now be glimpsed in the top-down versus bottom-up opposition of simulation and narrative forms proposed by Frasca. Narrative, as a bottom-up form, is understood to derive its significance in passing from the specific to the general situation, and simulation works by passing from the general model to specific instantiations of the model. The constant traffic between the general and the specific, and narrative and simulation, disturbs the clarity of this separation of the two forms. A simulation relies on narrative-based recordings of experience (such as in the example of forum theater), generalized from the specific in procedures of story construction, character development, stylistic and generic conventions, and so forth. Each specific narrative work likewise emerges only on condition of these generalizations, reproducing them as the basis and possibility of its specificity.

Of course, the proliferation of simulational cultural forms and their specific reworkings of the exterior archive of human experience is having an increasingly significant impact on the mnemotechnological milieu in general and narrative-based forms of cultural memory in particular, as many theorists of the information age have observed. The history of simulation's iterative reproduction of narrative is part of the history of technological modernity, a history best understood as the backstory of the more specific history of computer simulation described above.

To outline briefly this backstory, I would commence with the development of formalized military war gaming.[40] This was a key progenitor of computerized modeling and simulation principles and procedures. War gaming emerged as a new Enlightenment innovation in military officer training during the eighteenth century in Prussia and elsewhere. These practices drew on a rationalist enthusiasm for the schematic, mathematical simplification of complex real-world dynamics into abstract principles and procedures. Proponents of this new scientific approach to war found increasing support, and these new methods gradually impinged on existing training regimens based on making detailed study of the history of military conflicts and learning established techniques of strategy and tactics. War gaming could not have been devised without this existing tradition of historical study. The abstraction and reduction of war to war game rested on the historical and narrative record of previous military experience, and on its role as the basis for training future warriors. The understanding and interpretation of what was significant (or not) about the conduct of war contained within the heritage of military chronicles and other written records, theoretical tracts on strategy, military training manuals, and other documents made possible their selective reproduction in the form of war game models. Each assumption in the war game model is literally unthinkable without this historical heritage of narrative-based work on war.

The critical tool that is *September 12th*, when viewed from the most longitudinal perspective, is a reflective meditation on this backstory of military history and on its adoption in war game simulation practices that are now widely disseminated in commercial and amateur war game models. Only as such can it be a simulation tool for critical thinking. Simulation is a mutated adoption of the narrative mnemotechnical tool dedicated to the future in a specific, experimental, hypothetical manner, one that may be critically cited via a creative reproduction such as in *September 12th*. A constant theme of the history of war gaming is at the heart of this operation, namely, the tension between the historical record of warfare's unpredictable complexity and the effort to model it in a rational simulation that could bracket off part of this complexity for the purposes of predictive analysis. The dependence of each and every assumption in the war model on the historical archive of specific military conflicts produces this tension.

Like the narrative form that is a key part of its own backstory, simulation, as a new mnemotechnology, draws on the past with a view to the future. What Frasca calls its top-down process of modeling a general situation draws on and synthesizes the understandings arising from the heritage of bottom-up historical syntheses of past experience. If narrative gestures toward the general element in the specific case in fulfillment of its orientational function, simulation mobilizes the calculative reason of technoscientific modernity to schematically map out the general situation available for speculative hypothetical research.[41]

The undoing of the simplistic schematization of

Narrative ➔ Past
Drama ➔ Present
Simulation ➔ Future

means that simulation must be thought of as a new mnemotechnical form before its specific critical potential can be adequately apprehended. It must be understood as a process of exterior memorization dedicated to the orientation of the individual vis-à-vis his or her collective in time and space, here, today, and into the future. Articulated at this level of conceptual generality, this is what simulation shares with narrative and the theater. To recall our discussion of *Tekken Torture Tournament* and the *Painstation* projects, their theatrical staging of competitive gameplay is able to engage the spectator participants in just such an orientational reflective and speculative relation to computer gaming. Their critical potential is activated in the suspension of the habitual taking place of simulated conflict in contemporary entertainment culture.

Like theatrical and simulation-based experimental projects, narrative-based works can also generate a critical encounter with simulation. Although it also relies on a theatrical staging of simulation, the Blast Theory and Mixed Reality Lab project *Desert Rain* (1999–2004) is one whose critical force arises from an historical reflection on simulation's role in recording and understanding the real (Figure 8). This is achieved as part of the work's larger ambition to investigate the blurring of the distinction between the mediatized representation and the reality of the 1991 Gulf war.[42] One views the work only as a participant in a game in which one plays as part of a team of six. The team members are assigned the goal of finding a person whose identity is described on a magnetic swipe card they are given at the start of the game. The person must be found through cooperative action with other team members in navigating a virtual space. The simulation providing this activity is a VR-based modified military training simulation. Having successfully achieved the mission goals (or not, as was the case with my team's experience of *Desert Rain*), the team members move to a debriefing room via a passage covered in sand. This final space in the installation is a simulated hotel room with six monitors activated by the swipe cards. Testimony from the target personages, including a soldier in Iraq, a tourist, a peace worker, and a BBC journalist, concerning their experiences of the war, its history, and its aftermath, are played on the activated monitors.

This is a rich and complex work that explores the theme of the perceived virtuality of war in the era of contemporary media and virtual reality mediations. Its predominant mode of engaging participants is, I would argue, via

FIGURE 8 Photograph of projection onto the rain curtain with performer Ju Row Farr. Photograph by Fiona Freund. *Desert Rain*, 1999 (interactive game, installation, and performance). A collaboration with Blast Theory and the Mixed Reality Lab, University of Nottingham.

solicitation of historical reflection on the war and on its representation. The staging of the VR simulation, which is the centerpiece attraction of the project as a new media art installation, is devised so as to isolate that simulated experience from the passage to the debriefing space, in which historical accounts of war experience are represented. Ultimately, participants are asked to compare these accounts with their experience of the mediation of war in *Desert Rain* and in their own mediated historical experience. In what is no doubt a complex staging of the challenges faced by historical discourse in the era of contemporary media technologies—indeed, more complex than I have been able to indicate here—*Desert Rain* explores the struggle of narrative forms of understanding to operate in a simulated theater of operations.

It Ain't Necessarily So

Earlier I suggested that from a certain point of view, the limitations of Frasca's articulation of the future critical potential of simulation as the form of the future were perhaps necessary. While *September 12th,* his practical instantiation of this future potential, is a canny interference with the modeling of high-tech war simplistically reproduced in mainstream and amateur computer games, we have explored the manner in which Frasca's theorization of simulation as the form of the future lacks a critical encounter with the history of computer simulation technology. The predictive, hypothetical force of computer simulation is in no small way a legacy of the military technoscientific merger with the modern rational industrialization of planning, control, and regulation in the military-industrial and military-entertainment complexes. The entwining of these two trajectories is the accident par excellence of technological development in the logistical era of pure war. Given the pervasive and comprehensive dimensions of the fallout of this defining accident of the nuclear age, it may seem necessary to forget this heritage in looking to an alternative, critical future potential of simulation. I would suggest that, on the contrary, this heritage must be remembered as central to the proliferation of simulation in contemporary technoculture and hence to any adoption of it in the name of different futures.

Conclusion

The Challenge of Simulation

The *2009 Army Capstone Concept* is a short video released by TRADOC (U.S. Army Training and Doctrine Command) as a digestible summary of the Army's concept statement about what kind of capabilities the Army estimates it will require to "apply finite resources to overcome adaptive adversaries in an era of complexity and uncertainty."[1] This statement, based on the lessons of the first decade of the war on terror, revises the previous prediction that technology would provide "near perfect situational awareness" via "sensors, standoff capability and improved command and control." It outlines a project of incorporating cultural and historical knowledge and experience into strategic planning for a projected future of "persistent" and "irregular" conflict in the increasingly numerous failed cities of global capital's empyrean. It is not clear, however, whether we should take at face value this sober revision of the U.S military's confidence in its ability to deliver the "full spectrum dominance" envisaged in 1990s Pentagon-authored documents emanating from proponents of the "Revolution in Military Affairs" and later Pentagon-authored blueprints for coping with the insurgencies in Afghanistan and Iraq. Despite the lip service paid to the merits of historical and cultural studies, the video is liberally sprinkled with images of the latest high-tech weapon systems in use in these theaters. Prominent among these in the video are remote-controlled robots that carry out thousands of hours of missions on land and in the air.

Use of these robots for operations—for explosive ordnance disposal, automated antiprojectile base defense, and aerial reconnaissance, as well as weapons delivery platforms on the ground and in the air—has grown exponentially during the years of the war on terror. Used in a variety of contexts with varying degrees of remoteness between operators and their robotic projections into the battlefield, the emerging media icon of the robot wars is of the unmanned aerial vehicles (UAVs) such as the Predator (General Atomics Aeronautical Systems) being flown remotely over Afghanistan or Iraq by "pilots" situated in trailers set up at Nellis and Creech Air Force bases in Nevada. In contrast to the spirit, if not to the image track, of the *Capstone Concept* video, P. W. Singer argues that the rise of robotic war-fighting systems heralds the most significant and far-reaching transformation of war and military operations since the atomic bomb.[2]

The merits of and assumptions informing this prediction deserve a substantial analysis exceeding the scope of my concerns here. I begin the concluding chapter of this study with consideration of this undoubtedly significant weapons development because it demonstrates, among other things, the ever closer circuits of interchange between war, simulation, and technoculture in the time of the war on terror. As is immediately apparent in the media coverage of the reachback remote piloting systems at the Nevada bases, the control interface for the UAVs (and for other military robots) resembles the controller configurations of commercial game consoles such as the Xbox and Playstation systems. This is no accident; the systems have been developed this way for two reasons: first, to facilitate the training of operators by taking advantage of their familiarity with navigating and acting in the virtual spaces of video gameworlds, and second, to leverage the research and development work done by the commercial games industry in developing such interactive technics.[3] The technics and the technocultural milieu of video gaming are mutually inducted here for (inter)active service in the U.S. (and other allied Western) military's persistent global war on terror, along with those of the Xbox generation recruited to serve in its ongoing prosecution.

This mobilization of virtual simulational technics should be understood as another spiral of the complex interrelations between military and nonmilitary technological developments of virtualization examined in this book. In chapter 3, I examined computerized flight simulation, noting the difficulty of separating the military and entertainment origins of analog flight simulators and discussing the significance of Ivan Sutherland's work for the military and the commercial development of digital virtual reality. It is thus difficult to read the military's appropriation of game console technics as a poaching of technology from one domain to another. It is better approached as another step in a compositional dynamic of military-technocultural becoming where the relation between the two is not isolated or extraneous, but constitutive of their different but co-implicated trajectories.

The challenge of this book has been to get a better critical grasp on this complex dynamic in order to contribute to improving critical work on contemporary media and technocultural developments. The video game deployment of remote-controlled weapons systems crystallizes the stakes of this challenge. Through its virtualization of the distant place where the robot stands ready to act on the world, the controlling system projects the simulational technics of cold war research and development out from the training and testing facilities and over the territory of the designated enemy combatant. As I noted in chapter 1, this trajectory was launched in the 1990s in the wake of SIMNET's success in training Persian Gulf war tank units via the dissemination of portable mission simulation systems to deployed forces. With the UAVs and other robot warriors, however, simulation breaches the narrowing gap between training and execution. If combat means a contest between two or more opposed people, then these simulational technics effectively anticipate it and preempt its occurrence. The robotic prosecution of war is in a sense its disappearance into something else—something like the thing simulation models in order to control. The strategic-military implications of this are what Singer mainly has in mind in his claim about the importance of robotic weapons. From our perspective, this robotic redefinition of war must be analyzed as part of the broader dynamics relating war, simulation, and technoculture. The relationship between military and commercial video gaming technics so evident in these robotic systems then assumes its full significance. It is from this point of view that I have approached video games as phenomena central to our technocultural future.

Mnemotechnical Experience: Rethinking the Narrative Versus Simulation Opposition

I have argued in this book that beyond explicitly serious undertakings, such as the projects we examined in the previous chapter, computer games are always already worthy of serious critical and theoretical interrogation. As forms of contemporary entertainment, they are part of the technocultural organization of contemporary existence. Entertainment and leisure activities provide many answers in today's so-called postscarcity age to the question about what to do next. This is immediately apparent when one considers the global scale, investment levels, and diversity of interests of the major media corporations dominating the computer games industry. The stakes of entertainment are high indeed. Computer games are forms that operate precisely by playing out and playing with serious modes of cultural production, including daily work routines, the production of war, the management of resources in logistical scenarios, technoscientific experimentation, and social and personal relationship development. Serious, experimental, or pedagogical computer game projects are particular modalities of this playing with the real tasks of living, doing, and making. As numerous examples in this study have shown, commercial computer games are another, and instances of gameplay that comment reflectively on, ironize, satirize, or otherwise engage critically and speculatively with the serious activities of life are available through the entertainment that games provide.

To take advantage of this critical potential of video game technocultural production and its diversions, it is essential to approach video games from a perspective that comprehends their significance as forms native to the computer age. This book has sought to discover what is specific about computer games as simulational forms at the forefront of contemporary technoculture. The technological platform for simulation, the digital electronic computer, is the defining technology of the digital age. Its emergence out of the cold war mobilization of technoscientific research and development is something that any critical engagement with computer games must first address; its ongoing implications must also be considered.

Virilio has cogently characterized the post–World War II era of pure war as the accidental consequence of wartime mobilization. In pure war, the exceptional, temporary passage to total mobilization mutates into a temporally unlimited preparation for an impossibly hot instant of total nuclear war. The undoing of any definitive distinctions between war and peace, logistics and strategicopolitical discourse, military and domestic/commercial economics, and technoscience is the ongoing damage of this accident.

The anticipatory, deterrent vector of the pure war logistical tendency to preempt the enemy undermines the differences between wars of national liberation and U.N. police actions, national defense and homeland security operations, invasion and preemptive counterterrorist measures. James Der Derian describes another face of this confusion between war and simulation when he examines the increasing ambiguity of the scope and nature of simulation training operations he witnessed at the U.S./NATO Combat Maneuver Training Center in Southern Germany at the height of the Bosnian conflict in the 1990s. He describes the shifting characterizations of training missions that involved military forces in complex situations that included "civilians in the area of operations, the press, local authorities, and private organizations."[4] The training exercises he observed for these "Military Operations Other than War" changed designation so that they became simulations of "Operations Other than War" and, ultimately, "Stability Operations."[5] Der Derian captures the ambiguity of the nature of the operations being simulated:

> In other words, the "White Paper" [outlining the purpose and nature of these training simulations] was this year's model for the high-tech, post–cold war simulations and training exercises that would prepare U.S. Armed Forces for pre-peacekeeping noninterventions into those postimperial spaces where once- and wannabe-states were engaged in postwar warring.[6]

The further into the post–cold war era, the more difficult it becomes to designate unambiguously any military operations as war (or postwar warring) in the traditional strategicopolitical sense of this concept. The relative clarity of the distinction between absolute, total nuclear conflict (as the ultimate form of war that monopolizes the category of war) and other limited conflicts fades from view.

Following the lead of Virilio and of other contemporary cultural theorists examined in this study, I argue that simulation has transformed real war just as it has transformed the real of economics, politics, education, and cultural practice in general. The rise of robot war is one of the most apparent indications of this transformation. To develop a critical framework to approach these transformations, it is necessary to consider simulation as a decisive modification of the mnemotechnical recording and processing of experience discussed in the previous chapter.

To recap, philosopher of technology Bernard Stiegler describes media forms of all kinds as mnemotechnologies—that is, exterior memory supports that ground human historical experience by preserving and making available experiences that we who live today have not ourselves lived. Any mnemotechical form arises from a selective process of (re)construction that is not equal to real experience. These mnemotechnical forms condition—and have always already conditioned—experience, and as such are its condition of possibility. A pure opposition between simulation and real experience is, in this view, untenable. Rather, it is a question of distinguishing simulation from lived experience and simulation from other mnemotechnical forms, without posing these questions in terms of an unequivocal oppositionality.

The complication of the relation between simulation and the real needs to be understood not as a radically new development through which a new representational and interactive media form suddenly uproots the ground of the real. Instead, the novelty of the contemporary era of simulation should be approached as a shift in the prevailing relations between mnemotechnical forms and the experience that they condition by selectively reproducing the archive of its past occurrence and providing a basis for anticipating its future course.

What is it that simulation brings to this dynamic of life lived on the basis of its mnemotechnical conditions? The contrast with narrative is the most pertinent and widely adopted means for articulating this specificity. The ludology debate in games studies circulates around this theme. Stories represent experience inasmuch as they record a particular selection, evaluation, and therefore judgment of experience that arises from a particular individual (or individuals), in a particular moment of cultural individuation. The narrative interpretation machine discussed in chapter 4 produces a work that produces in turn questions about its truthfulness to the way things were and are in the world of the reader's experience. This experience is prefigured, as Paul Ricoeur has it, through a lifetime of narrative entailments.[7] These questions about the story concern the merit of its interpretation of experience—questions that involve the work in a process of comparison with and potential reappraisal of the reader's existing historical and cultural coordinates. In other words, these questions engage the readers/viewers with their future by tasking them with the challenge of determining and legitimating their criteria of evaluation.

Understanding the narrative work and being certain of one's judgment about its judgment of experience means knowing how to take its meaning today in the present moment of reading. It is knowing whether or not to rethink one's past judgments, decisions, and actions, and therefore anticipating knowing how to think and act in the future. In reading a story, the reader is always engaged in a process of (re)legitimation that is directed both at the self and the text. Legitimation is, as Jacques Derrida has decisively argued, a performative act that animates every interpretation precisely as this potential retroactively evaluates the past—in and through the available recording of that past—from a future present.[8]

With simulation, experience is not recorded in the same manner as in a narrative. A simulation is produced through a process of modeling. To rephrase Gonzalo Frasca, the selective reiteration of the factical record of experience produces a model that is the reduction of a more complex system into a less complex system designed to operate for a particular purpose.[9] The purpose dictates the process of evaluating the simulation in its design phase, wherein the selective reproduction of experience in and as the model is accomplished. In his influential work (in simulation industry circles) on designing computer simulations, Robert G. Sargent describes this evaluation process as having three stages: validation, verification, and accreditation of the model.[10] Elaborating on Sargent's description and commenting on his diagrammatic representation of this process, Roger Smith states,

For the purposes of VV&A the simulation development process is divided into the problem space, conceptual model, and software model with definite transitions and quality evaluations between these stages as shown in Figure 2 [reproduced below as Figure 9, with Smith's minor terminological changes from Sargent's original diagram]. Validation is the process of determining that the conceptual model reflects the aspects of the problem space that need to be addressed and does so such that the requirements of the study can be met. Validation is also used to determine whether the operations of the final software model are consistent with the real world, usually through experimentation

and comparison with a known data set. Verification is the process of determining that the software model accurately reflects the conceptual model.
Accreditation is the official acceptance of the software model for a specified
purpose. A software model accredited for one purpose may not be acceptable
for another, though it is no less valid based on its original design.[11]

Questions of truthfulness, legitimacy, and significance posed by an accredited simulation can only concern the fitness of the simulation "for a specified
purpose." This purpose will revolve around study of a defined "problem
space" within "the real world," study that would take the form of Espen
Aarseth's ergodic engagement with the simulation intended to result in the
discovery of possible solutions (epiphanies) that would eliminate the problem (aporia) in the problem space.[12]

At the serious (as opposed to entertainment) end of the simulation business of military-industrial, economicologistic, and related applications, these
hypothetical solutions would be tested in the real world with a view to obviating the need for any future reformulation of the problem space—such, at
least, is the dominant, instrumental view of the goal of simulation. A less
positivist, more cynical view of the simulation industry's operation may be
closer to the mark. This would see a typical late capitalist enterprise seeking
the perpetual growth of consumption of its product via the marketing of an
endless stream of new and improved versions arising from a perpetually iterative design process.[13]

In any event, the design of a simulation effectively preempts the questioning of the significance and legitimacy of its record of experience other
than from an instrumental perspective. That which narrative works generate
as an integral part of the dynamics of their reception is not a designed outcome of simulation in the commercial mainstream. These questions have
been posed and answered in advance in the design phase of the simulation.
The answers inhere in the model as schematic representation of the problem
space, itself a schema of the real world that poses the problem in response to
which the simulation has been produced. A simulation is therefore a system
that must foreclose the question of the nature and legitimacy of its reproduction of experience before it can function effectively as a problem-solving
technics. The validation of the conceptual model must be concluded before

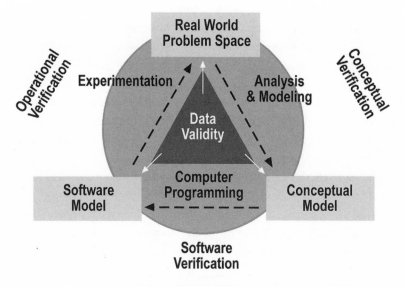

FIGURE 9 Verification, validation, and accreditation cycle of simulation design;
reproduced with the permission of Robert G. Sargent.

the verification or accreditation stages of design can be finished. An accredited simulation will elicit, as the core of its reception by the user, an implicit
affirmation of its conceptual model signaled by his or her cybernetic engagement in the simulation's software model of the problem space. Ian Bogost
puts it succinctly in characterizing video games as exemplars of "procedural
representation" produced in the simulational modeling of processes. Game
design is all about choices and selections afforded by the model: "choices are
selectively included and excluded in a procedural representation to produce
a desired expressive end."[14]

Ideology and Simulation

As many cultural and media theorists have argued, narrative forms can also—
and in mainstream audiovisual culture, routinely do—construct interpretations of experience that attempt to preempt questioning of their legitimacy.
The mainstream could be understood as a preemptive force constituted
by the cumulative effect of the coordination and coincidence of cultural and

media works sharing similar interpretations.[15] Here we are in the terrain of theories of hegemonic cultural production, ideological apparatuses, dominant and preferred readings, and so forth. Computer simulation, and computer games as simulations, could be included in readings of culture arising from this terrain as the most recent examples of the reproduction of dominant cultural values in mainstream media.[16] Yet this could miss the crucial aspect of the simulational form we are concerned with here.

Manovich's discussion of the standardization of cognition evident in the development and celebration of computer-mediated interactivity can help us pinpoint both this aspect and this risk. His analysis is not unrelated to the novelty of computer simulation inasmuch as simulation is a principal *causa finalis* of the design of computer interactivity. He contextualizes this "modern desire to externalize the mind" in the design of objective, rational systems of machine–user interface and operation as part of the

> demand of modern mass society for standardization. The subjects have to
> be standardized, and the means by which they are standardized have to be
> standardized as well. Hence the objectification of internal, private mental
> processes, and their equation with external visual forms that can be easily
> manipulated, mass produced, and standardized on their own.[17]

But Manovich misses the full implications of his analysis when he expresses the effects of this standardization found in new media interactivity in terms of the ideological critique of culture. He characterizes the externalization of thought in preprogrammed, new media interactivity as an "updated version" of Louis Althusser's concept of "interpellation" in which "we are asked to mistake the structure of somebody else's mind for our own."[18] In Manovich's argument, this "somebody" is the designer of the new media work. This is something of a misreading—or at least a partial, limited reading—of Althusser's work on ideology and subjectivity. It focuses on ideology as a misrecognition of the individuality of one's own "internal, private mental processes" that is caused by an external, material process. This focus leaves intact the integrity of the interiority of the subject's "internal, private mental processes" in positing a mistaken identification by the new media user with the "mental trajectory of the new media designer"—as if one could find oneself thinking the other individual's (interior) thoughts as if in the other's head.[19] Such a misidentification is only possible on the basis of the material, technical new media form. The profound complexity of this exterior, mnemotechnical vehicle with the interior mental processes of the user is missing from Manovich's account. Manovich is right to describe the design of interactivity as a process in which the "subjects have to be standardized, and the means by which they are standardized have to be standardized as well." The most radical consequence of this, however, would be found in the alteration of the nature of "internal, private mental processes" implied in this standardization of the means of standardization.

The novelty of new media interactivity would consequently have to be considered beyond the positing of a "new kind of identification [with the new media designer] appropriate for the information age of cognitive labor."[20] Computer simulation highlights the novelty in its preemptive strike against interpretation in favor of a will to accomplishment. Jos de Mul, comparing play and narrative forms of temporal engagement, explains the rise to prominence of computer games as a function of their correspondence to the *Homo volens* that defines modern humanity. For "Willful Man," the "projective dimension" of human temporal engagement tends to overshadow the interpretative engagement with the past thanks to the "powerful means" of modern technology.[21] Through these means, the user of an interactive simulation is solicited to engage with the model as one whose internal mental processes are always already oriented to the accomplishment or discoveries it prefigures. Engagement, play, learning, and training take place when the user is in place. The user does not adopt the mentality of the simulation designer(s) in the course of interacting with the work in the same way that he or she may identify with the characters in a movie or follow the film's enunciation of a directorial instance. As producer of the simulation's eventualities in specific hypothetical situations, the user will have adopted the simulation's modeling of the general situation in the act of becoming the user, who is required to author the production of the experience him- or herself.

In other words, the interpellation effected by the user's interactive engagement in a simulation is best understood as resulting in a confusion not with the mind of the simulation designer, but with the mentality of simulation as a material, mnemotechnical process. In relation to computer games as simulations, James Newman comments that one plays a computer game to learn how to "think like a computer."[22] Newman goes on to describe this as a process of coming to synthesize one's experience of the gamespace in what I would call a managerial or logistical perspective through which all the interacting elements can be perceived and controlled effectively. Newman draws on the work of Ted Friedman, who has argued for the potential for computer games as an "aestheticized" form of computer simulation to communicate different "structures of thought" from those transmitted by existing media.[23] "The way computer games teach structures of thought—the way they reorganize perception—is by getting you to internalize the logic of the program."[24] In *Civilization* (Microprose, 1991), for instance, the player does not identify with the many roles one must perform, such as "king, general, mayor, city planner, settler, warrior, and priest. . . . so much as with *the computer* itself."[25]

Friedman views this process of internalization as intrinsically cybernetic. The constant feedback between player and simulation is the core mechanism through which "the line demarcating the end of the player's consciousness and the beginning of the computer's world blurs."[26] In realtime games like the first-person shooter I examined in chapter 5, those closest to the primal scene of cybernetics in Wiener's wartime research, the player's engagement in the speed race of information processing is a commitment to thinking like a computer and at the speed of a computer—or, at least, in response to the speed at which the computer can calculate the responses of the simulation to the player's input.

In view of the relation between mnemotechnics and experience, I would argue that the large-scale adoption of computer simulation in contemporary audiovisual culture tends toward an implicit conformity to the schemas of interpreting the problem space of the real world programmed into the prevailing simulational forms. Through this tendency, the capacity to critically engage in the dynamic of transformative inheritance of the past through selective reproduction of the artifacts and mnemotechnical archives of recorded experience is threatened. In other words, the preemption of interpretative engagement with the simulation's selective recording of experience tends to deter its functioning as a mnemotechnical form per se, inasmuch as mnemotechnics do not simply make the past available, but make possible the reinvention of the past through the possibility of performative counter interpretations of the factical archive in the present. The reinvention of the past is the possibility of the reinvention of the future programmed in the past as given. The preprogramming of interpretation necessary to simulation as instrumental form to be used by the computer user tends to close off this possibility.

Border Insecurities: The Networks of Military, Commercial, and Technocultural Becoming

The ability of the simulation form to standardize the recordings of experience for the purpose of user involvement is a significant contributing factor to a major shift in what Stiegler calls the perpetual "disorganization and re-organization of the organic" by the technological memory retained outside the body in the technical "organization of the inorganic."[27] Today the validated model of the simulation design process is major proponent of this shift. The validated model predetermines the possible outcomes of technoscientific mediation of cultural and political developments in terms of solutions to the problems selectively reproduced in the schematic modeling of reality. The culture of what Stiegler calls "generalized simulation" would be, in Virilio's terms, a pure war milieu in which deterrent anticipation was the primary temporal orientation.[28] The diffusion of war into peacetime evoked in Virilio's term would be exemplified in the performative violence of the validation process. This not only enacts an always violent legitimation of a simulation's selective interpretation of experience, but also preempts challenges to its legitimacy as a standard procedure of simulation design.

The science of cybernetics, emerging as I discussed in chapter 1 out of Wiener's efforts to invent a predicting machine for use as a preemptive weapon system, appears as a signal example of the diffusion of this logistical process. Its consequent and ongoing transformation of social, political, and technocultural existence cannot be overestimated. Cybernetics had the anticipatory control of eventuality as its target, working toward it in a conflictual dynamic with the new potentialities it constantly throws up.[29]

The quasi-intentional, artificial life forms that Seth Giddings discusses are an example of these new potentialities.[30] The science of artificial life, developing as a branch of artificial intelligence, has found various aesthetic

computer game nonplayer characters and in game systems more
g. y. These forms have, as Giddings notes, in some instances contributed to the ongoing advance of the science.[31] Giddings proposes that the
player's engagement in gameplay with these artificial life-forms amounts
to a paradigmatic instance of the emerging technoculture of the cybernetic
circuit of emergent networks of human and nonhuman development. If this
is so, then the predominant mobilization of this dynamic in the military-
entertainment complex follows the deterrent anticipatory logic we have
identified as the logistical engine of this complex of war and technoculture.
Giddings's signal example of this paradigmatic phenomenon—its military
dimension unremarked upon—is the popularity of the Gameboy Advance
game, *Advance Wars 2* (Nintendo, 2003), a turn-based battle strategy game
that involves play against computer-controlled units to achieve territorial
military goals.[32]

The "re-organization of the organic" performed by computer simulation
technologies orients the human toward the future in what I have called a
deterrent anticipatory mode. They provide an interactive, technical form for
thinking in a standardized, standardizable, problem-solving fashion. In doing
so, they contribute to wider dynamics operative in contemporary mainstream technoculture. These dynamics are evidenced in the recent escala-
tion of global technological developments in the age of terror toward greater
security from unexpected attacks in unanticipated forms, toward counter-
measures for asymmetrical responses to preemptive military actions, to a re-
invigorated logistical overriding of traditional politicostrategic discourse in
the advanced nations. The part played by simulation in these dynamics is
not a minor one, as the analyses of Virilio, Der Derian, and others closer to
the terrain of video game studies demonstrate. Roger Stahl's *Militainment,
Inc.* and Nick Dyer-Witherford and Greig de Peuter's *Games of Empire* have
made important contributions to analyzing the part played by video game
design, marketing, and adoption by different player constituencies in the
network of interconnections between military, commercial, and technocultural becomings.[33]

At the level of recent American geopolitics, the security of the perime-
ter between democracy and dictatorship, freedom and tyranny, civilization
and religious fanaticism, war and terror, "with us" and "for terrorism" is the

perceived stake of this work to anticipate the dangers of the future. Samuel Weber's account of the constitutive anxiety over the security of the border between theater and its other (the real) discussed in the previous chapter reminds us of the theatrical, performative nature of this massive effort of orientation toward security in the time of the war on terror.[34] The integrity of what can be preserved this side of the border is at stake, and it is the maintenance of this that justifies (and requires) violent actions toward the others threatening the continued integrity of the community, and the suspension of ethical dispositions and legal/juridical responsibilities toward the others.[35] Securing the future of the homeland justifies the sacrifice of democratic rights, civil liberties, and rights to privacy, as well as the lives and limbs of citizen-soldiers, not to mention those targeted as enemies.[36] Above all, it requires the communal sacrifice of the possibility of other futures than that programmed in and as the ongoing anticipation of external threats to security.

But this very effort, in its intensity and technoscientific systematicity— including its massive investment in simulation technologies of training and prediction, as well as the preemptive control of situations—cannot guarantee its own success. One might consider this effort as a secular iteration of the sacrificial impulse legitimized in terms of the religious imperative to preserve what is holy from corruption.[37] Derrida states that the holy (*heilig* in German) is what is whole, intact, healthy.[38] Derrida describes such sacrificial gestures as an autoimmune response of the religious community, one which is an instance of the

> death-drive that is silently at work in every community, every *auto-co-immunity*, constituting it as such in its iterability, its heritage, its spectral tradition. Community as *common auto-immunity:* no community [is possible] that would not cultivate its own auto-immunity, a principle of sacrificial self-destruction ruining the principle of self-protection (that of maintaining its self-integrity intact), and this in view of some sort of invisible and spectral survival. This self-contesting attestation keeps the auto-immune community alive, which is to say, open to something other and more than itself: the other, the future, death, freedom, the coming or the love of the other, the space and time of a spectralizing messianicity beyond all messianism.[39]

As I demonstrated in relation to online game communities, Jean-Luc Nancy argued in a similar way that the identity of the community can never be produced in its final form. The violent effort to produce the community by exclusions, sacrifices, and struggle can, as a work of self-realization, only lead to (more) violence, (more) war. I argued that this work of self-production is characteristic of online game communities and that the predominant forms of being and acting in such communities serve to reinforce norms of identification. Players play in a virtual space of contestation performing routines of self-realization. Responses to exceptional and idiosyncratic variations of these routines highlight the normative, autoimmune tendency of the insecure community to foreclose its (future) survival. This does not, of course, guarantee the exclusion of idiosyncratic, singular iterations of the routines of communal reproduction. On the contrary. As Derrida says, the autoimmune response is also, paradoxically, what keeps the community open to change, to otherness, to a "spectralizing messianicity" that will save it from itself.

Having returned via online game community to the question of computer gaming in relation to these wider dynamics of contemporary technoculture, let us repose the question of what can be said about computer games in general in the context of our discussion of computer simulation in general. If computer simulation must be thought in relation to the preemptive, anticipatory dynamic of the contemporary technocultural orientation, what of computer games as the mass entertainment manifestation of simulation? I have argued that computer games reproduce this anticipatory dynamic in and as gameplay. That is to say, they replay it, but this also means they play with the experience of this dynamic of today's technocultural insecurity. As games, they replay the urgent dynamic of racing ahead of eventuality in a fun form only supposedly free of real, serious consequences. As Johan Huizinga demonstrated, play is culturally antecedent; the serious only emerges subsequently in the record of human languages.[40] Forms of play are consequently set apart but never irrevocably sundered from a fundamental relation to the serious. One is tempted to understand computer games in this light as offering a temporary release from or an inoculation against the anxieties arising from the prevailing existential conditions of technocultural postmodernity, not the least of which is the anxiety about the sacrifices called for by the community in the maintenance of its technoscientific preemption of future contingency.[41] This understanding falls short, however, of both the challenge and the potential of computer games to engage players in the future of contemporary technoculture.

Endgame: The Challenge of Simulation

To play with the experience of something can also be to interfere with it in some fashion. Computer games possess this potential insofar as they are entertainment forms that take place in the suspending of routines of serious activity. I noted in chapter 2 the French root of entertainment—*entretenir*, "to hold between"—to point to this potential to interrupt the routine temporal ordering of existence that entertainment reserves in its very punctuation of everyday productive endeavor. We might conclude by asking what can be done otherwise with this racing ahead of simulation, of which computer games are an entertaining expression? Computer games allow the possibility to experience otherwise the logistical preemptive strike on the future in its potentiality. After Virilio, I would call this an experience of accidentality, the unforeseen eventuality that accompanies every program, every invention, every orderly implementation of a technological advance.

We have seen some of the ways that games open up this replay of deterrent anticipation, of the predominance of what we analyzed in chapter 5 as a certain kind of targeting. Aberrant gameplay and player adoptions of commercial games, commercial releases commenting ironically on the generic conventions of the first-person shooter mode of play, critical and alternative games, and artistic practices mobilizing game technologies or intervening in the usual routines of player community autoproduction—all these play in different ways in the space provided by video game entertainment. More recently, games studies scholarship has seen work coming from activist designers and researchers about the critical potential of video games. Ian Bogost has argued for the rhetorical potential of the expressive power of video games as processual forms. Game design is about authoring—via computer programming—rules of behavior for dynamic models of real or imagined systems or phenomena.[42] He argues for the considerable potential of procedural rhetoric to be recognized beyond the habitual marginalization of video games as either frivolous entertainment forms or the reduction of their rhetorical power to established models of verbal or visual rhetoric.

Mary Flanagan's *Critical Play: Radical Game Design* is more explicitly addressed to the game design and development community. It advocates incorporation in the iterative game design cycle of a process of engagement in and reflection on the cultural and political values that are embedded in our current play frameworks and technology practices.[43] It proposes an alternative critical play design model that builds "values goals" into the model development process and into considerations of designing for diverse play styles and even for their potential subversion.[44]

Both of these contributions to approaching the critical and rhetorical potential of the simulation-based video game form are important for their insistence on addressing the specific formal and technological characteristics of video games and positioning them in relation to existing media technicities. Formulas for programming this idiosyncratic, critical potential are always going to run the risk of missing this potential. Worse—and perhaps this is the ultimate, and permanent, threat to the promise of computer games—the novel, idiosyncratic, inventive, and nascent critical reproductions of the technics of simulation that computer games offer run the constant risk of recruitment to the service of the mainstream program industries in their ongoing expansion, one that tends to promote unceasingly the preemption of criticality. By the same token, this program is susceptible to accidentality, and its efforts to map out its progress cannot, perhaps, guarantee immunity in the future they prescribe.

Consequently, the involvements of players with computer games is key here. However powerful the logistical impulse to preemptive control of experience realized in the game design, players open up the possibilities for specific, idiosyncratic adoptions of its entertaining playtime. However, to make something of a game via participatory co-creation of its realizable potential is not necessarily to undermine the deterrent impetus of digital technoculture.[45] As I have argued, we need to think beyond the promotion of participatory media culture or player sociality as if in itself individual player adoption of a computer game technics toward self-expression or community formation is automatically democratic or critical, automatically antithetical to the predominant anticipatory tendencies of computer simulation. The critical potential of inhabiting the suspension of the serious must be realized in a battle for criticality against the overarching tendency of the

program industries to standardize and predetermine the
and utilization of their products. Nevertheless, one can pla
co-create, vigilantly, responsively, selectively, watching for,
coming the bugs, artifacts, mods, critical and creative reading
tions, and other accidental becomings that alter what we car
what games do with us, and what they give us to think abc
doing with them now and tomorrow.

→ Apply to cosmopolitanism.

NOTES

Introduction

1. Roger Stahl, *Militainment, Inc.: War, Media, and Popular Culture* (New York: Routledge, 2010), 3.

2. Ibid., 110.

3. Nick Dyer-Witherford and Greig de Peuter, *Games of Empire: Global Capitalism and Video Games* (Minneapolis: University of Minnesota Press, 2009), xix.

4. Ibid., 29.

5. Gilbert Simondon, cited in Adrian Mackenzie, *Transductions: Bodies and Machines at Speed* (London: Continuum, 2003), 16.

6. Mackenzie, *Transductions*, 17.

7. Ibid., 18.

8. Paul Virilio and Sylvère Lotringer, *Pure War*, trans. Mark Polizzotti and Brian O'Keefe (New York: Semiotext(e), 1997), 24.

9. Espen Aarseth and Patrick Crogan, "Games, Simulation and Serious Fun: Interview with Espen Aarseth," *Scan* 1, no. 1 (January 2004), http://www.scan.net.au.

10. See Friedrich Kittler's account of Turing's famous hypothesis in *Literature, Media, Information Systems,* ed. John Johnston (Amsterdam: Overseas Publishers Association, 1997), 148: "After 1937, computing, whether done by men or by machines, can be formalized as a countable set of instructions operating on an infinitely long paper band and the discrete signs thereon. Turing's concept of such a paper machine, whose operations consist only of writing and reading, proceeding and receding, has proven to be the mathematical equivalent of any computable function. Universal Turing machines, when fed the instructions of any other machine, can imitate it effectively."

11. Gonzalo Frasca, "Simulation 101: Simulation Versus Representation," http://www.jacaranda.org/frasca/weblog/articles/sim1/simulation101d.html.

12. Constance Penley and Andrew Ross, *Technoculture* (Minneapolis: University of Minnesota Press, 1991), xii.

13. Philip K. Lawrence, *Modernity and War: The Creed of Absolute Violence* (London: Macmillan, 1997), 62.

14. On my secondhand IBM clone purchased in 1990 to word-process (onto analog cassette tape) my postgraduate research results, Fighter Pilot was an unexpected and much-loaded diversion from the routines of serious scholarship.

15. See http://www.barbie-dressupgames.com.

16. Kittler, *Literature, Media, Information Systems,* 156.

1. From the Military-Industrial to the Military-Entertainment Complex

1. Mia Consalvo, "It's No Game: News Commentary and the Second Gulf War," available in the Digital Library of the Digital Games Research Organisation, http://www.digra.org/dl/display_html?chid=http://www.digra.org/dl/db/05163.33172.

2. On the connection between computer development and ballistics, see Paul N. Edwards, *The Closed World: Computers and the Politics of Discourse in Cold War America* (Cambridge, Mass.: MIT Press, 1996), 45–47.

3. On the transformation of scientific research during the war, see Manuel De Landa, *War in the Age of Intelligent Machines* (New York: Zone Books, 1991), 147–48; Edwards, *Closed World,* 52–55; and Andy Pickering, "Cyborg History and the World War II Regime," *Perspectives on Science: Historical, Philosophical, Social* 3, no. 1 (1995): 1–48.

4. On Turing's involvement in British efforts at code breaking, see Edwards, *Closed World,* 18. De Landa, for his part, has this to say on the success of Turing and the British cryptological team: "Turing himself worked as a cryptologist during the war and was instrumental in breaking the Nazis' Enigma code, a feat that greatly contributed to German defeat by allowing Allied armies to follow Nazi radio communications in detail" (*War in the Age of Intelligent Machines,* 129).

5. Edwards, *Closed World,* 114.

6. Peter Galison, "The Ontology of the Enemy: Norbert Wiener and the Cybernetic Vision," *Critical Inquiry* 21 (Autumn 1994): 228–66.

7. Ibid., 229.

8. Ibid.

9. Ibid., 242.

10. Ibid., 250 (Galison's emphasis).

11. Edwards, *Closed World,* 103.

12. Ibid., 99–100.

13. Ibid., 76.

14. Ibid., 94.

15. Ibid., 107 (Edwards's emphasis). Edwards earlier identifies Ronald Reagan's 1980s Strategic Defense Initiative (SDI, also known as Star Wars) as the continuation of this desire for (and fantasy of) a predictive, protective container against nuclear attack. We can add to this George W. Bush's resurrection of this via the Star Wars 2 research program.

16. Pickering, "Cyborg History," 8.

17. Edwards, *Closed World*, 104.

18. On the "fabulous" nature of nuclear war, see also Paul Virilio and Sylvère Lotringer, *Pure War*, trans. Mark Polizzotti and Brian O'Keefe (New York: Semiotext(e), 1997); Jacques Derrida, "No Apocalypse, Not Now (Full Speed Ahead, Seven Missiles, Seven Missives)," trans. Catherine Porter and Philip Lewis, *Diacritics* 14 (Summer 1984): 20–25; and Ken Ruthven, *Nuclear Criticism* (Melbourne: Melbourne University Press, 1993).

19. Benjamin Woolley, *Virtual Worlds: A Journey in Hype and Hyperreality* (Oxford: Blackwell, 1992), 51.

20. Pickering, "Cyborg History," 21.

21. Timothy Lenoir and Henry Lowood, "Theaters of War: The Military-Entertainment Complex," in *Collection—Laboratory—Theater: Scenes of Knowledge in the 17th Century,* ed. Jan Lazardzig, Ludger Schwarte, and Helmar Schramm (New York: Walter de Gruyter Publishing, 2005), 427–56.

22. Ibid., 435–39.

23. Ibid., 437.

24. See ibid., 434–35: "General Norman Schwarzkopf and his staff prepared at the U.S. Central Military Command in Florida for a potential conflict in this [Middle Eastern] region by playing scenarios of the war game *Operation Internal Look* designed by Gary Ware. Ware had compiled enormous amounts of data—cartographic and military—on Kuwait and Iraq, and immediately after the invasion of Kuwait, the war gamers shifted *Internal Look* to running variations of the now 'real' scenario. . . . As a prediction, *Operation Internal Look* got good marks. Despite some shifts in the initial balance of forces, the 30-day simulated air and ground campaign was pretty close to the real sequence, although the percentage of air and ground action was slightly different. The ground battle pretty much unfolded as forecasted. Lessons learned from *Internal Look* shaped the defensive plan for Desert Shield, and drove home the power of computer simulation in preparing for war."

25. Stephen Biddle, in "Victory Misunderstood: What the Gulf War Tells Us about the Future of Conflict," *International Security* 21, no. 2 (Fall 1996): 139–80, argues that the exceptionally high loss ratio of Iraqi to U.S. forces in the battle was a result of a combination of U.S. technical superiority and mistakes made by the defending Iraqi forces (150).

26. Lenoir and Lowood, "Theaters of War," 440.

27. Ibid., 441.

28. Ibid.

29. Ibid. These sentiments are enthusiastically echoed in F. Clifton Berry Jr., "Re-creating History: The Battle of 73 Easting," *National Defense,* November 1991, 6–56.

30. J. C. Herz, *Joystick Nation: How Videogames Ate Our Quarters, Won Our Hearts, and Rewired Our Minds* (Boston: Little, Brown, 1997); Ed Halter, *From Sun Tzu to Xbox: War and Videogames* (New York: Thunder's Mouth Press, 2006); Roger Stahl, *Militainment, Inc.: War, Media, and Popular Culture* (New York: Routledge, 2010); Nick Dyer-Witherford and Greig de Peuter, *Games of Empire: Global Capitalism and Video Games* (Minneapolis: University of Minnesota Press, 2009).

31. One of the first major game/training simulation outcomes of the Institute for Creative Technologies (ICT) was a series of combat command simulations codeveloped with private contractors, Pandemic Studios and Sony. *Full Spectrum Warrior* (Pandemic Studios, 2004) was the commercial release version of a game developed from the beginning as both a commercial and military product. The initial Xbox platform commercial release of the game contained the military training version, which could be unlocked with an access code readily available online. See Dyer-Witherford and de Peuter, *Games of Empire,* 97–122, for a detailed account of the game's development through the auspices of the ICT and the controversy that arose around its codevelopment in the light of criticism from military users of its ineffectiveness as an urban counterterrorist training system.

2. Select Gameplay Mode

1. T. L. Taylor and Beth E. Kolko, "Boundary Spaces: *Majestic* and the Uncertain Status of Knowledge, Community and Self in a Digital Age," *Information, Communication and Society* 6, no. 4 (2003): 497–522.

2. Daniel Bell, *The Coming of Post-Industrial Society: A Venture in Social Forecasting* (London: Penguin Books, 1976), Jean-François Lyotard, *The Postmodern Condition: A Report on Knowledge* (Manchester: Manchester University Press, 1986), Fredric Jameson, *Postmodernism, or The Cultural Logic of Late Capitalism* (London: Verso, 1991).

3. Jean Baudrillard, *Simulations,* trans. Paul Foss et al. (New York: Semiotext(e), 1983).

4. Espen Aarseth, "Genre Trouble: Narrativism and the Art of Simulation," in *First Person: New Media as Story, Performance, and Game,* ed. Noah Wardrip-Fruin and Pat Harrigan (Cambridge, Mass.: MIT Press, 2004), 45–55; and Gonzalo Frasca, "Videogames of the Oppressed: Critical Thinking, Education, Tolerance, and Other Trivial Issues," in Wardrip-Fruin and Harrigan, *First Person,* 85–94.

5. T. L. Taylor, *Play between Worlds: Exploring Online Game Culture* (Cambridge, Mass.: MIT Press, 2006).

6. Mark Poster, "Theorizing Virtual Reality: Baudrillard and Derrida," in *The Information Subject* (Amsterdam: G+B Arts International, 2001), 117.

7. Ibid.

8. Rex Butler, *Jean Baudrillard: The Defence of the Real* (London: Sage, 1999). In a comment reproduced on the jacket of the book, Baudrillard says that Butler seems to understand him better than he does himself.

9. Baudrillard, *Simulations,* 3.

10. Lyotard, *Postmodern Condition.* I discuss Paul Virilio's thesis in this book's introduction. Virilio and Sylvère Lotringer, *Pure War,* trans. Mark Polizzotti and Brian O'Keefe (New York: Semiotext(e), 1997).

11. See Baudrillard, *Simulations, In the Shadow of the Silent Majorities: or, The End of the Social* (New York: Semiotext(e), 2007), and *Fatal Strategies* (London: Pluto Press, 1990).

12. Butler cites Baudrillard's experience of the abysm of his critical doubling of simulation when in an interview Baudrillard says the "giddiness I'm talking about ended up taking hold of me. I stopped working on simulation. I felt I was going totally mad" (*Jean Baudrillard,* 7–8).

13. Baudrillard's later work often evinced a much sharper, renewed engagement in this more critical encounter with real eventuality. See, for instance, the much maligned, and misunderstood *The Gulf War Did Not Take Place,* trans. Paul Patton (Sydney: Power Publications, 1995), and his essay on 9/11, *The Spirit of Terrorism and Requiem for the Twin Towers* (London: Verso, 2002).

14. Poster, "Theorizing Virtual Reality," 124.

15. Ibid., 135.

16. Jameson, *Postmodernism;* Bill Nichols, "The Work of Culture in the Age of Cybernetic Systems," *Screen* 29, no. 1 (Winter 1988): 22–46.

17. Martin Heidegger, *Being and Time,* trans. John Macquarrie and Edward Robinson (Oxford: Basil Blackwell, 1962).

18. Bernard Stiegler, *Technics and Time, 1: The Fault of Epimetheus,* trans. Richard Beardsworth and George Collins (Stanford, Calif.: Stanford University Press, 1998), 159.

19. Ibid., 177.

20. See, for example the U.S. Entertainment Software Association Web site (http://www.theesa.com) for a typical overview of the facts and figures circulating that indicate the scope and magnitude of computer games revenue, market penetration, and so forth as compared with other major media forms.

21. See Angela Ndalianis, *Neo-Baroque Aesthetics and Contemporary Entertainment* (Cambridge, Mass.: MIT Press, 2004), for an insightful discussion of this accelerating cross-mediality of entertainment forms.

22. Edward Castronova, *Synthetic Worlds: The Business and Culture of Online Games* (Chicago: University of Chicago Press, 2005), 8.

23. Gonzalo Frasca, "Simulation Versus Narrative: Introduction to Ludology," in *The Video Game Theory Reader,* ed. Bernard Perron and Mark J. P. Wolf (New York: Routledge, 2003), 233.

24. Jesper Juul, *Half-Real: Video Games between Real Rules and Fictional Worlds* (Cambridge, Mass.: MIT Press, 2005), 43.

25. Bernard Stiegler, *Technics and Time 3: Cinematic Time and the Question of Malaise,* trans. Stephen Barker (Stanford, Calif.: Stanford University Press, 2009), 108.

26. Ibid., 120.

27. Bernard Stiegler, *Acting Out,* trans. David Barison et al. (Stanford, Calif.: Stanford University Press, 2008), 89.

28. Paul Virilio, "The Accident Museum," in *A Landscape of Events,* trans. Julie Rose (Cambridge, Mass.: MIT Press, 2000).

29. Johan Huizinga, *Homo Ludens: A Study of the Play Element in Culture* (London: Paladin, 1970), 65: "The Play-concept as such is of a higher order than is seriousness. For seriousness seeks to exclude play, whereas play can very well include seriousness."

30. This should come as no surprise in the wake of Freud's metapsychological speculations in "Beyond the Pleasure Principle" concerning the little game of Fort-Da played at his feet one day by his nephew (in *The Standard Edition of the Complete Psychological Works of Sigmund Freud,* vol. 18, trans. James Strachey [London: Hogarth Press, 1955]). On the relation between betting and the future as the end, see also Jean-Michel Rabaté, "The 'Mujic of the Footure': Future, Ancient, Fugitive," in *Futures of Jacques Derrida,* ed. Richard Rand (Stanford, Calif.: Stanford University Press, 2001), 179–200.

31. Birgit Richard, "Norn Attacks and Marine Doom," in *Ars Electronica: Facing the Future—A Survey of Two Decades,* ed. Timothy Druckrey (Cambridge, Mass.: MIT Press, 1999), 339–40.

32. I am indebted to Alan Cholodenko for this observation.

33. Max Horkheimer and Theodor Adorno, *Dialectic of Enlightenment,* trans. John Cumming (London: Verso, 1997), 131.

34. Lev Manovich, *The Language of New Media* (Cambridge, Mass.: MIT Press), p. 210.

35. Shuen-shing Lee, "'I Lose Therefore I Think': A Search for Contemplation Amid Wars of Push-Button Glare," *Game Studies* 3, no. 2 (December 2003), http://www.gamestudies.org/0302/lee/.

36. Ibid.

3. Logistical Space

1. Benjamin Woolley, *Virtual Worlds: A Journey in Hype and Hyperreality* (Oxford: Blackwell, 1992), 51.

2. Andy Darley, "From Abstraction to Simulation: Notes on the History of Computer Imaging," in *Culture, Technology and Creativity in The Late Twentieth Century,* ed. Philip Haywood (London: John Libbey, 1990), 53.

3. See Timothy Lenoir and Henry Lowood, "Theaters of War: The Military-Entertainment Complex," in *Collection—Laboratory—Theater: Scenes of Knowledge in the 17th Century,* ed. Jan Lazardzig, Ludger Schwarte, and Helmar Schramm (New York: Walter de Gruyter, 2005), for a substantial account of this reformulation of the postwar military-industrial complex.

4. See Woolley, *Virtual Worlds,* 43; and Erkki Huhtamo, "Encapsulated Bodies in Motion: Simulators and the Quest for Total Immersion," in *Critical Issues in Electronic Media,* ed. Simon Penny (New York: State University of New York Press, 1995), 167.

5. Huhtamo, "Encapsulated Bodies in Motion," 167.

6. See Paul Virilio, *War and Cinema: The Logistics of Perception,* trans. Patrick Camiller (London: Verso, 1989), for such an analysis of cinema's development.

7. See Virilio, *Negative Horizon,* trans. Michael Degener (London: Continuum, 2005), 105–19.

8. Alan Cholodenko, introduction to *The Illusion of Life: Essays on Animation,* ed. Alan Cholodenko (Sydney: Power Publications, 1991), 21.

9. The Army pilots were employed at the time in transporting the U.S. mail, also linking flight simulation to a key communications network, both military and non-military, at its very outset. See Carl Lapiska, Larry Ross, and Don Smart, "Flight Simulation: An Overview," *Aerospace America,* no. 31 (August 1993): 14.

10. Woolley, *Virtual Worlds,* 43.

11. See Ken Pimentel and Kevin Teixeira, *Virtual Reality: Through the New Looking Glass* (New York: Intel/Windcrest/McGraw-Hill, 1993), 34.

12. James L. Davis, "Virtual Systems: Generating a New Reality," *Aerospace America,* no. 31 (August 1993): 26.

13. See Pimentel and Teixeira, *Virtual Reality,* 35, Woolley, *Virtual Worlds,* 41, and Howard Rheingold, *Virtual Reality* (London: Mandarin, 1992), 88–91. The corporation Evans & Sutherland remains a leading supplier of high-end military simulators.

14. Woolley, *Virtual Worlds,* 53.

15. Ibid.

16. Ibid., 55.

17. Lapiska et al., "Flight Simulation," 16.

18. Lenoir and Lowood, "Theaters of War."

19. Ibid., 436.

20. Lapiska et al., "Flight Simulation," 15 (my italics).

21. Virilio, *War and Cinema,* 86.

22. Lenoir and Lowood, "Theaters of War," 444.

23. Manuel De Landa, *War in the Age of Intelligent Machines* (New York: Zone Books, 1991), 105.

24. De Landa assesses the significance of this for the later development of the "American system" of manufacture and the formulation of the "scientific principles of management." De Landa, *War in the Age of Intelligent Machines,* 30–31.

25. See Lenoir and Lowood, "Theaters of War," 449–50.

26. Virilio, *War and Cinema,* 96.

27. Paul Virilio and Sylvère Lotringer, *Pure War,* trans. Mark Polizzotti and Brian O'Keefe (New York: Semiotext(e), 1997), 23.

28. Ibid., 24.

29. De Landa gives a concise account of the history of this rise of logistics, from the theoretical contest between Jomini's logistical vision for the conduct of war and Karl von Clausewitz's reactive insistence on the radical unpredictability that haunts any military action and the consequent necessity to articulate it with political and diplomatic negotiation at every step (*War in the Age of Intelligent Machines,* 84–104).

30. Michael Benedikt, introduction to *Cyberspace: First Steps,* ed. Michael Benedikt (Cambridge, Mass.: MIT Press, 1991), 20.

31. Benedikt, *Cyberspace: First Steps,* 21.

32. Ibid., 21.

33. Ibid., 1–2.

34. Benedikt's essay in the same book, "Cyberspace: Some Proposals," betrays the powerful influence of flight simulation on his vision. Anticipating the formulations of new media theorist Lev Manovich, cyberspace is, for Benedikt, "just a gigantic, active and spatially navigable database" (149). Concepts of flight permeate his descriptions

of this navigation, as in his discussion of a hypothetical cyberspatial experience in which one encounters an "unidentified flying data object" (157), and his suggestion that leaving cyberspace should be facilitated by an "autopilot" (172). Numerous allusions to the TV series *Star Trek: The Next Generation* (158, 169, 178) further indicate to what extent his conceptualization of cyberspace is linked to a model drawing heavily on that of flight simulation, inasmuch as *Next Generation* relies heavily for its appeal on its mainly computer-generated visual simulations of space flight and space combat. We might also note here the subsequent pervasive influence of *Next Generation*'s cyberspatial VR amusement system, the holodeck, as a model for speculations on the future of new media and a reference point for critical examinations of the discourses supporting immersive experience technologies. Janet Murray's *Hamlet on the Holodeck: The Future of Narrative in Cyberspace* (Cambridge, Mass.: MIT Press, 1997) is only one of the best-known and detailed examples of the latter.

35. Cholodenko, *Illusion of Life,* 21.

36. I will return to this process of the relegation of contextual elements such as geopolitical, critical, and other properly historical factors to a marginal (but not insignificant—rather, significantly marginal) role in flight sim computer games (and computer games in general) in the following chapter.

37. Judith Roof, "Depth Technologies," in *Technospaces: Inside the New Media,* ed. Sally R. Munt (London: Continuum, 2001), 26.

38. Ibid.

39. Ibid., 25.

40. Mark Poster says as much when he states that virtual reality technology "places in question the fixity and naturalness of the human perceptual apparatus" through its integration of machine-generated optical sensations with the human eye. "Theorizing Virtual Reality: Baudrillard and Derrida," in *The Information Subject* (Amsterdam: G+B Arts International, 2001), 118.

41. Roof, "Depth Technologies," 25.

42. See Roof, "Depth Technologies," 32–33, for an economical summary of 3-D computer graphics design and its basis in the Cartesian x-, y-, and z-dimensional grid.

43. I have examined Virilio's project in these terms in more detail in "The Tendency, the Accident and the Untimely: Paul Virilio's Engagement with the Future," in *Paul Virilio: From Modernism to Hypermodernism and Beyond,* ed. John Armitage (London: Sage, 2000).

44. Davis, "Virtual Systems," 28.

45. Virilio, *War and Cinema,* 59 (Virilio's emphasis).

46. Ibid., 79.

47. "The Battle of 73 Easting" project is discussed in chapter 1.

48. Lenoir and Lowood, "Theaters of War," 442.

49. Adaptations of these distributed interactive simulation protocols are at the basis of the online game worlds of massively multiplayer online role-playing games, first-person shooter online gameplay mode, and any online gameplay mode (including, of course, flight-simulation games) that involves the realtime interplay of multiple players across the Internet in a common "world" space.

50. Bernard Stiegler, *Technics and Time 2: Disorientation,* trans. Stephen Barker (Stanford, Calif.: Stanford University Press, 2009), 2.

51. Ibid.

52. In this regard, the adoption by participants of nonterritorial online community associations and identities in computer gaming and other networked new media contexts is a major theme of critical research in the field, one which we will consider in chapter 6.

4. Military Gametime

1. The terrorists' use of American flight training facilities, including jet flight simulators and commercial flight sim games, is well known. A (perhaps more fantastical) report describes the experience of an American businessman traveling in Egypt before the 9/11 attacks who was told in a conversation with a Cairo shopkeeper that *Flight Simulator* (presumably the Microsoft game) was popular in Egypt, and that this was because an attack on New York with "planes used as bombs" was expected in September or October. Dave Eberhart, "Egyptians Knew of Planned 9-11 Attacks Last August, Says Banker," *Newsmax.com,* Wednesday May 29, 2002, http://www.newsmax .com/archives/articles/2002/5/29/71547.shtml.

2. I note in this regard the proliferation of reality TV programming on commercial television in many countries. The dominance of this programming today, with its obvious correspondences to experimental simulation and interactive, ludic forms of entertainment—forms that have their own histories in television programming (and the radio formats that television remediated)—could be understood in terms of the increasing centrality of interactive simulational practices in contemporary technoculture.

3. Andy Darley, "From Abstraction to Simulation: Notes on the History of Computer Imaging," in *Culture, Technology and Creativity in The Late Twentieth Century,* ed. Philip Haywood (London: John Libbey, 1990), 39.

4. *Microsoft Combat Flight Simulator: WWII–Europe Series* (Microsoft, 1998) was the first in the series. *Microsoft Combat Flight Simulator 3: Battle for Europe* (Microsoft, 2002) was the third; its historical reference was also to the air war in Europe, with a focus on the post-Normandy ground attack campaign of the Allies and the Luftwaffe's

response. A number of add-on mission sets have also been released for games in the series by Microsoft and licensed publishers.

5. Lev Manovich, *The Language of New Media* (Cambridge, Mass.: MIT Press, 2000), 223.

6. Ibid., 233.

7. Ibid., 217.

8. The decision by the Microsoft Games division team not to model the attack on Pearl Harbor as part of the mission package is curious but perhaps understandable from a marketing point of view. It did not stop Microsoft from licensing a third party, JustFlight, to design a set of add-on missions for *Microsoft Combat Flight Simulator 2*, based on the Pearl Harbor attack and on hypothetical alternative scenarios. Indeed, since the release of *Microsoft Combat Flight Simulator 2* in 2000, and of Bay's film in 2001, several flight sims of the Pearl Harbor attack have been released commercially.

9. See the Chaps Squadron Web site (http://www.chapshq.com). I will take up the theme of game modification in more detail in chapter 7 and in the conclusion.

10. See the official *Microsoft Combat Flight Simulator 2* Web site (http://www .microsoft.com/games/combatfs2/articles_RAAF.asp).

11. *Microsoft Combat Flight Simulator 2: World War II Pacific Theater Pilot's Manual* (Microsoft Corporation, 2000), 3.

12. Tom Engelhardt, *The End of Victory Culture: Cold War America and the Disillusioning of a Generation* (New York: Basic Books, 1995).

13. J. C. Herz, *Joystick Nation: How Videogames Ate Our Quarters, Won Our Hearts, and Rewired Our Minds* (Boston: Little, Brown, 1997), 212.

14. Manovich, *Language of New Media*, 222.

15. Ibid., 214. The principle of transcoding, described by Manovich as "the migration of computer based forms back into culture at large," is a key concept in his study of new media forms and their impact on contemporary culture.

16. Most notable among these supporting media works is the National Geographic–produced documentary, *Beyond the Movie: Pearl Harbor* (2000), distributed as television programming on the National Geographic Channel and subsequently released on DVD.

17. See the official *Pearl Harbor* film's Web site (http://video.go.com/pearlharbor/).

18. In this way, the game negotiates the tension William Uricchio discusses in war gaming between the historical and hypothetical, the factuality of the simulated past, and its undermining via its experimental recreation for the purposes of simulation. See "Simulation, History, and Computer Games," in *Handbook of Computer Game Studies,* ed. Joost Raessens and Jeffrey Goldstein (Cambridge, Mass.: MIT Press, 2005), 331–32.

19. Engelhardt, *The End of Victory Culture.*

20. Japanese box office records cited from Stephen Cremin's online *Asian Film Bulletin* 79 (July 21–22, 2001), available via e-mail subscription to aflbulletin@mac.com. With regard to the critical reception of *Pearl Harbor,* see, for example, Geoffrey Macnab, "Pearl Harbor," *Sight and Sound* 11, no. 7 (July 2001): 49, and Macnab, "Bunk, but Unlikely to Bomb," *Independent,* March 23, 2001, 12; Neil McDonald, "Swashing and Buckling," *Quadrant* 45, no. 7 (July 2001): 85–89; Ian Buruma, "Oh! What a Lovely War," *Guardian,* May 28, 2001, suppl., 2–3; and Ed Rampell, "Pearl Divers Toy with Reality," *Variety* 292, no. 11 (April 30, 2001): 1.

21. David Thomson, "Zap Happy: World War II Revisited," *Sight and Sound* 11, no. 7 (July 2001): 34–37.

22. Ibid., 35.

23. Ibid., 36. Thomson mentions the *Star Wars* series of films (George Lucas) and *Starship Troopers* (Paul Verhoeven, 1997) in this regard.

24. This "smart bomb" perspective was replaced in coverage of the second Iraq war by the embedded vision of journalists accompanying advancing military units. This new perspective on the conflict positioned the telespectator more like a player-character in a first-person shooter or adventure game and less like the disembodied point of view controlled by a remote commander. One could read here an aesthetic figuration of the passage from the pre- to post-9/11 U.S. geostrategic policy.

25. Angela Ndalianis, "Special Effects, Morphing Magic, and the 1990s Cinema of Attractions," in *Meta Morphing: Visual Transformation and the Culture of Quick-Change,* ed. Vivian Sobchack (Minneapolis: University of Minnesota Press, 2000), 259.

26. Barbara Robertson, "War Effort," *Computer Graphics World,* June 2001, 29.

27. Christian Metz, "Notes toward a Phenomenology of the Narrative," in *Film Language: A Semiotics of the Cinema* (New York: Oxford University Press, 1974), 16–28.

28. Hayden White, "The Value of Narrativity in the Representation of Reality," *Critical Inquiry* 7 (1980): 5–23. See also White, *The Content of the Form: Narrative Discourse and Historical Representation* (Baltimore: Johns Hopkins University Press, 1989).

29. Paul Ricoeur, "Narrative Time," *Critical Inquiry* 7 (1980): 179. For an extended analysis of narrative and temporality, see Ricoeur, *Time and Narrative,* 3 vols. (Chicago: University of Chicago Press, 1984–1988).

30. Ricoeur, "Narrative Time," 174.

31. Paul Ricoeur, *Time and Narrative,* vol. 1, trans. Kathleen McLaughlin and David Pellaur (Chicago: University of Chicago Press, 1984), 67.

32. White, "Value of Narrativity," 23.

33. From this perspective, I would identify *Pearl Harbor* as one of the cycle of hybrid effects/"new sincerity" films (to cite Jim Collins) initiated by the box office success of *Titanic* (James Cameron, 1997). See Patrick Crogan, "(Dis)ingenuity: James Cameron's *Titanic*," *Metro Education*, no. 17/18 (March 1999): 17–18.

34. A dialectic of spectacle and narrativity has animated film history and its theorization since the advent of cinema. For instance, see Tom Gunning, "An Aesthetic of Astonishment: Early Film and the (In)credulous Spectator," in *Viewing Positions: Ways of Seeing Film*, ed. Linda Williams (New Brunswick, N.J.: Rutgers University Press, 1995). Gunning's influential revision of the largely "primitivist" understanding of early film as immature and deficient precursor to narrative cinema proposed that film's first predominant form was that of an aesthetic of "astonishment." Narrative form became dominant in mainstream cinema only subsequently, and never completely eradicated the spectacular modality of cinematic entertainment.

35. Thomas Doherty, *Projections of War: Hollywood, American Culture and World War II* (New York: Columbia University Press, 1999), 2. See also Geoff King, "Seriously Spectacular: 'Authenticity' and 'Art' in the War Epic," in *Spectacular Narratives: Hollywood in the Age of the Blockbuster* (London: I. B. Tauris, 2000).

36. See Thomas Schatz, "The New Hollywood," in *Film Theory Goes to the Movies*, ed. Jim Collins, Hilary Radner, and Ava Preacher Collins (New York: Routledge, 1993).

37. Bay quoted in "Pearl Harbor: More or Less," *Air Power History*, no. 48 (Fall 2001): 39.

38. Robertson, "War Effort," 22.

39. Andy Darley, *Visual Digital Culture: Surface Play and Spectacle in New Media Genres* (London: Routledge, 2000), 150.

40. Espen Aarseth, "Aporia and Epiphany in *Doom* and *The Speaking Clock*: The Temporality of Ergodic Art," in *Cyberspace Textuality: Computer Technology and Literary Theory*, ed. Marie-Laure Ryan (Bloomington: Indiana University Press, 1999), 32.

41. Ibid.

42. Espen Aarseth, *Cybertext: Perspectives on Ergodic Literature* (Baltimore: Johns Hopkins University Press, 1997), 5. Aarseth establishes the ground of his distinction between narrative and ergodic work in this text by insisting on the material differences between the ergodic work and the narrative textual form. He argues that while an ergodic work, or what he terms a "cybertext," "is a machine for the production of a variety of expression," a nonergodic work is given in the single form of a "linear expression" (3). The work done by the user of this nonergodic form is "trivial"—for example "eye movement and the periodic or arbitrary turning of a page" (2). Consequently, the "semantic ambiguity of a linear text" should not be confused with the "variable expression of the nonlinear text" (3).

43. Aarseth, "Aporia and Epiphany," 37.

44. Ibid.

45. Ibid., 38.

46. Ibid.

47. Ibid., 39. To illustrate this point, Aarseth discusses a "poetic generator" software creation, John Cayley's *The Speaking Clock*, as an alternative ergodic form that has a more open-ended function—namely, the creation of a potentially endless series of poetic articulations.

48. Ibid.

49. This indeterminacy is an abiding theme of James Der Derian's *Virtuous War: Mapping the Military-Industrial-Media-Entertainment Network* (Boulder, Colo.: Westview Press, 2001).

50. Manovich, *Language of New Media*, 278.

51. Aarseth, "Aporia and Epiphany," 37.

52. Manovich, *Language of New Media*, 210.

53. Ibid.

54. Ricoeur, *Time and Narrative*, 67.

55. Paul Virilio, *War and Cinema: The Logistics of Perception*, trans. Patrick Camiller (London: Verso, 1989), 59 (Virilio's italics).

56. Philip K. Lawrence, *Modernity and War: The Creed of Absolute Violence* (London: Macmillan, 1997), 62.

57. Ibid., 70.

58. Ibid., 72.

59. Even if the dream of remote control resulted in the doctrine of mutually assured destruction, the dream itself dies hard, as is evidenced by the Strategic Defense Initiative (dubbed "Star Wars") program of the Reagan era, its resuscitation as Star Wars 2 by the second Bush administration in the wake of 9/11, and the exponential growth in the deployment of robotic weapons systems today.

60. Paul Virilio, *Strategy of Deception*, trans. Chris Turner (London: Verso, 2000), 4.

61. Ibid., 7.

62. Manovich, *Language of New Media*, 264.

63. Jacques Derrida, *Of Grammatology*, trans. Gayatri Chakravorty Spivak (Baltimore: Johns Hopkins University Press, 1976), 144.

64. See Barry Atkins, *More than a Game: The Computer Game as Fictional Form* (Manchester: Manchester University Press, 2003), for a discussion of the nature of the historical discourse articulated by a World War II realtime strategy game series, *Close Combat* (Atomic, 1997–2000).

65. Ricoeur, "Narrative Time," 178.

66. Ricoeur, *Time and Narrative*, 77.

5. The Game of Life

1. Samuel Weber, *Targets of Opportunity: On the Militarization of Thinking* (New York: Fordham University Press, 2005).

2. Peter Galison, "The Ontology of the Enemy: Norbert Wiener and the Cybernetic Vision," *Critical Inquiry* 21 (Autumn 1994): 228–66.

3. Espen Aarseth, "Aporia and Epiphany in *Doom* and *The Speaking Clock*: The Temporality of Ergodic Art," in *Cyberspace Textuality: Computer Technology and Literary Theory*, ed. Marie-Laure Ryan (Bloomington: Indiana University Press, 1999), 32.

4. Ibid., 38.

5. Espen Aarseth, *Cybertext: Perspectives on Ergodic Literature* (Baltimore: Johns Hopkins University Press, 1997), 92.

6. Aarseth, "Aporia and Epiphany," 39.

7. See Galison, "Ontology of the Enemy," 252–53, on Wiener's globalization of this "technological *apercu*" (that for "an antiaircraft operator, the enemy really does act like an autocorrelated servomechanism") "into a new age for humanity and a general philosophy of human action." In *Cybernetics; or, Control and Communication in the Animal and the Machine* (Cambridge, Mass.: MIT Press, 1948), Wiener explains his scientific discovery of the principles for analyzing and regulating human and nonhuman behavior through communication and control systems as the latest transformation in the simulacrum of the human, succeeding the clockwork and steam engine–inspired notions of human being in preceding technological eras.

8. Weber, *Targets of Opportunity*, 12.

9. Les Levidow and Kevin Robins, "Towards a Military Information Society?" in *Cyborg Worlds: The Military Information Society*, ed. Les Levidow and Kevin Robins (London: Free Association Books, 1989), 159.

10. Ibid., 159.

11. Ibid.

12. Galison, "Ontology of the Enemy," 236.

13. Ibid., 237.

14. Ibid.

15. Ibid.

16. Ibid.

17. Ibid., 240.

18. Galison draws on Wiener's later formulation in *The Human Use of Human Beings: Cybernetics and Society* (New York: Avon Books, 1950) of two kinds of "devils" confronting humans—the Manichean, rationally calculating one and the Augustinian devil of blind chance and disorder—to characterize cybernetics as one of the three key Manichean sciences to emerge from the military technoscientific mobilization of

the war years (Galison, "Ontology of the Enemy," 232). The other two were operations research (which led onto systems analysis, systems theory, and a range of logistical modeling and predictive techniques) and game theory (whose influence on nuclear war simulation and strategic and diplomatic doctrine is well documented). In Galison's view, they were united in their shared vision of the enemy as a calculating, adaptable opponent knowable effectively only via his or her techniques and technics: "This was an enemy at home in the world of strategy, tactics, and maneuver, all the while thoroughly inaccessible to us, separated by a gulf of distance, speed, and metal" (233). Consequently, the knowledge sought through these Manichean sciences is meaningful only in and as its instrumental, practical application to technical responses to this enemy object.

19. N. Katherine Hayles, *How We Became Posthuman: Virtual Bodies in Cybernetics, Literature, and Informatics* (Chicago: University of Chicago Press, 1999), 68. See Hayles 67–73 for an account of the Macy Conferences debates around the "the man in the middle."

20. Andy Darley, *Visual Digital Culture: Surface Play and Spectacle in New Media Genres* (London: Routledge, 2000), 150: "What counts far more [in *Quake*] is the actual playing, and this involves a certain kind of *kinaesthetic performance* that becomes almost an end in itself" (Darley's italics). Darley is talking about the relegation of narrative involvement to a marginal position in action games, something he suggests is also the case "for most computer games." This strangely virtual, computer-mediated bodily performance is the core of the immersive effect in games in Darley's analysis. I would qualify his position here by saying that the performance is almost an end in itself inasmuch as the gamer is having fun with an interactive computer system that reproduces for entertainment purposes the highly teleological technics developed initially in Wiener's targeting project, the AA predictor, and related military technoscientific ventures.

21. Bernard Stiegler, *Acting Out,* trans. David Barison et al. (Stanford, Calif.: Stanford University Press, 2009), 70.

22. Douglas D. Noble, "Mental Materiel: The Militarization of Learning and Intelligence in U.S. Education," in Levidow and Robins, *Cyborg Worlds,* 19. This was precisely the question posed by Wiener at the conclusion of the AA predictor project. His experiments had shown that the AA predictor worked quite well in anticipating the flight path of the operator for which it had the data of previous flights, but it was ineffective if another operator flew the apparatus. He calculated that a far greater database of simulated or actual flights was needed to enrich the statistical basis and quality of the programming of the predictor. But this also led him to the foundation of cybernetics as the science tasked with the goal of modeling and anticipating human behavior

as systematically teleological. Galison states that the "core lesson that Wiener drew from his antiaircraft work was that the conceptualization of the pilot and gunner as servomechanisms within a single system was essential and irreducible" (Galison, "Ontology of the Enemy," 240).

23. Noble, "Mental Materiel," 19.

24. Henry Jenkins and Kurt Squire, "The Art of Contested Spaces," in *Game On: The History and Culture of Videogames,* ed. Lucien King (London: Laurence King, 2002), 65. Given their general characterization of computer games in terms of play in contested spaces, the failure of the authors to include war gaming or military technoscientific developments in simulation or virtualization in their list of the major influences on commercial computer gaming depictions/constructions of space is yet another both extraordinary and typical instance of the will-to-forget war's centrality to contemporary technoculture.

25. Tom Athanasiou, "Artificial Intelligence, Wishful Thinking and War," in Levidow and Robins, *Cyborg Worlds,* 121.

26. Paul Virilio, *War and Cinema: The Logistics of Perception,* trans. Patrick Camiller (London: Verso, 1989), 58. More precisely, Virilio is making a synecdoche of a specific form of computer program developed in artificial intelligence research, one designed to derive answers from an expert knowledge database.

27. For an explanation of the mathematical conceptions informing early cybernetics and communications engineering formulations of information, see Hayles, *How We Became Posthuman,* 53; and Mark C. Taylor, *The Moment of Complexity: Emerging Network Culture* (Chicago: University of Chicago Press, 2001), 107–10. Taylor explains the relations between Shannon's notion of information, emerging out of his work on improving electronic signal communications, and Wiener's cybernetics-inspired formulations. Taylor shows how Wiener and Shannon concurred that what at first sight seem to be contrasting notions of information—one a mathematical expression of noise (uncertainty) in a communications set up (Shannon) and the other a measure or determination of the delimitation of uncertainty in the dynamic of a communication feedback loop (Wiener)—are in fact varying perspectives on the same cybernetically conceived phenomena.

28. Paul Virilio, *The Information Bomb,* trans. Chris Turner (London: Verso, 2000), 141.

29. Weber, *Targets of Opportunity,* 21.

30. Stafford Beer cited by Levidow and Robins, "Towards a Military Information Society?" 166. See my discussion of SAGE in chapter 1.

31. Galison, "Ontology of the Enemy," 253.

32. See Aarseth, "Aporia and Epiphany," 37–38.

33. Military weapon-based combat shooter games with a science fiction or horror theme continue to be made, such as *Resistance: Fall of Man* (Sony Computer Entertainment, 2006). Moreover, it should be noted here that survival horror games have developed into a major genre in the last decade. They rely heavily for their shock and scare effects on the possibilities of putting players into the first- and third-person modes of gameplay that situate them within the game milieu. See Ewan Kirkland's analysis in "*Resident Evil's* Typewriter: Survival Horror and its Remediations," *Games and Culture* 4, no. 2 (2009): 115–26, of the genre's canny utilization of the technical system and remediated techniques from the horror film genre to deliver its uncanny thrills.

34. Barry Atkins has examined the critical counterfactual potential of computer games in *More than a Game: The Computer Game as Fictional Form* (Manchester: Manchester University Press, 2003), in relation to a realtime strategy game series, *Close Combat* (Atomic, 1997–2000).

35. Simon Penny, "Representation, Enaction, and the Ethics of Simulation," in *First Person: New Media as Story, Performance, and Game,* ed. Noah Wardrip-Fruin and Pat Harrigan (Cambridge, Mass.: MIT Press, 2004); Frank Lantz and Eric Zimmerman, "Rules, Play, and Culture: Checkmate," *Merge* 1, no. 5 (Summer 1999): 41–43.

36. Penny, "Representation, Enaction," 76.

37. Ibid., 76.

38. Ibid., 77. In *On Killing: The Psychological Cost of Learning to Kill in War and Society* (Boston: Little, Brown, 1996), Grossman compared the use by U.S. Army and police forces of firearm training simulators to the kind of conditioning in shooting human targets available through shooter video games.

39. Penny, "Representation, Enaction," 82.

40. Ibid.

41. In relation to gun-related violence in general in the United States as compared to that in other countries, Michael Moore's documentary, *Bowling for Columbine* (2001), presents an argument that emphasizes the importance of ideological and cultural factors specific to a U.S. social context in understanding the far higher rates of shootings in that country, factors to do with interethnic relations, American conceptions of the individual and property rights, and the American welfare system.

42. Jeffrey Goldstein, "Violent Video Games," in *The Handbook of Computer Game Studies,* ed. Joost Raessens and Jeffrey Goldstein (Cambridge, Mass.: MIT Press, 2005), 341–58. See also the "Brief *Amici Curiae* of Thirty-Three Media Scholars" in *Interactive Digital Software Association, et al. versus St. Louis County, et al.,* September 24, 2002, http://www.fepproject.org/archives/violence.html.

43. Goldstein, "Violent Video Games," 342.

44. Ibid., 350.

45. Penny, "Representation, Enaction," 81.

46. Ibid., 76.

47. Tanya Krzywinska and Geoff King have a similar criticism of Grossman's claims about the conditioning effect of commercial shooter games in *Tomb Raiders and Space Invaders: Videogame Forms and Contexts* (London: I. B. Tauris, 2006), 200.

48. David Nieborg, "Mods, Nay! Tournaments, Jay!" in *Fibreculture*, no. 8 (2006), http://journal.fibreculture.org/index.html. See also Sue Morris, "Co-Creative Media: Online Multiplayer Computer Game Culture," *Scan* 1, no. 1 (January 2004), http://www.scan.net.au/scan/journal/display.php?journal_id=16), for a discussion of the co-creative gamer community that developed around *Doom*.

49. The dynamic of end-user reinvention and its anticipation and incorporation by system designers (military, entertainment, and military-entertainment) is far from unidirectional. For an excellent overview and articulation of the participatory culture approach and its theoretical and political stakes, see Joost Raessens, "Computer Games as Participatory Media Culture," in Raessens and Goldstein, *Handbook of Computer Game Studies*, 373–88.

50. Virilio characterizes military technology as the apparently contradictory production of accidents; see Chris Dercon, "An Interview with Paul Virilio," trans. Daphne Miller, *Impulse* (Summer 1986): 36. This explains the centrality of military prerogatives to technological development (and in particular to modern technology), inasmuch as "every technology produces, provokes, programs a specific accident." Paul Virilio and Sylvère Lotringer, *Pure War*, trans. Mark Polizzotti and Brian O'Keefe (New York: Semiotext(e), 1997), 38.

51. Hayles, *How We Became Posthuman*, 26. Hayles argues that rather than an opposition, what we could call a transductive relation between pattern and randomness exists in which new patterns emerge out of changed conditions of randomness and vice versa. Hayles provides in this text a substantial historical analysis and critique of the passage of cybernetics from wartime invention to influential postwar cross-disciplinary theoretical discourse; see in particular her chapters 3 and 4.

52. Ibid., 104.

53. Ibid., 131–59.

54. Taylor, *Moment of Complexity*, 99–123.

55. Ibid., 112–13.

56. Jonathan Dovey and Helen Kennedy's *Game Cultures: Computer Games as New Media* (London: Open University Press, 2006) represents an attempt to develop aspects of a remobilization of cybernetic thought influenced by Donna J. Haraway's work on the cyborg as a viable model for undermining patriarchal technoculture. In

their analysis of female gamers and game cultures, they see the critical and ironic potential of women inhabiting the masculine-constructed position of tech savvy power gamer, master of the cybernetic control node in action games genres, including first-person shooters.

6. Other Players in Other Spaces

1. The "dead_in_iraq" project is documented on Joseph DeLappe's Web site, http://www.unr.edu/art/delappe/DeLappe%20Main%20Page/DeLappe%20Online%20MAIN.html. The project commenced in March 2006; DeLappe describes it as a partly "fleeting, online" memorial to the service personnel killed and partly as a "cautionary gesture." See also Roger Stahl, *Militainment, Inc.* (New York: Routledge, 2010), 128–30, for another account of DeLappe's project. For Stahl, dead_in_iraq juxtaposes two "accessible aspects of war culture" in a confronting way that poses questions about the "relationships between citizens, media and war" (130).

2. This is in contrast to marketing and unit sales—unlike the typical commercial release computer game, *America's Army* is available as a free download. The success of *America's Army* as a game has led, inevitably perhaps, to financial and commercial exploitation of its significant popularity. For instance, in 2007 Ubisoft released a licensed Xbox 360 spin-off of the game in a commercial extension of the hitherto military-developed and published series entitled *America's Army: True Soldiers* (Ubisoft, 2007).

3. The exemplary nature of online multiplayer game communities as forms of contemporary and emerging computer networked sociality in an era of complex online/off-line social engagements is argued by a number of writers, including T. L. Taylor, *Play between Worlds: Exploring Online Game Culture* (Cambridge, Mass.: MIT Press, 2006); Edward Castronova, *Synthetic Worlds: The Business and Culture of Online Games* (Chicago: University of Chicago Press, 2005); and Castulus Kolo and Timo Baur, "Living a Virtual Life: Social Dynamics of Online Gaming," *Game Studies* 4, no. 1 (November 2004), http://www.gamestudies.org/0401/kolo/.

4. On the concept of emergent forms of gaming, as opposed to classic closed games with set progression toward clearly defined and regulated objectives, see Jesper Juul, *Half-real: Video Games between Real Rules and Fictional Worlds* (Cambridge, Mass.: MIT Press, 2005), 72–78.

5. *The Sims Online* extends the hugely successful single-player game into an online form. Both Celia Pearce in "Story as Playspace: Narrative in Games," in *Game On: The History and Culture of Videogames,* ed. Lucien King (London: Lawrence King, 2002), 116, and Mary Flanagan, in *Critical Play: Radical Game Design* (Cambridge, Mass.: MIT Press, 2009), 48–61, have approached *The Sims* as belonging to a tradition of dollhouse play.

6. See, for instance, Paul Virilio and Sylvère Lotringer, *Pure War,* trans. Mark Polizzotti (New York: Semiotext(e), 1997); Paul Virilio, *Speed and Politics: An Essay on Dromology,* trans. Mark Polizzotti (New York: Semiotext(e), 1986); Paul Virilio, *Strategy of Deception,* trans. Chris Turner (London: Verso, 2000); and Paul Virilio, *Ground Zero,* trans. Chris Turner (London: Verso, 2002).

7. Richard Coyne, "Cyberspace and Heidegger's Pragmatics," *Information Technology and People* 11, no. 4 (1998): 338–50.

8. Martin Heidegger, *Being and Time,* trans. John Macquarrie and Edward Robinson (Oxford: Basil Blackwell, 1962).

9. Coyne, "Cyberspace," 339.

10. Ibid., 339.

11. For an introduction to the literature around this debate, see Günther Neske and Emil Kettering, eds., *Martin Heidegger and National Socialism: Questions and Answers,* trans. Lisa Harries (New York: Paragon House, 1990); Heidegger, *The Heidegger Controversy: A Critical Reader,* ed. Richard Wolin (Cambridge, Mass.: MIT Press, 1993); Jacques Derrida, *Of Spirit: Heidegger and the Question,* trans. Geoffrey Bennington and Rachel Bowlby (Chicago: University of Chicago Press, 1989); Jean-François Lyotard, *Heidegger and "The Jews,"* trans. Andreas Michael and Mark S. Roberts (Minneapolis: University of Minnesota Press, 1990); and Philippe Lacoue-Labarthe, *Heidegger, Art and Politics: The Fiction of the Political,* trans. Chris Turner (Oxford: Blackwell, 1990).

12. Heidegger, *Being and Time,* 103 (German pagination).

13. See ibid., 69–72, on the opposition of readiness-to-hand (*Zuhandenheit*) and presence-at-hand (*Vorhandenheit*).

14. Ibid., 103.

15. See Bernard Stiegler, *Technics and Time 2: Disorientation,* trans. Stephen Barker (Stanford, Calif.: Stanford University Press, 2009), 2, on his mobilization of Bertrand Gille's notion of disadjustment.

16. Heidegger, *Being and Time,* 104–5; see note 2 on page 138 of the Macquarrie and Robinson translation.

17. Ibid., 105.

18. Ibid., 107.

19. Heidegger, *Being and Time,* 107–8.

20. See, for example, Kolo and Baur, "Living a Virtual Life"; Julian Holland Oliver, "The Similar Eye: Proxy Life and Public Space in the MMORPG," in *Computer Games and Digital Cultures: Conference Proceedings,* ed. Frans Mayra (Tampere, Finland: Tampere University Press, 2002), 171–84; and Sue Morris, "Co-Creative Media: Online Multiplayer Computer Game Culture," *Scan* 1, no. 1 (January 2004): http://scan.net

.au/scan/journal/. T. L. Taylor's work, alone and in coauthorship with Mikael Jakobsson, has focused on this area. Her book, *Play between Worlds,* is her major statement on the nature of online gaming sociality based on her ethnographic research in the MMORPG, *Everquest.*

21. Heidegger, *Being and Time,* 105 (Heidegger's italics).

22. See Martin Heidegger, "The Question Concerning Technology," in *The Question Concerning Technology and Other Essays,* trans. William Lovitt (New York: Harper and Row, 1977), 3–35. The "action" of the mode of revealing of modern technology, *Gestell* ("enframing") is translated as "challenging-forth" (from *Herausfordern,* "to challenge," 14). I prefer Samuel Weber's translation in "Upsetting the Setup: Remarks on Heidegger's 'Questing after Technics,'" in his *Mass Mediauras: Form, Technics, Media* (Sydney: Power Publications, 1996), of *Herausforderung* as "driving- or goading-forth" (69).

23. Jeff Malpas, "Uncovering the Space of Disclosedness: Heidegger, Technology and the Problem of Spatiality in *Being and Time,*" in *Heidegger, Authenticity, and Modernity: Essays in Honor of Hubert L. Dreyfus,* ed. Mark Wrathall and Jeff Malpas (Cambridge, Mass.: MIT Press, 2000), 227.

24. See Heidegger, "Overcoming Metaphysics," in *Heidegger Controversy,* 84. In relation to the terms of his existential analysis in *Being and Time,* we could propose that the other players are typically encountered as "the They"—in German, *Das Man* (in French, *On*), the everyday, "primordial" being of other *Dasein* given in common linguistic constructions such as "They think that . . . ," "They say . . . ," one that serves to cover over more authentic encounters with others in the time of one's existence. See Heidegger, *Being and Time,* 113–14.

25. See Stiegler, *Technics and Time 1: The Fault of Epimetheus,* trans. Richard Beardsworth and George Collins (Stanford, Calif.: Stanford University Press, 1998), in particular chapter 4; and Derrida, *Of Spirit.*

26. See, for instance, Hubert Dreyfus, "Heidegger on Gaining a Free Relation to Technology," in *Technology and the Politics of Knowledge,* ed. Andrew Feenberg and Alastair Hannay (Bloomington: Indiana University Press, 1995); Malpas, "Uncovering the Space of Disclosedness"; Weber, "Upsetting the Setup"; Stiegler, *Technics and Time 1.*

27. Heidegger, *Being and Time,* 107.

28. Samuel Weber notes that *Raum,* "somewhat like English *room,* articulates this notion of singular plurality, negotiating between 'space' and 'place.'" *Targets of Opportunity: On the Militarization of Thinking* (New York: Fordham University Press, 2005), 130.

29. Coyne, "Cyberspace," 341.

30. On local area network gaming, see Melanie Swalwell, "The History and Development of Lan Groups: An Australasian Case Study," in *Other Players*, ed. Miguel Sicart and Jonas Heide Smith, online proceedings (IT University of Copenhagen, 2004), http://www.itu.dk/op/papers/swallwell.pdf. In relation to the sociality of arcade and home-based situations where gameplay takes place in situations of shared physical proximity of players and spectators, see James Newman, "The Myth of the Ergodic Videogame: Some Thoughts on Player–Character Relationships in Videogames," *Game Studies* 2, no. 1 (July 2002), http://www.gamestudies.org.

31. Taylor, *Play between Worlds*, 91.

32. Timothy Lenoir and Henry Lowood, "Theaters of War: The Military-Entertainment Complex," in *Collection—Laboratory—Theater: Scenes of Knowledge in the 17th Century*, ed. Jan Lazardzig, Ludger Schwarte, and Helmar Schramm (New York: Walter de Gruyter Publishing, 2005).

33. Oliver, "Similar Eye," 181–82.

34. Joost Raessens insists on this point in his discussion of media interactivity in "Computer Games as Participatory Media Culture," in *The Handbook of Computer Games Studies*, ed. Joost Raessens and Jeffrey Goldstein (Cambridge, Mass.: MIT Press, 2005), 373–88. "Interactivity," he says, needs "an individual relation with, for example, a television or computer screen. Even computer games that are played with several people over a local network or the Internet are based on this starting point" (379).

35. See Taylor, *Play between Worlds*, 38, where Brad McQuaid, original producer and codesigner of *Everquest*, is quoted concerning the deliberate building in of player cooperation into the game. McQuaid offers this definition of community: "community is relationships between players, whether it [*sic*] be friendly or adversarial, symbiotic or cooperative" (38).

36. To reiterate our closeness to Heidegger here, as part of our positioning against his work that is at once close up and moving away, I would cite Darin Barney's "The Vanishing Table; or, Community in a World That Is No World," in *Community in the Digital Age*, ed. Andrew Feenberg and Darin Barney (Lanham, Md.: Rowman & Littlefield, 2004), in which he draws on some comments from Heidegger's postwar work, *Discourse on Thinking*, to characterize the impacts on modern electronic and digital information and communications technology on modern community formation. These comments take us back to *Being and Time's* remarks about the new de-severing performed by radio. "Already in 1955," writes Barney, "Martin Heidegger could observe: 'All that with which modern techniques of communication stimulate, assail and drive man—all that is already much closer to man today than his fields around his farmstead, closer than the sky over the earth, closer than the change from night to day,

closer than the conventions and customs of his village, than the tradition of his native world.' Under these conditions—arguably accentuated by digital technology—if community is to exist at all, it will exist in a form appropriate to 'the illusion of a world that is no world'" (40).

37. Jean-Luc Nancy, *The Inoperative Community*, trans. Peter Connor et al. (Minneapolis: University of Minnesota Press, 1991), 4.

38. Ibid.

39. Ibid.

40. Ibid., 5.

41. Ibid.

42. See J. C. Herz, "Gaming the System: Multi-Player Worlds Online," in King, *Game On*, 86–96, on the spontaneous development of clans among the community of online *Quake* players. Herz is one of the writers to describe online game sociality as "tribal" (93).

43. Holin Lin, Chuen-Tsai Sun, and Hong-Hong Tinn, "Exploring Clan Culture: Social Enclaves and Cooperation in Online Gaming," in *Level Up: Digital Games Research Conference*, ed. Marinka Copier and Joost Raessens (Utrecht: University of Utrecht and DiGRA, 2003), 288–99. The authors thematize cooperative player strategy in general in the online worlds under consideration as risk management.

44. Ibid., 297.

45. Ibid., 292.

46. Taylor, *Play between Worlds*; Morris, "Co-Creative Media"; Kolo and Baur, "Living a Virtual Life"; Talmadge Wright, Eric Boria, and Paul Breidenbach, "Creative Player Actions in FPS Online Video Games: Playing Counter-Strike," *Game Studies* 2, no. 2 (December 2002), http://www.gamestudies.org/0202/wright/.

47. Morris, "Co-Creative Media."

48. On the incitement to become a productive consumer, see Lev Manovich, *The Language of New Media* (Cambridge, Mass.: MIT Press, 2000), 221–25.

49. Heidegger, *Question Concerning Technology*, 27.

50. See Manovich on the "myth" of computer-mediated interactivity in *Language of New Media* (57).

51. See Castronova, *Synthetic Worlds*, 9, where MMORPGs are cast as "waystations between the late twentieth century and the future. . . . From this point of view, synthetic worlds are simply intermediate environments: the first settlements in the vast, uncharted territory that lies between humans and their machines" (8). The extension of a long history of American colonial frontier discourse could not be more emphatically marked here, as the perspective from which to analyze the social-cultural possibilities for settling this "territory" arising from current MMORPG practice. In a

more circumspect vein, Espen Aarseth in "Games, Simulation and Serious Fun: An Interview with Espen Aarseth," *Scan* 1, no. 1 (January 2004), http://www.scan.net .au/scan/journal/, has this to say about the future being mapped out in online games: "They're [game designers] making new rules which are going to affect the way we communicate online. So we have games today and massive online societies tomorrow just like with the MUDs but on a much larger scale. . . . In thirty years from now we will see very interesting results of that development, how these systems that began as games develop a whole new state of etiquette, social rules, strategies for large scale human interaction which is going to have a big impact on the rest of society."

52. Wright et al., "Creative Player Actions" (my emphasis).

53. Taylor, *Play between Worlds*, 82–83.

54. Scott Lash, *Critique of Information* (London: Sage Publications, 2002), 39–40.

55. Ibid., 39.

56. Ibid., 40.

57. This theme pervades Stiegler's *Technics and Time 1*. See, for instance, "Prometheus' Liver," 185–203.

58. This consciousness of the community of others is not, according to Nancy, that of an individual. It is only experienced "in and through the community." Nancy, *Inoperative Community*, 19.

59. Ibid., 27.

60. Weber, *Targets of Opportunity*, 105.

61. Adrian Mackenzie, *Transductions: Bodies and Machines at Speed* (London: Continuum, 2002), 145–70.

62. Ibid., 169.

63. See Josephine Starrs's account of *Quake4U* in "Game Hack," *Scan* 1, no. 1 (January 2004), http://scan.net.au/scan/journal/display_synopsis.php?j_id=25. One could consider here the similar project, in a single-player mode, of Brody Condon's *Adam Killer* mod of *Half-Life*. Shuen-shing Lee describes how Condon "installs a photograph of his friend Adam Frelin as the opposing figure in the game and has it duplicated, stuffing the scenario full." "'I Lose Therefore I Think': A Search for Contemplation Amid Wars of Push-Button Glare," *Game Studies* 3, no. 2 (December 2003), http://www.gamestudies.org/0302/lee/.

7. Playing Through

1. Gonzalo Frasca, "Simulation Versus Narrative: Introduction to Ludology," in *The Video Game Theory Reader,* ed. Bernard Perron and Mark J. P. Wolf (New York: Routledge, 2003), 233.

2. See the C-level Web site, http://c-level.org/tekken1.html.

3. See the art collective //////////fur//// art entertainment interfaces' Web site, http://www.painstation.de.

4. //////////fur//// art entertainment interfaces' Web site, http://www.pain station.de/new/gameplay.html.

5. Design and the Elastic Mind, http://www.moma.org/interactives/exhibitions/ 2008/elasticmind/#.

6. Shuen-shing Lee, "'I Lose Therefore I Think': A Search for Contemplation Amid Wars of Push-Button Glare," *Game Studies* 3, no. 2 (December 2003), http:// www.gamestudies.org/0302/lee/.

7. For instance, the performance and conceptual art practices of the Australians Mike Parr and Stelarc, and the French artist Orlan.

8. Erkki Huhtamo, "Encapsulated Bodies in Motion: Simulators and the Quest for Total Immersion," in *Critical Issues in Electronic Media,* ed. Simon Penny (Albany: State University of New York Press, 1995), 167.

9. Samuel Weber, *Theatricality as Medium* (New York: Fordham University Press, 2004).

10. Ibid., 314.

11. See Paul Virilio, *Bunker Archeology,* trans. George Collins (New York: Prince-ton Architectural Press, 1994), 41.

12. See chapter 5 for a discussion of the "man in the middle."

13. Bernard Stiegler, "Technoscience and Reproduction," *Parallax* 13, no. 4 (2007): 29–45.

14. Weber, *Theatricality as Medium,* 315.

15. For a rigorous elaboration of this proposition, see Stiegler's reading of Heideg-ger's notion of facticity in *Technics and Time 1: The Fault of Epimetheus,* trans. Richard Beardsworth and George Collins (Stanford, Calif.: Stanford University Press, 1998), 215–19.

16. //////////fur//// art entertainment interfaces' Web site, *Painstation* concept page, http://www.painstation.de/index_old.html, now taken down.

17. Frasca, "Simulation Versus Narrative," 233.

18. Gonzalo Frasca, "Simulation 101: Simulation Versus Representation," http:// www.jacaranda.org/frasca/weblog/articles/sim1/simulation101d.html.

19. See, for instance, Sherry Turkle, "Our Split Screens," in *Community in the Digi-tal Age,* ed. Andrew Feenberg and Darin Barney (Lanham, Md.: Rowman & Littlefield, 2004); Slavoj Žižek, *The Plague of Fantasies* (London: Verso, 1997); Jean Baudrillard, *Simulations,* trans. Paul Foss et al. (New York: Semiotext(e), 1983); and Espen Aarseth, "Genre Trouble: Narrativism and the Art of Simulation," in *First Person: New Media as Story, Performance, and Game* (Cambridge, Mass.: MIT Press, 2004).

20. Espen Aarseth and Patrick Crogan, "Games, Simulation and Serious Fun: An Interview with Espen Aarseth," in *Scan* 1, no. 1 (January 2004), http://www.scan.net.au.

21. Stiegler, *Technics and Time 1*, 159.

22. Gonzalo Frasca, "Videogames of the Oppressed: Critical Thinking, Education, Tolerance, and Other Trivial Issues," in *First Person: New Media as Story, Performance, and Game* (Cambridge, Mass.: MIT Press, 2004), 86. The problems begin when Frasca repeats affirmatively Aarseth's own gesture in *Cybertext: Perspectives on Ergodic Literature* (Baltimore: Johns Hopkins University Press, 1997) of adopting cybernetics without reflecting on the implications of selecting its universalizing, generalizing principles.

23. Weber, *Theatricality as Medium*, 314.

24. Frasca, "Videogames of the Oppressed," 87.

25. Available on the Newsgaming Web site, http://www.newsgaming.com.

26. See the Newsgaming Web site, http://www.newsgaming.com/games/index12.htm.

27. Lee, "I Lose Therefore I Think." Lee analyzes another Frasca game, *Kabul Kaboom!* (Frasca, 2001), http://ludology.org/games/kabulkaboom.html, in similar terms.

28. *Donkey John,* http://www.donkeyjohn.com/donkeyjohn/. See the text by the producer of *Donkey John,* Joe Boughton-Dent, "Video Games Killed the Political Czar," *M/C: A Journal of Media and Culture, M/C* Reviews section, October 2005, http://reviews.media-culture.org.au/, now taken down.

29. A deal was finally settled between the two nations in 2005, years after negotiations had commenced.

30. In *Persuasive Games: The Expressive Power of Videogames* (Cambridge, Mass.: MIT Press, 2007), Ian Bogost characterizes such alternative or political games as lacking a real engagement with the "procedural" rhetorical potential of the video game form (50).

31. See the Web sites for these games: *Under Siege,* http://www.underash.net/en_download.htm; *Under Ash,* http://www.underash.net/emessage.htm.

32. M. Adnan Salim (general manager, Akfarmedia) on the *Under Ash* Web site.

33. Turkle quoted in Frasca, "Videogames of the Oppressed," 87–88.

34. Newsgaming's *Madrid* (2004), http://www.newsgaming.com/games/madrid/, made as a response to the terrorist bombings of the train network in Madrid, is a "game" about the rituals of mourning and their inevitable inadequacy as models of behavior/response to real traumas. In what is a futile struggle, the player must keep alight the candles of a large group of mourning figures by clicking on them when they

(frequently) go out. A kind of frantic affect is experienced by the persistent player as a critical echo of the frenetic involvement in similar games where the pleasure is in delaying the inevitable defeat by the game.

35. Frasca, "Videogames of the Oppressed," 89.

36. In adopting a notion of theater and simulation as tools for use in a particular critical project, Frasca repeats the classic metaphysical devaluation of the technical being vis-à-vis the organic, natural, human being. The inanimate tool, incapable of authoring its own development, application, or evolution, awaits the autonomous human user to provide its essential purpose, application, and innovation. Frasca's isolation of "simulation in general" from its specific history and dynamic of development corresponds with and is in a sense performed in this identification of simulation as a neutral tool awaiting specific, alternative utilization from its habitual mobilization. This book has approached the question of gaming and simulation technology from a position informed by the critical theorization of technology (given us to think in the work of such writers as Martin Heidegger, Paul Virilio, and Bernard Stiegler), a position that takes issue with this classic metaphysical—and itself technical—preemptive gesture of separating the tool as dead technics from the living (see Stiegler, *Technics and Time 1*, 1).

37. See the discussion of narrative as interpretation machine in chapter 4.

38. Bernard Stiegler, *Technics and Time 3: Cinematic Time and the Question of Malaise*, trans. Stephen Barker (Stanford, Calif.: Stanford University Press, 2009), 8. The archaic, transcultural characteristic of narrative is something identified by many theorists of narrative, including Roland Barthes, Mieke Bal, Christian Metz, Hayden White, and Paul Ricoeur. On this point, see Jos de Mul, "The Game of Life: Narrative and Ludic Identity Formation in Computer Games," in *The Handbook of Computer Games Studies*, ed. Joost Raessens and Jeffrey Goldstein (Cambridge, Mass.: MIT Press, 2005), 253–54.

39. Frasca, "Videogames of the Oppressed," 88.

40. See Patrick Crogan, "Wargaming and Computer Games: Fun with the Future," in *The Pleasures of Computer Gaming: Essays on Cultural History, Theory and Aesthetics*, ed. Melanie Swalwell and Jason Wilson (Jefferson, N.C.: McFarland, 2008), for a more detailed analysis of this history.

41. In "Videogames of the Oppressed," Frasca explains the difference between fixed narrative form and the "dynamic essence" of video games, citing this as the reason why "videogames are not a good realm for historic events or characters or for making moral statements" (86). This has not stopped numerous commercial games from being based on historical events (battle sims, adventure and role-playing games, and flight and vehicle simulations) and exploring counterfactual historical scenarios in different degrees of tolerance in regard to their variation from the historical record. In

doing so, they faithfully reproduce a major application of military war gaming simulation and training, namely, the replaying of past battles as a means of learning from the mistakes of former warriors.

42. See the *Desert Rain* page on the Blast Theory Web site, http://www.blastthe ory.co.uk/bt/work_desertrain.html.

Conclusion

1. The TRADOC Web site is http://www.army.mil/info/organization/unitsand commands/commandstructure/tradoc/. The video and the full Capstone Concept document are downloadable there. The video is also available at http://www .vimeo.com/7066453.

2. P. W. Singer, *Wired for War* (New York: Penguin, 2009), 10.

3. Ibid., 68. See also Roger Stahl, *Militainment, Inc.: War, Media, and Popular Culture* (New York: Routledge, 2010), 91.

4. James Der Derian, *Virtuous War: Mapping the Military-Industrial-Media-Entertainment Network* (Boulder, Colo.: Westview Press, 2001), 59, citing the "Coordinating Draft of the 7th Army Training Command White Paper of Mission Training for Military Operations Other than War."

5. Ibid., 58.

6. Ibid., 59.

7. This is what Paul Ricoeur, in *Time and Narrative*, vol. 1, trans. Kathleen McLaughlin and David Pellaur (Chicago: University of Chicago Press, 1984), calls mimesis "a preunderstanding of the world of action, its meaningful structures, its symbolic resources, and its temporal character" that grounds the composition of story plots (54).

8. See Jacques Derrida, *Acts of Religion,* ed. Gil Anidjar (New York: Routledge, 2002), 228–98. Derrida's discussion of the aporetic nature of the self-legitimizing gestures of any legally established state or status quo remarks upon its implications for a discussion of the performative power of the interpretation of any text whose significance is already well established via institutional practices, traditions, and so forth, including those conventional interpretations that serve to reaffirm and relegitimate the established one.

9. Gonzalo Frasca, "Simulation 101: Simulation Versus Representation," http:// www.jacaranda.org/frasca/weblog/articles/sim1/simulation101d.html.

10. Robert G. Sargent, "Verification and Validation of Simulation Models," in *Proceedings of the 2005 Winter Simulation Conference, Orlando, FL, December 2005,* ed. M. E. Kuhl, N. M. Stieger, F. B. Armstrong, and J. A. Jones (Piscataway, N.J.: Institute of Electrical and Electronics Engineers, 2005), 130–43.

11. Roger Smith, "Simulation: The Engine behind the Virtual World," available at the Model Benders Web site, http://modelbenders.com/papers/Papers.html.

12. See our discussion in chapter 4 of Aarseth's model of ergodic temporality within the cybernetic realm of ergodic works such as computer games.

13. Mary Flanagan characterizes the predominant model of video game design as such an iterative cycle of development, testing, and revision. See *Critical Play: Radical Game Design* (Cambridge, Mass.: MIT Press, 2009), 254.

14. Ian Bogost, *Persuasive Games: The Expressive Power of Videogames* (Cambridge, Mass.: MIT Press, 2007), 45.

15. Miriam Batu Hansen expresses some unease with the term "mainstream cinema," noting that "in addition to the connotation of quasi-natural flow, it suggests a homogeneity that locates side-streams and counter-streams on the outside or margins, rather than addressing the ways in which they at once become part of the institution and blur its boundaries." "The Mass Production of the Senses: Classical Cinema as Vernacular Modernism," in *Reinventing Film Studies,* ed. Christine Gledhill and Linda Williams (London: Arnold, 2000), 339. Leaving aside the demands Hansen places on a single descriptor to address the complexities of the institution, process, and diversity it names, I suggest that the connotation of a "quasi-natural flow" is apt to the naturalizing dynamic of mainstream cultural forms.

16. See, for example, Geoff King and Tanya Krzywinska, *Tomb Raiders and Space Invaders: Videogame Forms and Contexts* (London: I. B. Tauris, 2006). In chapter 4, "Social, Cultural and Political Dimensions," they examine these in relation to both the content of computer games and the "core gameplay," identifying "social-cultural-ideological meanings" emerging from both of these aspects of games (168).

17. Lev Manovich, *The Language of New Media* (Cambridge, Mass.: MIT Press), 60.

18. Ibid., 61.

19. Ibid.

20. Ibid.

21. Jos de Mul, "The Game of Life: Narrative and Ludic Identity Formation in Computer Games," in *The Handbook of Computer Games Studies,* ed. Joost Raessens and Jeffrey Goldstein (Cambridge, Mass.: MIT Press, 2005), 261.

22. James Newman, "The Myth of the Ergodic Videogame: Some Thoughts on Player–Character Relationships in Videogames," *Game Studies* 2, no. 1 (July 2002), http://www.gamestudies.org/0102/newman/.

23. Ted Friedman, *Electric Dreams: Computers in American Culture* (New York: New York University Press, 2005), 139.

24. Ibid., 137.

25. Ibid., 136.

26. Ibid., 138.

27. See Bernard Stiegler, *Technics and Time 2: Disorientation*, trans. Stephen Barker (Stanford, Calif.: Stanford University Press, 2009), 160.

28. Bernard Stiegler, *Technics and Time 3: Cinematic Time and the Question of Malaise*, trans. Stephen Barker (Stanford, Calif.: Stanford University Press, 2009), 195.

29. This dynamic is no better articulated than in Samuel Weber's reading of the contradictory unsecuring movement that Heidegger evokes in relation to the movement of *Gestell* underlying modern technics in "Upsetting the Setup: Remarks on Heidegger's 'Questing after Technics,'" *Mass Mediauras: Form, Technics, Media*, ed. Alan Cholodenko (Sydney: Power Publications, 1996), 70: "The translation of *Entbergung* as *unsecuring* thus foregrounds what I take to be the decisive question that emerges from Heidegger's quest [for the essence of technology]: how a movement of unsecuring comes to evoke as its response its diammetrical opposite—the frantic effort to establish control and security. The effort is all the more 'frantic' or 'furious' (*rasend*) because it is constantly goaded on by the unsecuring tendency of technics as such."

30. Seth Giddings, "Playing with Non-Humans: Digital Games as Techno-Cultural Form," in *Worlds in Play: International Perspectives on Digital Games Research*, ed. Suzanne de Castell and Jennifer Jason (New York: Peter Lang, 2007), 115–28.

31. Ibid., 126.

32. Ibid., 125. Giddings compares the ALife units in *Advance Wars 2* to the cellular automata invented by John Conway for the famous *Game of Life* (1970), a breakthrough in ALife research and its popularization. In this regard, see also Birgit Richard, "Norn Attacks and Marine Doom," in *Ars Electronica: Facing the Future—A Survey of Two Decades*, ed. Timothy Druckrey (Cambridge, Mass.: MIT Press, 1999), 339–40.

33. Roger Stahl, *Militainment, Inc.;* Nick Dyer-Witherford and Greig de Peuter, *Games of Empire: Global Capitalism and Video Games* (Minneapolis: University of Minnesota Press, 2009).

34. See, in this regard, Weber's discussion of the links between war, terrorism, and spectacle in the post-9/11 milieu in *Theatricality as Medium* (New York: Fordham University Press, 2004), 326–35. The Western media stage the spectacle of the war on terror (in concert with the ever-expanding forces of the state) to encourage the viewer "to '*look forward*' [toward "Enduring Freedom," as their military operation in Afghanistan is officially known by the United States] and simultaneously *forget the past;* encouraged to identify with the ostensibly invulnerable perspective of the camera registering as blips the earth-bound destruction [of the caves of Tora Bora] tens of thousands of feet below" (335).

35. Daniel Ross, in *Violent Democracy* (Cambridge: Cambridge University Press, 2004), has documented and analyzed these profoundly ambivalent, contradictory,

and violent gestures toward the future of democracy perpetrated by the United States military, political, and legal systems (and their allies in the Coalition of the Willing) in the war on terror in Afghanistan and Iraq, as well as in the homeland.

36. Dyer-Witherford and de Peuter cite Michael Hardt and Antonio Negri's *Multitude: War and Democracy in the Age of Empire* (London: Penguin, 2006) on the shift from defense to security: "Whereas 'defense' involves a protective barrier against external threats, 'security' justifies a constant martial activity equally in the homeland and abroad." (*Games of Empire*, 100). Of course, Paul Virilio's book *L'Insécurité du Territoire* [Territorial Insecurity] (Paris: Editions Stock, 1976) anticipated the recent phenomenon of generalized security and its theorization by some years.

37. Derrida, *Acts of Religion*, 86.

38. Ibid., 84.

39. Ibid., 87.

40. Johan Huizinga, *Homo Ludens: A Study of the Play Element in Culture* (London: Paladin, 1970), 65: "The Play-concept as such is of a higher order than is seriousness. For seriousness seeks to exclude play, whereas play can very well include seriousness."

41. McKenzie Wark's *Gamer Theory* (Cambridge, Mass.: Harvard University Press, 2007), advances a position about the pleasures of video gameplay that amounts to a cynical reprise of this reading of the escapist dimension of video game entertainment, or, rather, a reprise of this reading for the cynical game player disenchanted with the illusion of control and agency provided by contemporary interactive technoculture.

42. Bogost, *Persuasive Games*, 28–30.

43. Flanagan, *Critical Play*, 252.

44. Ibid., 257.

45. Joost Raessens puts it this way: "Computer games are not just a game, never just a business strategy for maximizing profit, but always also a battlefield where the possibility to realize specific, bottom-up, heterogeneous forms of participatory media culture is at stake. "Computer Games as Participatory Media Culture," in Raessens and Goldstein, *Handbook of Computer Games Studies*, 384.

INDEX

mimesis, Ricoeur's concept of, 205n7

miniaturization, flight simulation development and, 42–43

mise-en-abyme, simulation and, 24–26, 181n12

Mitchell, William, 82

mnemotechnical experience, Stiegler's concept of: critical engagement and, 168–69; experimental game projects and, 153; narrative vs. simulation opposition, 159–65

modernity: hyperstandardization of sociality and, 129; online gaming and, xxiv; technoculture and, xx–xxi

Morris, Sue, 106, 126–27

multimodal games, 19–20

Multitude: War and Democracy in the Age of Empire, 208n36

Museum of Modern Art, Design and the Elastic Mind exhibition and Web site, 136

Nancy, Jean-Luc, 111, 125, 127–28, 131, 172

Napoleon: Total War computer game, 67

narrative: computer games and co-option of, xxiii, 30; computer war gaming and role of, 61–64, 80–83; future trends in computer gaming and, 143–54; game modifications of, 83–85; mnemotechnical experience and, 159–65; in special effects films, 67–76, 189n34

Nazi Party, Heidegger's involvement with, 115

Ndalianis, Angela, 69

Negri, Antonio, xv, 208n36

networked community, online gaming and, xxiv

networked simulation training, SIMNET program and, 12–18

"New Hollywood," special effects films and, 72–73

Newman, James, 168

new materialism, computer simulation and, 26–27

new media projects: computer gaming and, 135–55; interactivity and subjectivity in, 166–69

Newsgaming, xxiv–xv, 146–49, 203n34

Nichols, Bill, 27

Nieborg, David, 105–6

Noble, Douglas D., 95

nuclear deterrence hypothesis, emergence of, 81–83

Oliver, Julian Holland, 123

online gaming: community and social networking and, xxiv, 22–27; distributed interactive simulation protocols and, 186n49; future predictions concerning, 30; networking of individual players and, 121–28; nonterritoriality and, 58, 186n52; player and/as space in, 114–21; as recruitment propaganda, 111–13; technoculture and, xxiv; unworking of networking and, 128–34. *See also* massively multiplayer online role-playing games (MMORPGs)

Operation Internal Look, 179n24

Operation Iraqi Freedom, media coverage compared with computer gaming, 1–2

PATRICK CROGAN is senior lecturer in film and media and cultural studies at the University of the West of England, Bristol.

(*continued from page ii*)